A Sociology of Industrialisation: an introduction

DAVID BROWN
and
MICHAEL J. HARRISON

M

First published 1978 by
THE MACMILLAN PRESS LTD
London and Basingstoke
Associated companies in Delhi Dublin
Hong Kong Johannesburg Lagos Melbourne
New York Singapore and Tokyo

Printed in Hong Kong

British Library Cataloguing in Publication Data

Brown, David
A sociology of industrialisation. – (Macmillan business management and administration series).
1. Industry – Great Britain – Social aspects
2. Great Britain – Industries – History
I. Title II. Harrison, Michael J.
301.5′5′0941 HC255

ISBN 0–333–23558–4
ISBN 0–333–23559–2 Pbk

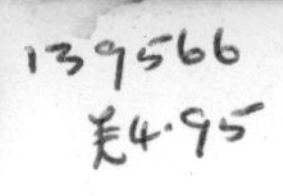

Sociology of Industrialisation: an introd...

Also in the Macmillan Business Management and Administration Series, edited by Alan Hale

Published

David Brown and Michael J. Harrison: A Sociology of Industrialisation – an introduction

Terry Green and John Webster: Managing Mathematically

Arthur Hindmarch, Miles Atchison, and Richard Marke: Accounting – an introduction

Forthcoming in 1978

Peter Haine and E. E. J. Haidon: Computers in Business

Peter Ribeaux and Stephen Poppleton: Psychology and Work – an introduction

Editor's Introduction

This series is a direct outcome of the opportunities and challenges created by the rapid expansion of higher and further education in the past decade.

The expansion involved changes in the structure of advanced education, through the CNAA, the Polytechnics, the Regional Management Centres and the professional bodies which encouraged staff to develop new and experimental teaching. Substantial changes have taken place in the definition, scope and methodologies of the social, administrative and management sciences leading to modifications in the presentation of these subjects. Many new full-time students and staff have questioned traditional approaches and methods and have established more open discussion and debate on their courses. Demands for qualified manpower led to an expansion in part-time education and increased questioning by students in full-time jobs of the relevance of their studies.

Each of these developments has had a profound impact on the structure and content of courses and given fresh impetus to the discussion and modification of curricula and teaching methods in polytechnics, universities and colleges of further education. The editor and authors of the books in this series have made a deliberate attempt to respond to these changes.

The books set out to provide a comprehensive and up-to-date introduction to the ideas and methods of their subjects for specialist and non-specialist students in fields such as business and management studies, social science and administration. Their aim is to help students who have little or no previous knowledge of them to achieve a mastery of the scope and basic techniques of their subjects and to use them critically and with imagination for further study or for practical professional applications. They also seek to make some contribution to discussions of teaching and learning problems in their field.

Many introductory books present their subjects as a coherent body of knowledge of which the logic is self-evident and the concepts and methods clear to the careful reader. Students do not always find this so. Confronted as they are by a well-established discipline which has developed a particular method that may not bear any obvious relationship to the way in which they have been accustomed to think or to realities as they see them, students often have difficulty in comprehending the significance and detail of the forms of analysis it employs.

The editor and authors of the series felt that they should not take for granted the 'self-evident logic' of their subjects, but try to demonstrate to readers the ways in which their disciplines provide an effective framework for the analysis of problems in their field. When abstractions or concepts are introduced their functions and limitations are explained. Where methods or techniques are described the authors show why they take the form they do and the ways in which they may be used for particular tasks of analysis.

Students often criticise courses because their subjects or parts of them do not have any obvious, or immediate, practical applications. They may present what appear to be unnecessarily complicated ways of dealing with quite straightforward problems or, paradoxically, they may be regarded as over-simplifying or ignoring difficulties which are experienced in real situations. Criticisms of this sort are due to misunderstandings about the nature of subjects. Systems of knowledge provide generalisations which are derived from a variety of abstractions and models. Some of these yield tools of description and analysis that have direct applications. Others suggest ways of looking at problems that, however fruitful, may have only limited or indirect applications.

The authors have tried to make clear the relevance of their subjects. Where concepts and methods have direct applications they show how, and under what circumstances, they can usefully be applied. Where they are of indirect use they show how a process of simplification may isolate and draw attention to the important characteristics of a complex problem, or how the study of complicated or abstract aspects of a problem may throw fresh light on it.

The authors have rejected a view, reflected in many basic textbooks, that students at an introductory level should concentrate on 'learning up' the information and techniques of their subjects and not be troubled with discussions of concepts and analytical method. This 'descriptive' approach, which divorces the study of techniques from that of conceptual and analytical structures, makes it more rather than less difficult for students to appreciate how a technique has developed, why it takes a particular form and how it functions. As a result students can spend a considerable time trying to understand, with limited success, a method of describing and presenting information or a method of analysis and fail to achieve any real facility in using it. The discussion of concepts and analytical method also acquaints a student with some of the difficulties and controversies surrounding the ideas and techniques he is studying. Without such knowledge he is unlikely to appreciate their limitations or establish any real ability to discriminate between alternative approaches and methods.

One of the more important aims of education is to develop a student's capacity to formulate and solve theoretical and practical problems. It is clear that few business and administrative problems are in practice separable into the neat categories represented by disciplines such as economics, accounting, law, sociology, psychology and computing. But most courses are based on combinations of studies in these and similar discrete disciplines which are rarely effectively integrated. It is recognised that the development of bodies of knowledge which provide rigorous rather than superficial integrative approaches will be a long and difficult task. The editor and authors of the books in this series are aware of this problem and within their limitations have attempted to indicate points at which contributions from other disciplines are necessary to the analysis of the problems with which they are dealing. It is thus hoped that in the long run the series will make some contribution to the development of interdisciplinary approaches.

The problems outlined above are common in the teaching and learning of many subjects which, although emerging historically as systems for analysing and solving practical problems, have developed advanced methodologies and a logical order of presentation that may not bear an obvious relation to the practical problems with which they are supposed to be concerned.

Sociology has proved in recent years to be an outstandingly popular field of interest for both students and 'laymen'. This may be partly due to a growing awareness of the significance of social relationships and structures as factors in understanding human activities and problems and partly to concern about developments and problems in contemporary society. But all too frequently those who approach the subject have difficulties in grasping its scope and complexity. It prescribes neither objective solutions nor simple programmes. It may appear to put forward unusually complex concepts to explain apparently simple phenomena, to employ unnecessarily specialised terminology or even to be a mere extension of radical, left-wing political science. In its analysis of human behaviour and structures sociology is concerned to make explicit the assumptions, which may be historically and socially determined, through which social systems and action have evolved, and this may confront students not only with a rigorous discipline but with the problems of making major adjustments to their own frames of reference. The authors have sought to provide a rigorous foundation in industrial sociology in a form that the student who masters the book will not only have a grasp of specific problems and methods in this field but also a basis for a more adequate understanding of the nature of contemporary sociology.

The editor and authors of the books in this series are conscious of their limitations in attempting to implement their ideas in writing and teaching and do not suppose that their presentation will solve students' learning problems. They do not ignore the critical importance of motivation and sustained and disciplined study as factors in effective learning. But they felt that if subjects were presented in a way that made their form and justification explicit rather than implicit this would aid teaching and learning.

In seeking to achieve their aims the books in the series have been subjected to a great deal of critical scrutiny. Each is written by more than one author. This has enabled authors to combine a comparison of views with a considerable, and sometimes uncomfortable, degree of mutual criticism. The editor and authors have all, in recent years, had considerable experience of designing and teaching new CNAA honours degree, diploma or professional courses. Their manuscripts have been discussed with colleagues in education and the professions and have been tested in classes with students.

My thanks as editor are owed to the authors who responded to my request to write the books in the form that I have outlined. This has involved them in an extremely demanding process. The fact that we shared some basic assumptions about education and learning was of great help. The editors and staff of Macmillan with whom we have worked have showed great patience and could not have done more in difficult dircumstances to encourage the series. My thanks are also due to George Brosan, Maurice Peston and Bruce May, who through many discussions have significantly influenced my educational ideas, and to my wife Diane, who has kept a discerning eye on my activities and the progress of the series.

ALAN HALE

ACKNOWLEDGEMENTS

The authors and publishers wish to thank the following, who have kindly given permission for the use of copyright material:

George Allen & Unwin (Publishers) Ltd and the University of California Press for an extract from page 367 of *British Factory – Japanese Factory* (1973) by Ronald Dore.
Cambridge University Press for material from *Household and Family in Past Time* (1972), edited by P. Laslett.
Penguin Books Ltd and Harper & Row Inc. for a table on page 158 from *Emile Durkheim, His Life and Work, A Historical and Critical Study*, by Steven Lukes (Allen Lane 1973/Peregrine Books 1975) © Steven Lukes, 1973.

Contents

Introduction

This book is the product of several years' experience teaching sociology both to sociology students and to non-sociologists, particularly business studies students. The central organising perspective used is the notion of the free market, and the way it has developed, especially in the British context, indeed perhaps only to its fullest extent in nineteenth-century England. The main idea is to show the ways in which the structures arise which constrain the social activities of individuals and therefore to demonstrate the need for an awareness of what causes these structures to develop and change. The emphasis on structure is complemented by a treatment of ideology and legitimation which relates systems of social justifications to these underlying structures. This perspective in our view is important not only to an understanding of sociology as a discipline but also to an understanding of what sociology has to offer to business studies students. The emphasis is clearly not on practical problem solution in such areas as organisational design, motivating the work-force or selecting new recruits. The major objective is to alert students to wider issues about the nature of society and the changing context of business. It is seen as the appropriate underpinning for further study in industrial sociology, industrial relations and, in other contexts, for sociological theory as well.

We recognise that this approach 'ignores' many of the key concepts, such as role, socialisation, community, etc., which are central to most introductory sociology textbooks. However, the continuity we hope we have achieved should more than compensate those who wish to understand problems of industrial enterprises in their contemporary social and political environments. In the cause of brevity we have also omitted several topics currently occupying the limelight in sociology. For example, we have not made an explicit analysis of the changing role of women in industrial society. This is not out of malevolence, but a belief that the application of the class/market model presented here can account for such changes, and that the understanding of the basic processes of market society must come first.

We might well have extended our treatment to illustrate how the ideology of the nuclear family became used as an ideological justification for the exclusion of women from certain privileged labour markets. The Factory

Acts, Ten Hours Act, and the acts regulating hours of work, particularly night-work, can be seen as state interventions to ensure that women were kept out of certain sectors of the labour force and confined to positions chiefly concerned with the reproduction of labour power. Market society depended upon a plentiful supply of labour prepared and able to work, such a labour force depended upon a particular pattern of exploitation of women via unpaid housework. This text has chosen not to look at sex as the critical variable: that remains an essential second step in analysis if we wish to understand the functioning of particular social arrangements in contemporary society. The major issues we raise and discuss are thought to effect everybody, although particular qualities of groups, of which sex is one, obviously mediate the consequences of the changes outlined.

Finally a definite attempt has been made to relate the sociological approach to the problems tackled by positive economics. We believe that while sociology has a distinctive emphasis, it does not have a distinctive area of investigation, but in its various areas overlaps with economics, law, politics, psychology and history. Without accepting the thesis that economic requirements determine the forms of social arrangements we have considered that this provides the appropriate organising argument to integrate the major sociological theories about the nature of advanced society.

The text is a genuine collaboration and we have discussed and reworked each chapter together to endeavour to ensure that a unified perspective emerges. We hope this comes out. The number of people who have influenced our thinking is considerable, particularly students who have suffered earlier versions of this approach; we have learnt much from them.

1
Sociology and Industrial Behaviour

Why and in what ways is a sociological perspective important to students of the business world? The argument here will be that the sociological perspective can be useful in two ways. First, certain concrete problem situations within the context of business organisations are only understandable in the light of the social context of the participants and their pictures of the social world. Second, the sociological perspective suggests that the methods of producing goods and services are not totally determined by criteria of technical efficiency but are also critically affected by the historical period in which they emerge, the systems of ideas, priorities and values present in the wider social setting and by the interests of the parties who benefit from these particular arrangements. It is not the purpose of this book to write a critique of current business practices or, equally, a defence of those practices, but rather to examine the way these practices are related to other factors in society. Why and how far profit-maximisation has become important as a principle of economic organisation is the problem from the sociological viewpoint, not whether it is morally right or wrong. The problem of the values of sociologists and in particular of the authors of this introduction to sociology will be returned to after the attempt has been made to communicate a feel for some of the problems sociology can help illuminate, and some of the different styles sociologists use in their analyses.

Piece-work and girl workers

Business organisations are concerned with the transformation of raw materials and labour resources into some form of good or service. It is of critical importance for competitive businesses that the amount of raw materials, labour and capital resources used in the production of these goods and services should be minimised, and whatever perspective is adopted, if everything else is equal, it is obviously better to use less labour than more to produce a given output. The problem is to determine what strategies are available to the organisation to obtain the greatest production from their labour resources. Or to rephrase this, how can organisations motivate their work-force and bring together the workers' interests and managerial interests in high output? The simplest approach has argued that if pay is linked to output so that higher output brings higher pay, people see that it is in their interests to produce more as this leads to higher earnings, which can be exchanged for the goods and services they value. The most straightforward system for linking pay to performance is straight piece-work: a certain amount is paid for every item processed. The clothing industry uses this type of system, and a worker's wage is calculated by taking the number of pieces of work done – garments finished, buttonholes made, or hems put up might be the pieces of work – and multiplying the price for one piece by the number produced. The theoretical assumptions underlying wage systems of this kind are very simple, namely people are interested in making more money and will put out more effort at work if they see that it leads to higher earnings. Both these assumptions seem to be commonsense assumptions and do not involve any problems; actually the behaviour of people at work is only very rarely understandable in terms of such a simple model of motivation.

For a variety of reasons piece-work and bonus schemes which offer more money for more output have become particularly well established in Lancashire, especially among those industries employing large numbers of female employees. This is mainly a legacy of the cotton industry in this area. In a great number of firms these systems of payment appear to work fairly well and the simple psychological model that people work to earn money and will work harder if they can earn more money is supported. In certain circumstances, however, some groups of workers do not seem to respond in the usual way. How can this deviation be explained. Millward (1968) studied three firms in this area, two engaged in the electronics industry and a data processing organisation. The workers involved in the study were all women and it emerged that for a certain group of these women the bonus schemes did not seem to be working in the manner intended. Within the groups of young girls, many workers were not attempting to increase their earnings by increasing output but seemed to be content to aim for relatively low output and earnings targets. What was it about these girls that made the 'money model of motivation' not very helpful as an explanation of their behaviour with respect to levels of output under the bonus system? The answer is very simple: the model of motivation, implicit in the payment schemes, designed to encourage higher production, took no account of the customs of the neighbourhood from which the firms drew their young labour forces. The girls were not acting irrationally, nor did they attach any less value to money than other workers in the firm; the difference lay in the way in which the effort and money wage were related for these girls.

Among young people in these areas, but obviously elsewhere as well, the community had certain customs which regulated the disposal of the girl's earnings while she still lived at home. Essentially, for the first couple of years after leaving school, and particularly in the first few months, when earnings are a low percentage of adult earnings, the girls in these areas adhered to the custom of 'giving in' their wages to their mothers. For the first months at work the girls did not have rights to their pay packets but took them home and handed them over unopened; their mothers would then return to them pocket money. The money a girl received back from her mother was unlikely to vary radically according to her earnings, indeed, it was much more usual for the pocket money to be a fixed amount or vary according to the girl's needs rather than her earnings. It was only when girls made the step from 'giving in' their wage packets to 'going on board', or negotiating a fixed weekly contribution to their mothers for their board and lodging, that the payment system began to have any effect on effort.

The reason the simple model of money motivation is inadequate in this situation is that the person putting in the effort and the person receiving the payment or reward for greater effort are not the same person. Shimmin says,

> Thus in areas where it is customary for young girls to hand the whole of their wages to their mothers, receiving in return a fixed sum as pocket money, it has been found that incentive payment systems are inappropriate unless steps are taken to ensure that each girl actually receives her bonus earnings, e.g. by giving her two wage packets each week, one containing her basic wage to give to her mother, and the other containing her bonus to keep for herself. (1962, p. 124)

The recommendation implicit in this quotation from Shimmin highlights the problem of the values of the social scientist even at the most elementary level. If the business firm adopts such a policy of two wage packets it is undermining the customs of the local community which favours the continuing dependence of the child during its first months at work. The sociologist cannot in his role as sociologist make this choice; he can only present evidence of the likely consequences of changes one way or the other. The problem is not, however, this simple as the sociologist must necessarily select what he studies and what aspects he emphasises and here the role of his private values cannot be ignored. The sociologist, having only limited resources and relatively unlimited potential avenues of exploration, has to make a choice about what he studies and how he studies it. Certain understandings exist between sociologists which suggest that the sociologist should seek to make explicit the ways in which his own values have influenced his selection of topics of research. It is certainly important to know why the sociologist has selected his problem as this aids in the evaluation of the generality of his conclusions. It is not very sensible, however, to argue that because the values of sociologists are not one's own that their findings are not true. The question should rather be whether there is anything about the explanation which suggests that certain important factors at work in the situation under examination have been ignored or underemphasised.

To return to the Lancashire lasses, the main idea of this example is to show that simple psychological models are often inadequate on their own as explanations of behaviour. The behaviour of these girls at work can only be understood if an adequate account is taken of the ways they are treated at home. More generally, sociology alerts one to look for the ways in which the demands placed on people by their participation in one part of their social life are affected by the demands placed on them by their participation elsewhere. People occupy a series of positions, at work, at home, among groups of friends, for example. When they are at work they are faced by one set of people who expect them to behave in certain ways, and who, if these expectations are met, will then behave in definite ways towards them. The example shows the way in which expectations of the girls in their roles as workers and as daughters are incompatible with one another.

All this seems like common sense, there is no need for sociology, it is all just common sense! Certainly, now that this custom of handing the wage packet over has been described, it needs no peculiarly sociological sophistication to see why the bonus schemes were not working as intended. This misses the point; it was only by the application of a sociological concept, in this case the idea that behaviour at work depends on status at home, that the evidence came to light which explained why the girls did not respond according to the simple model which claims the opportunity to earn more money will draw forth more effort.

Street Corner Society

The next explanation seems to fly in the face of common sense, and also suggests a slightly different way in which a sociological perspective can be used to help understand a certain pattern of behaviour. W. F. Whyte describes the activities of an Italian street-corner gang in Boston during the late 1930s and early 1940s (Whyte, 1955). He went to live in the community where the street-boys lived and sought to become actively involved in their day to day life. Despite his Harvard University background, Whyte was accepted in the neighbourhood, and particularly by one group of street-corner boys, and he describes and suggests explanations for the behaviour he observed. In the last example, the research problem was fairly narrowly defined, and the emergence of particular pieces of information allowed certain ideas to be tested. This example is drawn from a different type of investigation, a much broader and less structured investigation in which ideas and theories are generated rather than rigorously subjected to critical appraisal. The behaviour to be examined here is the bowling activities of the gang of street-corner boys, who were all young men aged between twenty and thirty-five, living in an Italian neighbourhood in one of the rundown areas of the central city. Bowling involves the rolling of a ball down a special alley at a set of ten pins with the object of knocking down as many of them as possible with two balls. The game is won by the individual or team that knocks most pins down with a given number of balls. It is a game which requires a certain amount of skill in the control of the ball and knowledge of what sort of bowl with the ball will knock down pins or skittles standing at the other end of the alley. It would seem that bowling is a skill that comes with practice, and at which certain people, by virtue of greater skills, will normally be expected to beat other people with lesser skills.

At the beginning of one winter Doc, the leader of the Norton Street Gang, arranged a bowling match against the Italian Community Club, whom the Nortons considered to be distinctly 'high-tones' and somewhat snobbish and conceited. Doc selected a team from among the gang and the Nortons went on to score a decisive victory over the Italian Community Club. This caused considerable jubilation and began a period of intensive activity in the bowling alley. Over the winter the gang met two or three times a week and picked teams among themselves; they played for the price of the game, which ensured that everyone was interested in making the teams as even as possible. Over the winter activity climaxed in a series of Saturday night individual challenge matches and matches against other cliques and gangs. A regular team emerged for these inter-group matches and other members of the gang had a chance to bowl only if a regular member was absent. This aroused feelings of resentment among the excluded bowlers, some of whom felt that they could beat some of the regular team bowlers. A special challenge match was arranged and despite the early prominence of the leading advocate of changing the team, the regular team all outperformed the challengers. Then Alec, the leading challenger, offered a challenge to Long John, who was a regular first teamer, and succeeded in beating him on several successive occasions. However, on subsequent match occasions Long John continued to play for the team, and after some support from Doc, the gang leader, managed to halt Alec's progress and defeat him as often as not in individual matches.

Why should this behaviour at the bowling alley interest the sociologist? Whyte shows it is interesting as an example of the dynamics of leadership in the gang and the effects that status in the group have on level of performance. The group did not emerge as a bowling club, the leaders were not chosen on the basis of the prowess at the alley, but despite this, the clique's leading personnel became the members of the first team on major match occasions and justified this by their superior performance when the pressure was on. The records for the winter showed a strong relationship between social position and bowling performance. As Whyte says, 'Bowling scores did not fall automatically into this pattern. There were certain customary ways of behaving which exerted pressure upon the invididual' (1955, p. 23). The failure of Long John, one of the group of leaders in the Norton Street Gang, to meet Alec's challenge is an interesting example of the interplay between status in the group and performance at a group activity and shows how leadership status can improve performance on valued group activities. Whyte argues,

> It is significant that, in making his challenge Alec selected Long John instead of Doc, Danny or Mike. It was not that Long John's bowling ability was uncertain. His average was about the same as that of Doc or Danny and better than that of Mike. As a member of the top group but not a leader in his own right, it was his social position that was vulnerable. (p. 22)

It was when Alec and Long John acted outside the group that it became possible for Alec to win. The other leaders, however, felt that Alec should not be allowed to beat Long John with such regularity. Accordingly Doc talked to Long John: 'I talked to him. I made him see that he *should* bowl better than Alec. I persuaded him that he was really the better bowler. Now you watch them the next time out' (Whyte, p. 22). After this Long John did manage to match Alec's performances.

Whyte shows the ways in which the giving and withdrawing of support by the leaders, coupled with the extent and ferocity of their heckling, were sufficient to make sure that the social structure of the group, its internal hierarchy of status, was reflected in performance in bowling. Again in this example the way in which the social organisation surrounds the individual's activities is critical to the understanding of why the individual acts as he does. In the first example, it was shown that roles in separate areas of an individual's life are interdependent and behaviour in one role may depend on demands made by another role. In this example it is shown how within one area of social life the expectations of appropriate behaviour are vital to the understanding of what is going on. When people deviate from the expected patterns of behaviour, or norms, associated with a role the people who interact with them in that role utilise sanctions, both negative and positive rewards, to bring behaviour back into line. The example also suggests that who controls the rewards is critical, or in other words the norms of a group may not be equally important to all members. The expectations which govern behaviour may be shared expectations, but the extent to which these expectations are equally distributed among members of the group is problematic, as is their belief in the justice of these expectations. In voluntary groupings presumably people leave if their behaviour is not perceived as sufficiently in line with what other members expect and the members make it uncomfortable to stay. Alternatively people may perceive these expectations of others as unjust; in this situation they may leave, if that is a possibility, or they may stay and seek to alter the internal organisation of the group.

Higher Civil Servants

The third example will be taken from Kelsall's (1956) study of higher civil servants in Britain. Kelsall was interested in the types of people who entered and achieved career success in the Administrative Class of the Home Civil Service. His problem stems from the sociologist's continuing concern to find out not only who has power in the community but by what routes they achieve their positions of preeminence. The Administrative Class of the Civil Service is immensely powerful as a result of its policy planning functions. While theoretically subject to ministerial control, the virtual monopoly of the knowledge necessary for decision making which the Administrative Class commands ensures that on many matters it is what the civil servant recommends that is decisive in forming government policy.

Kelsall sets out to examine the ways in which civil servants are selected and to see whether there have been any noticeable trends in the social origins of recruits to the Administrative Class since open competition was introduced by the Gladstone administration in 1870. In his own words,

> The purpose of the present study of this key profession is to provide answers to questions of the following kind. From which social strata is the Higher Administrative Class now being drawn, and what changes have taken place in this respect over the last eighty years or so? (p. 3).

In the interwar years there was a radical change in the procedure by which candidates for positions were assessed. Prior to the 1914–18 war the principle of selection was purely that of academic merit, candidates competed in a series of public examinations and vacancies in the Service were filled according to the order of marks obtained in these examinations. In the 1920s, an interview was added; initially canvassed as a viva voce, or verbal examination, to check that no 'mere smatterers' were admitted, it came to serve the following purposes:

> Qualities might be shown in this way which could not be tested in a written examination, but which should be useful to public servants. These apparently included alertness, intelligence and intellectual outlook; presence of mind and nervous equipoise were also important, and candidates who showed nervousness under interview conditions might, in fact, be held to lack a valuable quality. (Kelsall, 1956, p. 69)

The problem under scrutiny here is in what ways did such a change in the selection procedure operate to change the nature of the people admitted to the higher Civil Service? There were many objections to these changes in procedure, but most were politically naive and failed to halt their implementation. And indeed over the fifteen-year period of open competition between the wars the weight attached to the interview was substantially increased by reductions in the marks which could be obtained on the written examinations.

Kelsall attempts to assess the validity of the innovation. He presents evidence that suggests that there was no perceived need for the change among senior civil servants generally; they did not perceive any falling off of standards among new entrants. He then examines the success records of entrants in the period with the interview and the period before and finds that there is no appreciable difference in terms of the time taken to reach certain ranks and that the performance on the written examination was a considerably better predictor of future performance than the interview.

To return to the central question, did this change in recruitment procedures result in a change in the social characteristics of the intake of civil servants? Prior to the 1914–18 war the intake had been predominantly from Oxford and to a lesser extent Cambridge, and not surprisingly most of these candidates came from what are loosely called public schools. The idea that the interview was deliberately designed to reinforce this bias was dismissed. Sir Warren Fisher disposed of the idea thus: 'I think the information as to a person's origin is quite irrelevant. When I am looking at a fellow really I am not concerned with what his father was: I am concerned with what he is!' (Kelsall, 1956, p. 73). And in the absence of evidence to the contrary most people accepted that the selection procedures had no inherent bias. Evidence which might have challenged the whole basis of the interview was not systematically explored. The fact that candidates who presented themselves for interview on more than one occasion scored very appreciably different marks on the different occasions puzzled the people responsible for selection, but did not lead to questions about the reliability of the fifteen-minute interview.

In retrospect, however, the whole procedure looked suspect, because of the shortness of the interview, and the interview strategies – 'My own plan is to fish about for a topic in which the candidate is interested' – and the composition of the interview board – 'We try to choose people who have broad sympathies. . . . You get the advice of your friends; you get people you know. . . . You give them a trial trip.' All the evidence suggests that these interviews were most probably highly unreliable and not valid as predictors of future behaviour. That would not particularly matter if they were random in their effects, that is if the chance of a bad interview score was equal for all candidates. The data, however, suggests that in the interwar period the interview was probably tending to modify the type of school from which entrants came and in the direction of increasing the weight of the leading boarding schools. The possibility certainly exists that the interview introduced a systematic bias which favoured the socially advantaged group of public school graduates.

For one year, 1938, Kelsall obtained a sample of unsuccessful candidates, to supplement the samples of successful entrants on which the rest of his analysis is based. If he had had samples of successful candidates only it would have been impossible for him to eliminate the hypothesis that the predominance of public school boys was a result of a failure of other types of graduates to offer themselves for examination. With the data on interview and examination marks for the unsuccessful candidates as well as the successful candidates he was able to answer more directly some questions about the consequences of the interview. He split the sample of 278 British educated male candidates into two groups, one coming from secondary schools administered by local education authorities (which were generally grammar schools), the other from independent and direct grant schools (generally public schools). On this basis he found no appreciable difference in examination scores, nor did he when using boarding/non-boarding as the division. In 1938 at least there appeared to be no difference in examination performance on the basis of schools of origin. This picture is radically altered when scores on the interview are examined; here the socially advantaged groups, i.e. public schools and boarding, outperformed their rivals significantly. Public school candidates tended to get appreciably higher marks on the interview, especially if they had attended boarding schools. Finally, Kelsall compared the group who were selected as a result of the interview with those who were rejected on this basis. Of 76 successful candidates 18 would, on the basis of examinations alone, have been displaced by 18 others. Nearly 24 per cent of successful candidates, therefore, owed their success to the interview. Kelsall then proceeded to compare these two groups. There were more Oxford and Cambridge men in the interview successes, more boarding-school men, and fewer from local authority education schools. Although not statistically significant the direction of all these findings lends weight to the hypothesis that there was a systematic bias present. One last step corroborated this: the occupations of the fathers of these candidates was obtained from birth registration records and arranged according to the Registrar-General's Social Classes, it was then found that 13 of the successful interviewees had fathers in Classes I and II while only 7 in the unsuccessful group came from these categories and this difference is statistically significant, i.e. beyond the normal bounds of chance variation.

Kelsall has thus established a very strong case for the argument that the change in selection procedures had the unintended consequence of further intensifying the tendency to select higher civil servants from a particularly narrow group of educational channels and a homogeneous social background.

Obviously if one is concerned about equality of opportunity or the responsiveness of the State to the needs of the working class this shift towards recruiting more exclusively from the upper classes may be seen as retrograde. But, however these findings are interpreted, the sociological perspective has demonstrated that there were factors at work, determining who was selected, which altered the intentions of those who constructed the selection mechanisms in ways of which they were unaware. This example does, however, highlight one problem which sociology faces: many situations which are of interest to the sociologist are not open to his investigation; the discovery of latent characteristics of social processes may threaten the continuity of those processes, or alternatively the characteristics of the social processes may be known to the powerful, but denied to the powerless and the powerful may not desire the breakdown of this insulation. In circumstances like this, where the sociologist is denied access to situations in ways which permit him to use his most sophisticated techniques of analysis, he must proceed to use methods of less elegance and vigour if he considers the problem sufficiently important. Sociologists are hostages of the society in which they live: they are not entirely free to poke where they will and turn over all the stones they would choose. Thus Kelsall was allowed statistics on unsuccessful candidates for only one year, and that was for a period nearly twenty years earlier. The systematic non-availability of information must bias the sociologist's approach. Sociologists tend to have suspicious minds and the danger is that the blockages in the flow of data become obsessive and the sociologist comes to see every closed door as shutting him out from the important processes by which power in his society is exercised. The problem of the sociologist's values should be understood in this light.

Payment Systems and Systems of Belief

The fourth example brings back into focus the problem of payment systems. In an article Hilde Behrend (1959) asks a series of questions about the mechanisms which serve to justify the continued use of incentive schemes. Behrend conducted a survey of firms using payment by results schemes. She notes that statistical data on the relative productivity of labour under payment by results and straight time rates which are capable of sustaining rigorous scrutiny do not exist. The major reason is that because pay system design is critical to operating success, differences in the incentive system are virtually impossible to isolate. The most common problem is that changes in payment systems take place as accompaniments to changes in methods, including perhaps the introduction of methods study. She found that despite the lack of hard evidence to support their contentions most managers in her sample believed payment by results raised labour productivity; some were even prepared to offer estimates of by how much! She concludes,

> It thus appears that in most firms the use of incentive schemes rests on faith in – rather than proof of – the effectiveness of financial incentives; the results *expected* from payment by results have acquired the status of *achieved* results in spite of the lack of factual proof of the achievement. (p. 138)

This poses the problem of why, in the absence of evidence to confirm their efficiency, management attaches such importance to these incentive schemes. Behrend outlines the way that the belief system arises which supports the use of such schemes; the lack of evidence to support the instrumentality of the schemes leads to a heightened sense that an ideology, or acceptable explanation, is necessary. The argument proceeds on three postulates: first, that standards of effort can be altered, second, that financial motives are more important than non-financial motives, and finally, the best way to harness the financial motive is to link pay to output. These postulates, however, are combined in such a way, in the minds of many managers, that 'payment by results' seems natural and synonymous with 'financial incentives'. Moreover the belief in this argument seems to develop into a concomitant belief that workers have different *habitual* standards of effort on piece rates than on time rates. This belief is not purely one held by management, it is one that many workers share. However, the reason they believe it is different; they believe that a different wage effort bargain has been struck and they feel morally obliged to perform at a higher level than previously. The proposition becomes not 'rates of output are higher' but 'rates of output *ought* to be higher'. In this way the status of the propositions has changed from three hypotheses united in a testable theory into three axioms in a body of beliefs. Exceptions are explained away and a mythical average worker is expected to behave like this; something is wrong with society in general or the worker in particular if he does not.

It is possible to argue that the last few years have seen the belief system implicit in payment by results transformed into a full-blown ideology which justifies behaviour in accordance with the basic postulates of the belief system. It could be argued that people today are more interested in money or financial incentives than ever before because they have come to accept the managerial ideology which suggests this is the legitimate motivation.

Behrend's problem highlights a different order of problems to those of the first three examples, where the major emphasis was on the way that external social factors help to determine the behaviour of the individual. This example suggests that the sociologist is also interested in the systems of beliefs which are current in society and which help members of the society to order reality into manageable units. These systems of beliefs are to a large extent shared, but one critical question is how far the system of beliefs common in a society is based on the interests and interpretations of one sector of that society which by its prominence transmits these beliefs to other sectors where they become justifications for preferring certain courses of action to others. Once again the problem of the sociologist's values is critical; to examine systems of belief in terms of a rationalistic calculus is unlikely to lead to the preservation of the beliefs. The sociologist is more likely to uncover the myths of society than to find eternal verities of human existence. If any examination of belief systems threatens their existence, the sociologist must be a radical or eschew the public exposition of research findings in this area. The next chapter returns to this problem and examines how sociology was born as a critique of the individualistic ethic of *laissez-faire*.

To summarise, in this introduction no attempt has been made at an exhaustive delineation of the boundaries of sociology. Rather than follow any of the three strategies suggested by Inkeles (1964) in his *What Is Sociology?* in this chapter we have attempted to provide a sample of sociology. It is hoped that the reader will find these problems interesting in themselves and be sufficiently impressed with the light thrown on them by these pieces of sociological research to believe that sociology can be useful in understanding business behaviour. It is easier to say when something is not sociology than it is to say when it is, certainly cut and dried rules cannot be laid down which distinguish between sociology and its nearest neighbours, history, anthropology, economics and politics. Sociology is interested in the stages by which the social formations under scrutiny came into existence, history is obviously concerned with similar processes. History is no longer merely the study of unique events, nor can sociology completely ignore the unique. Similarly sociologists are critically concerned with the distribution of both power and wealth, and it becomes difficult to delimit watertight areas for political scientists and economists to work in uncontaminated by the occasional foray by inquisitive sociologists. The distinction between anthropology and sociology is equally tenuous; anthropologists have been more interested in pre-literate societies and their methods of investigation have been refined to meet problems of research in this environment. This distinction on the basis of society studied or methods used is fragile and at many points sociologists and anthropologists are indistinguishable. To define sociology in terms of the Grand Masters is similarly fraught with difficulties. Who are the fathers of the discipline? Inkeles, for example, pays very scant regard to Marx and the influence of Marx; in the European context this appears ridiculous, but the critical point is that the founders of sociology are bound to be selected according to certain preconceptions about what good sociology should be.

Here the strategy suggested is that sociology is unified by two pervasive qualities, the rejection of the adequacy of common sense as an explanation for behaviour in society, and the belief that behaviour is determined by influences which are outside the individual. Sociology stands opposed to the commonsense proposition that the behaviour of people in groups can be explained in terms of the motivations and emotions of the individuals alone. All the examples used in this chapter suggest that to utilise a sociological perspective alerts the investigator to the possibility that events are systematically patterned in ways that are not clearly perceived by the participants. In the next chapters the position of commonsense explanations will be examined and it will be demonstrated that commonsense explanations tend to be rationalisations of current arrangements rather than accurate models of social behaviour.

Suggested Further Reading

Berger, P. L. (1963) *Invitation to Sociology*, chap. 1 (Harmondsworth, Middlx: Penguin Books).

Douglas, J. D. (1970) *The Relevance of Sociology* (New York: Appleton Century Crofts).

Durkheim, E. (1962) *Rules of Sociological Method*, ed. G. Catlin (Chicago: University of Chicago Press).

— (1964) *Division of Labour* (New York: Free Press).

— (1968) *Suicide: A Study in Sociology* (London: Routledge & Kegan Paul).

Inkeles, A. (1964) *What is Sociology?* chaps 1 and 2 (Englewood Cliffs, N.J.: Prentice-Hall.

Bibliography

Behrend, H. (1959) 'Financial Incentives as the Expression of a System of Beliefs', *British Journal of Sociology* (July 1959) pp. 137–47.

Inkeles, A. (1964) *What is Sociology?* (Englewood Cliffs, N.J.: Prentice-Hall).

Kelsall, R. K. (1956) *Higher Civil Servants in Britain* (London: Routledge & Kegan Paul).

Millward, N. (1968) 'Family Status and Behaviour at Work', *Sociological Review* 16, pp. 149–64.

Shimmin, S. (1962) 'Extra-mural Factors Influencing Behaviour at Work', *Occupational Psychology* 36, pp. 124–32.

Whyte, W. F. (1955) *Street Corner Society* (Chicago: University of Chicago Press).

2 Industrialisation as a 'Phenomenon'

It has been argued that one of the major contributions of the discipline of sociology to the student of business studies is its ability to make the student aware that certain concrete problems within the context of business organisations are only understandable in the context of the participants and their images of the social world. Additionally it has been argued that economic production is not just determined by considerations of technical efficiency but also by extra-economic factors with which anyone who wishes to understand the process of production should be acquainted. The central theme of the last chapter was the capacity of the discipline to provide explanations of problems and situations which are at variance with common sense.

'Common sense' is that which we 'take for granted'. The aim of this chapter is similar to that of the last. Since we live in an industrial society the socially acceptable behaviours and the definitions of reality given to us constitute part of our common sense. For instance, we assume when employed by an industrial firm that it should 'make a profit' and that it should utilise its factors of production towards this goal of profitability. It seems to out commonsense view that such actions are in some way 'natural' or part of 'human nature'. The theme of this chapter is to put forward the view that such seemingly 'natural' actions, as making a profit and optimally utilising resources, are not products of a universal human nature, but are products of specific historical and social conditions. Those everyday commonsense actions, such as 'going to work' and 'getting to work *on time*', are not everyday occurrences for those who live outside the orbit of industrialism, but revolutionary and often painfully acquired pieces of behaviour. Pre-industrial societies did not have the notion of 'going to work' because work was not a distinct activity separated from leisure, house and family. 'Getting to work on time' was not a similar experience because time as a closely calculated phenomenon did not exist, 'time' was the rhythm of nature, the movements of hunted animals and the comings and goings of the seasons. So unique is the world of technology that we take for granted, that to appreciate this uniqueness we must suspend our commonsense views of reality and define as 'problematic' those things which we so readily accept.

Many of the things that we take for granted in our industrial society, inanimate sources of power, rapid transportation, media of instant communication, the separation of work from leisure, are revolutionary innovations. The phenomenon called the 'Industrial Revolution' was a *total* break with all past human history, it implied that all the past accumulated commonsense of human experience was rendered redundant.

The first step should be to define what we mean by the concept of industry. The sociologist W. E. Moore defines the term 'industry' as 'the fabrication of raw materials into intermediate components or finished products by primarily mechanical means dependent on inanimate sources of power' (1965, p. 4). Thus industrial technology uniquely substitutes inanimate sources of power for the power derived from human exertion alone. It is true that water-power and wind-power had been used for thousands of years prior to the Industrial Revolution, but what is unique about the advent of steam power, and other mechanical sources of propulsion, is that they release mankind from direct dependence upon nature and her viscissitudes. Because man creates the machinery of power and utilises his knowledge of nature through abstract scientific theories, he is able to reduce his dependence and establish his control over nature. This is not to argue that pre-industrial man did not use technology to mediate between himself and nature, but that controllable inanimate sources of power constitute a radical break in man's history of struggle with his environment.

The anthropologist M. Herskovits argues: 'Between a people and their habitat stands their technology, . . . the more adequate the technology the less direct are the demands made by their environment on the daily life of the people' (1952, p. 73). The revolutionary aspect of industrial technology is the qualitative difference inanimate sources of power make to the insulation of man from his habitat. Such sources allow much greater scope in the location of enterprises and little dependence upon the weather; in short, daily life is no longer geared to the natural environment.

Since this crucial disconnection of daily life from the demands of the environment is a consequence of the advent of inanimate sources of power, we recognise that as a result of this production is freed to base itself upon methods of a large scale. Where wind, water, flood and storm are variables dictating the scope and scale of production, where human power is the primary source of energy, there are obvious limitations on the scale of production; for instance human power must be fed and thus; unless agriculture is mechanised, the feeding of non-agricultural labour power requires such vast labour itself that it sets immediate limits to the scale of non-agricultural production. For example, it could be argued that the ultimate dependence of Rome upon slavery as a source of agricultural production set stringent limits to the scope of Roman industry since a valuable piece of capital equipment such as a slave must consume considerable amounts to continue production and this leaves little over for investment in industry. Following Aron, we can define the possession of large-scale industry as the most characteristic form of production, as a central fact, common to all industrial societies (Aron, 1967, p. 73). We can explain the arrival of large-scale industry in terms of the advent of inanimate power and can see that both the technological and organisation variables are more or less common to all industrial societies. It should, therefore, prove fruitful to follow Aron's analysis of the implications of large-scale industry as the major source of production in a society, since these implications are also likely to be common to all industrial societies (Aron, 1967, pp. 73–4).

First among these implications is that the industrial enterprise is likely to be separated from the family. This is a factor we so much take for granted that it is part of our stock of common sense. However the progressive separation of the household budget from the industrial enterprise is one of the most significant breaks with the traditional world undertaken by modernity (Weber, 1968, p. 162). This separation is essential if the long-run predictability essential for the calculations of large scale enterprise is to be achieved. The lord of the manor in traditional feudal society 'used' most of the produce for consumption, in his economic behaviour he used the land as an extension of his own wishes.

The weaver in the domestic system employed his family and household as a single unit of production, the family's ability to produce and sell was simultaneously the strength and weakness of the family in the battle to survive – the household unit was the production unit. The Florentine merchant who spent his profits on building a family chapel was not considered to have 'put his hand in the till' as would be a modern company director who spent the company's profits on a private yacht, even if he were a large shareholder in the company. Indeed, many of the recent injunctions against the 'unacceptable face of capitalism' have been made because of infringements of the strict separation of the funds of the enterprise from those of the private individual and his family.

The second characteristic of large-scale production is the introduction of what Aron calls a 'technological division of labour'. Division or differentiation according to functional specialisation is a feature of all societies. Even the least complex societies possess some degree of differentiation even if only on the rudimentary basis of age and sex, i.e. men hunt, women gather and old men think. What is unique to industrial society is the determination of this division of labour by the technological nature of the task at hand. (See Chapter 3 for a contrast between industrial and traditional modes of differentiation and a discussion of the central importance of the concept, traditionalism, in sociological theory.) Each individual is restricted to a specific range of competence, with various degrees of extensiveness (see Friedmann, 1961, chaps 1, 4 and 6), which defines his behaviour, his pace of work, and to a large extent with whom he works. In short, the technical division of labour circumscribes the worker's world, at least his world of work. Technical division of labour means proscription by and subordination to technique. In the work situation the modern industrial worker 'is' what he technically 'does'. The peasant in a traditional society would quite likely combine within his work role the functions of sower and tiller of the land, cart-driver, animal husbandman, toolmaker, teacher of the young and, if little differentiation of the household has taken place, lover of his wife. His work role and his other roles are integrated. How great the contrast with the contemporary specificity of 'capstan-lathe operator' or 'cost accountant'!

Third, the increasing scale of the industrial enterprise, when combined with the large-scale substitution of inanimate sources of power, means that each worker requires a large amount of capital in order for the enterprise to remain 'viable'. This capital must be constantly renewed. The systematic and progressive replenishment of capital is common to all industrial societies.

Aron's fourth characteristic inherent in large-scale production confronts one of the most profound differences between industrial society and its precursors – it is the element of 'rational calculation' and the systematic extension of rational calculation to all realms of existence. It is here that sociology most impinges upon common sense. To make calculations as to which is the most 'economic' type of car, as to which is the most 'profitable' way to invest money, is not a part of human nature, but the product of specific historical circumstances to which we are the heirs. This is not to argue that greed, profiteering and avarice are not to be found universally, albeit in different degrees, in all known societies: what is unique about industrialisation is the extension of a particular mode of calculation to every realm of existence.

Prior to taking up this point on a substantive basis, it is necessary to make a methodological digression. Max Weber sought to build a 'typology' of the forms of action amongst humans that were most amenable to 'understanding'. Weber felt that we share as 'human beings' a capacity to act rationally, thus we can understand other human beings when they act most rationally. For instance, if you know that Fred seeks to catch the number 11 bus at 2.30 more than he wants anything in the world and he gets drunk by 2.00 p.m. and misses the bus, you may define Fred's actions as 'beyond understanding' and thus 'irrational'. The most 'typical' rational behaviour for people who want to catch 2.30 buses more than anything else in the world is not to get passing-out drunk. Weber recognised that actual individual actions consist of a multitude of motives, a mixture of different degrees of rationality. Furthermore, he recognised that there are different types, or different ways of being rational. Consequently, he constructed 'types' of the most typical modes of rationality. Indeed, in real life we do much the same ourselves. We build models in our mind of the most typical modes of action and act upon the expectations these yield. One may build a type, on the basis of past experience, of the following nature:

(1) Doors are oblong constructions with movable wooden centres.
(2) I want to maintain dignity and avoid pain.
(3) In order to gain the motives outlined in (2) I should move the wooden obstacle in (1).

This is a working typification built on an idealised notion of doors. It is a set of working expectations. It is only when one is confronted with something outside the typification – such as 'glass doors' – that one is forced to abandon the typification. What Weber intended was to build such typifications of actions in order that the sociologist could 'understand' other people's actions in so far as they came near, in their real world behaviours, to one of the constructed types of rational action. To go back to the previous example, if Fred had not got drunk he would have been more typically rational and thus more 'understandable' to the observer. The observer does not know all

Fred's inner motivations, like showing off to the barmaid or finding drinks from pewter pots irresistible; he does, however, know the most rational and thus most typical action and find that most understandable.

Weber's four ideal types of rational action were as follows:

(1) Affectual action – this is often of an irrational nature and thus not amenable to typical understanding. For instance, the 'reflexive' eyeblink is beyond the control and the consciousness of the actor and can hardly be seen as motivated or intended and thus cannot be understood. Since this type of behaviour is 'determined by the actor's specific affects and feeling states' it is often too individualised to build 'typifications'.

(2) Traditionally rational action is often on the border of rationality and irrationality. Since such traditional action is purely imitative, just doing what has always been done, and therefore is unreflective, it is in Weber's sense not 'understandable'. In fact a great amount of everyday action tends to be of this nature – indeed it might be more appropriately called 'a-rational' since it is neither affective nor reflectively rational However it can have varying degrees of self-consciousness since adhering to the past is a value in itself. For instance, the conservative might argue that the past was better for people than the present, therefore we should act as people did in the past. This would be a highly self-conscious and motivated attitude. Additionally the 'traditional rationality' type is useful as 'a limiting case', that is to say it is useful as a mark against which to contrast other types of rationality.

(3) Value rational action, to quote Weber, 'is determined by a conscious belief in the value for its own sake of some ethical, aesthetic, religious, or other form of behaviour, independent of its prospects of success.' If someone wants to go to college to 'learn wisdom' and does not consider that getting a degree is any sign of wisdom, he does not consider that it is important that he must earn money when he leaves college, does not consider the veneration of others for a wise man is important, then he holds the value of philosophy for its own sake. All is subordinated to the pursuit of the ultimate value of 'wisdom' at all costs, all else is left unconsidered. The acquisition of knowledge is an end in itself. The religious martyr who sacrifices his life for an ideal and the businessman who wants nothing but the intrinsic satisfaction of belonging to the most powerful corporation in the world at the cost of family and ulcerated stomach both pursue an ideal in itself. They do not calculate the ideal's cost but merely pursue it for its own sake.

(4) Instrumentally rational action is determined by expectations as to the behaviour of objects in the environment and of other human beings: these expectations are used as 'conditions' or 'means' for the attainment of the actor's own rationally pursued and calculated ends (Weber, 1968, pp. 24–6). Unlike the ultimate rationality of the value orientation, the calculative rationality of instrumentality is capable of assessing ends and abandoning them should the costs they entail be too high.

In reality, the concrete actor will embody a mixture of these motivations, for instance his ultimate value may be the 'service of God' and he may employ calculative instrumental rationality to work out the best means towards the service of God.

Weber's types of rationality do however enable us to see some important differences between traditional societies and our own. This is not to say that traditional societies consist solely of people employing exclusively traditional forms of rationality; however the constraints of traditional society did mean that there were limits to the scope of calculative rationality – for example, the fact that most relationships were of a face-to-face continuous nature meant that there were definite constraints upon viewing one's fellows as 'instruments', as objects, to be manipulated for one's own purpose. Since traditional belief systems tended to be oriented towards religious absolutes and since religiosity percolated all forms of social existence, then work itself became shrouded with mystical belief and actual means of doing things took on a sacred character which limited technical innovation. Horton, when comparing the thought structure of African primitive societies with the thought structure of Western science, says:

> What I take to be the key difference is a very simple one. It is that in traditional cultures there is no developed awareness of alternatives to the established body of theoretical tenets; whereas in scientifically oriented cultures such an awareness is highly developed. It is this difference we refer to when we say that traditional cultures are 'closed' and scientifically oriented cultures 'open'. (1970, p. 153)

Whilst it is obvious that there are great differences between an African tribal society and medieval feudalism, what they share is the similarity of cultural closure, the scope for an instrumental view of nature and society is limited by the very lack of alternatives. The revolutionary character of industrial society is that the mental structure of collective thought and the social relationships that people enter into are both 'open' in the sense that both theories about the world and sets of social relationships are but 'alternatives' to other competing theories and relationships. The key to social differentiation, which is a possible description of industrialisation, is that it leads to the break up of 'closure' both of belief systems and social relationships.

The anthropologist Mary Douglas puts the matter well when she says, 'One inevitable by-product of social differentiation is social awareness, self-consciousness about the processes of communal life' (1970, p. 111). To return to the point, if the feature unique to industrialism is the extension of a particular mode of calculation to all realms of existence then we must analyse the conditions which make this instrumental calculative society possible. It is only when there is a break-up of a 'closed' world that 'alternatives' become apparent, it is only possible to choose between alternatives, to weigh up the relative costs of actions, when there are alternatives available. Traditional society can be defined as a 'closed society' in that the choices of views of nature and society are circumscribed by tradition, 'what has been in the past', social roles are circumscribed by birth, appropriate actions defined by custom, all of which have the full weight of community sanctions behind them, and are thus unquestioned, and to think of alternatives constitutes a heresy. Take, for example, the view of the 'material world' held by a majority of 'thinking men' in the early period of feudalism. To them the material world of objects and things, even of nature and the forces of nature, was 'more than a mask, behind which took place all the really important things; it seemed to them to be a language, intended to express by signs a more important reality' (Bloch, 1961, p. 83). A consequence of this was that the observation of the material and natural world, in the scientific sense of measurement, control and calculation, was unimportant, interpretation and search for 'mystic meanings' were the crucial activities. To continue with Bloch's analysis, 'This attitude explains, in part, the inadequacy of men's knowledge of nature which, after all, was not regarded as greatly deserving of attention. Technical progress – sometimes considerable – was mere empiricism' (p. 83).

This is a revealing quotation since it suggests that in spite of considerable technical innovation during the feudal period, it was not considered to be of any great importance. The utilisation of such innovation would require the sort of action upon the world that has been defined as 'instrumental rationality', a willingness to manipulate objects, change them, work out the best, the most productive means of performing a task. In spite of the considerable innovation, such as the stirrup and strip agriculture in the period, it was considered 'mere empiricism', mere playing about with and observation of things, which had little significance. What was important was to look for 'signs' of a God-created cosmos behind the observable, to interpret rather than to act upon. It was a passive acceptance of that 'God-given' reality behind the material world, and to act upon the material world was at worst a heresy, an affront to the God-given order, and at best a futile occupation, since 'reality' was not amenable to man's manipulation. This was the view of thinking men in such a traditional society. Such views did not succeed in discouraging innovation but they did prevent 'innovation', through rational instrumental manipulation, dominating the social fabric. Since the aristocracy and the Church had a monopoly of power, they held a monopoly of the dominant modes of thought and thus could determine what was considered socially important (see Chapter 4). The highest state a man on earth could achieve was the life of monastic withdrawal, of detached contemplation, of 'other-worldly' matters beyond the material world. A society which values such things highest is unlikely to encourage and extend attitudes and actions which seek to change the material world through systematic manipulation of material things. It is precisely the areas which were most resistant to the pressure of traditionalism, the towns, which were the source of technical, social and economic innovation. For the towns were to some extent free from the power of the feudal aristocracy. Similarly, medieval society produced severe limits upon economic actions, constraining the extent of the rational calculative action which we take for granted in modern society.

In medieval society work was seen as sacred, as part of the God-given order, but profit was not. Consequently the pursuit of profit was viewed by the authorities as distinctly ungodly. 'Work was held in respect for its moral importance, as though for its own sake, but gain was to be restricted to what was necessary for upkeep, scaled according to social position' (A. von Martin, 1963, p. 83). Work in such a society was regarded as an ultimate value, each occupation had its place in a 'natural' God-given order, and man by filling this duty, was merely fulfilling his destiny 'in his place'. He should not calculate his worth for it was already prescribed by tradition. Consequently profit, the gain of surplus over the costs of production through the recombination of the factors of production, defies traditional regulation. Sudden profit could mean that the bearer could occupy other than his 'natural place' in society, it could mean change. Thus, gain should be fixed according to the social position of the receiver. Consequently prices, output, labour should all be regulated to ensure that reward should not exceed that which was appropriate to that position. Von Martin sums up this position from the writings of two Catholic divines: 'According to Alexander of Hales and St. Bonaventura, both Franciscans, trade which aims at profit and the accumulation of wealth was illegitimate; they only recognised trade which provided for sustenance and for works of charity' (p. 83).

Most traditional religious orders tended to forbid usury, the lending of money for profit. Since this is so greatly at variance with the actions of the most highly respected of modern institutions, the banks, it provides an excellent example of the revolutionary nature of instrumental calculation when compared to the constraints of the past. Max Weber points out that the Catholic Church, including the Pope, had no scruples about employing usury themselves but condemned it in others. Weber sees much more than hypocrisy in this action. It is not that the Church and its dignitaries were opposed to wealth, indeed wealth was highly valued. Weber sees the condemnation of usury as a reaction by the Church to a condition in which commercial transactions are fairly well advanced.

Weber summarises this antagonism between traditionalism and the notions of absolute rationality of the Church and the innovative rationality of economic calculation in the following way: '. . . every economic rationalisation of a barter economy has a weakening effect on the traditions which support the authority of the sacred law' (1968, p. 584). The reason for this rests upon the very impersonality of economic rationalisation. Religious ethics stress the purely personal relationships between men, whatever the nature of this relationship, whether between equals, or between master and slave. Since these personal relationships must be regulated, they must have rules, they are subject to ethical regulation dictated by the Church. Thus the religious opposition to the economic calculus was based on the very impersonality of the latter. The lending of money is a totally 'impersonal' transaction, money is loaned to anyone who can be expected to return it with an agreed amount of interest: there is no sentiment, no link other than the commercial transaction between the parties involved. The more such transactions become the 'normal' mode of transaction in a society, then the more relationships are based upon pure calculation. There is a massive reduction in the personal and ethically regulated and a concomitant increase in the impersonal and the instrumental. People are evaluated and considered for calculative reasons. Will he lend? At what rate? Can he pay back and when? Each is an instrument in the eyes of the other. Religious bodies, therefore, suffer a decline in their capacity for ethical regulation. Regulation becomes economic regulation, and individuals controlled by the economic calculus.

> The growing impersonality of the economy on the basis of association in the market place *follows its own rules*, disobedience to which entails economic failure and, in the long run, economic ruin. (Weber, 1968, p. 584, our emphasis)

We have seen that within feudal society there were considerable elements of instrumental rationality in terms of technological and economic innovation. Certain groups, especially in the towns, were the carriers of this willingness to treat the world and others as an instrument of manipulation, to be acted upon in an impersonal fashion. Since both commercial and technical innovations seemed to thrive in the late feudal period, we cannot see this 'instrumentalism' as unique to modern society. To repeat an earlier point, it is not the existence of this type of rationality that is unique to the modern world but its systematic extension into every walk of life.

There can be little doubt that the 'breakdown' of feudal institutions was necessary for the emergence of industrial society, in that the institutions and attitudes that are required for the systematic extension of instrumental rationality' to the totality of social life are incompatible with and could not survive, let alone, prosper, in the 'closed' traditionalistic context of feudalism. However, feudalism underwent a radical breakdown throughout the whole of Europe. Europe by the close of the sixteenth century had all but purged itself of its feudal structure. It is true that there were many remnants of a feudal age but the era of an order based upon warlike competition between branches of a landed aristocracy, of personalised bonds linking man to man, lord to master, man to the land, gave way to an era of centralised nation states and national competitive warfare and domination by a single absolute monarch with the aristocracy deprived of their monopoly of force through arms. With great variations this was the pattern throughout Europe. France, Spain, Sweden and the Holy Roman Empire all enjoyed periods of national supremacy in the age of the absolute monarchs. Merchants and traders were common in all the great states – yet it was England that was the first to undergo the process of industrialisation. The answer to this unique explosion is not to be found in the breakdown of feudalism, since this occurred throughout western Europe (see Chapter 4).

The argument so far has stressed the basic incompatibility between 'traditional' and 'modern' beliefs, institutions and modes of behaviour. It has attempted to reveal the revolutionary character of the modernity we so much take for granted. It has contrasted the gross characteristics of modern society with the gross characteristics of pre-modern societies in order to reveal just how much at variance is the modern condition with all past history.

To summarise these gross characteristics common to all industrial societies: first, a reliance upon inanimate sources of power in the process of production; second, large-scale industrial enterprises as the most typical modes of social organisation in the sphere of production; this entails the third feature, the radical separation of the industrial enterprise from the family; fourth, the crucial feature of the technical division of labour which in turn required that, fifth, large amounts of capital were subject to constant renewal. Such capital accumulation required the development of institutions and attitudes that facilitated the sixth basic characteristic of 'economic calculation' on a socially extensive basis.

Two points must be made. First, the presentation of these common characteristics of industrial society does not imply any chronological order; for example, it is not being argued that economic instrumentalism comes before or causes technological innovations, or indeed vice versa. It is not implying that large-scale production causes a division of labour. All that is being said is that these are perhaps the most common features of societies that have undergone a successful process of industrialisation. Second, it is not being argued that because all industrial societies share these characteristics they are 'the same'. Whilst it is obvious that the possession of these characteristics must enforce considerable similarity, it would be an error to assume that they outweigh the differences. The political importance of the question as to whether industrial societies become more alike, as to whether they converge in their similarities, will be discussed in a later chapter. What is stressed here is that the world can never be the same again since the advent of these changes. What is shared by all those nations who have undertaken the transformation is the triumph of instrumental rationality over traditional rationality. This does not mean that men in industrial societies 'know more', that they have more knowledge in a quantitative sense, but that men in industrial societies share a common view of the nature of reality – at least the pervasive view of the nature of reality is shared, whether men be communists, socialists, conservatives or liberals, in their day-to-day dealings in the world of work, which has become increasingly separated from private dealings, they share a commonsense world. Rationalisation does not mean that men know more, but 'It means that there are no mysterious incalculable forces that come into play, but that one can, in principle, master all things by calculation' (Weber, 1961, p. 139).

This revolutionary break with the past shared by all industrial societies means not just a change in beliefs and attitudes, it means that institutions which embody calculative instrumentalism achieve a degree of 'autonomy' of 'distinctiveness' never before realised in human society. The merging of the 'economic' and the 'technological' comes about in the form of capital; capital, which symbolises the impersonality of the modern world, and also symbolises the uniqueness of the modern world. Both scientific-technological and economic decision making share to the most extreme extent this instrumental orientation of calculating between alternatives, of viewing the world as impersonal, as a series of phenomena to be manipulated. Whatever the political regime the necessity for the economic and technological structure to be totally related and to have a high degree of independence from the other institutions of society, such as family, friendship groups, religious considerations, is a shared characteristic of industrial societies. The relationship between the technico-economic structure and political control is perhaps the major source of difference between industrial societies and these variations between them the major source of conflict between them.

Nevertheless, the emergence of a distinct phenomenon which we call an 'economy', of which technology in the form of capital is an essential part, is one of the truly modern breaks with the known past. We take this so much for granted that it would be a salutary exercise to consider a case of this emergence of a distinct 'economy' from the matrix of wider social relationships. England was the first nation to undergo industrialisation, thus the first to exhibit this historically unique phenomenon in an exaggerated form. The 'break' with feudalism can be viewed as a process in which economic relationships disentangle themselves from the wider social relationships of sentiment, traditional power, sacred considerations and personalised bonds. It was the particular nature of this break, the unique features of this overcoming of traditionalism that made England the first nation to undergo industrialisation.

Before undertaking such a task it is well to stress the uniqueness of the English experience; precisely because England was the first nation to industrialise there are obvious limits to which the path to industrialisation followed by England can be taken as a model for industrialisation elsewhere. The historian Harold Perkin puts the problem most cogently:

> It is easy to see, once the pattern and potentialities of industrialism had been exemplified in one tremendously successful case, why underdeveloped societies should seek development, and how industrial revolutions in Western Europe, America, Japan and Russia could be motivated by envy and engineered by imitation. But the pioneer country had no blueprint and no such patent motivation. (1969, p. 7)

Put very simply, once certain technological and economic devices have proven advantageous for a nation then other nations will import them: indeed, so successful was England that her competitors in the game of international power politics were forced to import such devices if they were not to be crushed by weight of sheer economic and technological supremacy (see Appendix). The individuality of the English path to industrialisation is that the 'take-off' into 'sustained economic growth' was not imposed from above by some unified élite with a cohesive plan of emulation, it was a once and for all set of events of a collectively unanticipated nature.*

Unfortunately, it is necessary to complicate the problem further. As previously argued, most of western Europe had to greater or lesser degrees undergone similar transformations to that of England. Traditional feudal patterns had been greatly eroded. The emergence of a centralised state, the

*It may well be that in order to avoid confusion certain definitions should be clarified. W. E. Moore, in his excellent book *The Impact of Industry*, gives some lucid definitions relevant to the present debate.

He says of the term 'economic growth' that it has the advantage of the fact that it 'can be precisely defined: increased real income per capita' (p. 5).

Of the term 'economic development' he argues that the term 'implies structural changes in addition to mere increases in output.' Such changes include economic as well as political and legal institutions (pp. 5–6).

He continues: 'The most comprehensive term for the changes we are concerned with is *modernisation*. . . . It means essentially becoming a member of the common pool of world knowledge and useful techniques, perhaps without drawing much and adding little, but still sacrificing many time-encrusted customs for the sake of real or visionary benefits.' (p. 6).

pacification of anarchic militaristic war-lords, the establishment of urban trade and commercial centres and the increased influence of money as a standardised mode of exchange were part of a familiar if variable pattern. Suffice to say that all these, when combined with a general increase in population which was common in most of western Europe by the mid-eighteenth century (see Chapter 4), are necessary conditions for industrialisation. That it was unique to England suggests that whilst necessary conditions, they were not sufficient. It may be that it was the particular combination of these conditions that gave Britain its uniqueness. For instance, whilst England had a strong monarchy, as did its European neighbours, and thus had the relatively stable state, so necessary for sustained investment for future profit, the British monarchy had undergone a considerable diminishment and limitation of 'absolute' power. The Civil War and the Act of Regicide had considerably limited the Crown's perogatives, which meant a diminished ability to 'restrain' trade and commerce in its own favour. The ultimate domination of the country through Parliament meant that those with capital to invest had a degree of control over the conditions of the nation in which they invested. The lack of a strong military, when compared with France, meant that central power of a political nature was limited and consequently 'local' government under the landed gentry could favour the ambitions of individualised trade and commerce rather than the glorification of the State and its monarch. It is not the aim of this chapter to 'explain' why England was the first to industrialise. However, it is the aim of this chapter to suggest ways in which England was unique in providing an example to the world of the powers of an economy detached from the personalised relations and bureaucratic apparatus of a monarchical state. This in itself was unique, since every subsequent case of industrialisation had the benefit of self-conscious application of technical know-how, social organisation and an awareness of the mistakes made by England. Central to the argument here is that, in spite of the unplanned nature of England's industrialisation and the planned nature of the industrialisation of other nations, in spite of the 'non-typical' nature of the English experience, it is of sociological importance. Why is this so?

First, the very unplanned nature of English industrialisation provides, with perhaps the exception of the experience of the United States, a unique example of the degree to which the technico-economic structure can achieve a degree of independence, of autonomy from the totality of social relationships. If, 'In traditional, pre-industrial societies, the organisation of work is so interwoven with the larger organisation of the society that they can only be separated analytically' (McKee, 1969, p. 435), then it seems, in modern society, this separation is not just analytical, for purposes of explanation, but real. Now one of the major claims of the sociology of economic life is that the sociologist can provide an extra dimension to the arguments used by the economist – that sociology can provide explicit information concerning the implicit assumptions used by the economist. The economist 'assumes' that his propositions would operate in the real world 'other things being equal'. The sociologist provides both information as to the limits and as to the conditions under which the economist's propositions do work. Since the notion of 'economics' as a distinct subject is associated with the rise of industrialisation it may be revealing to look at the conditions that simultaneously promoted these two interrelated phenomena. The study of the rise of industrial England provides a case in which the economy achieved a degree of independence and control over the rest of social life of an unprecedented degree. If the category of 'the Economic' (Dumont, 1972, p. 209) was a uniquely European phenomenon, the degree to which this category dominated the mind and actions of men was more extreme in England with the advent of industry than at any time before, or – and this is crucially significant – *since*.

Second, the impact of this unique separation of the 'economic' from the political and social has had an impact on man's views of himself and his social relationships way beyond the confines of the British Isles, the notion of a 'self-regulating economy' to which political and social relationships are subordinated, the notion of a society subscribing to the model of the free play of supply and demand has had political and social, as well as intellectual, implications which have structured conflicts decisively throughout the world.

Third, it was as a critique of this model of man in free market society and its perceived implications that sociology arose, both as a celebrant of the model, a critic of this model, and in many cases, an alternative to this model.

Fourth, the assumptions behind the belief in the model reveal much of the 'real' state of society that enabled men to believe in it so avidly. The constant conflict and contradiction between the belief in the model and the realities of social life do much to explain the dynamics of English society and the actions of the business community in Britain throughout the nineteenth and twentieth centuries.

Fifth, the empirical study of English history prior to the emergence of 'industrialisation', which is often dated around 1750, reveals that prior to this late date England was already a 'market society' in a unique sense, and this is the important link in explaining both why England was the first to industrialise and why the model was inappropriate elsewhere.

Perkin summarises this position in the following way:

> It was, therefore, the peculiar relationship of the English landed aristocracy to society and hence the State which created the political climate for the germination of industrialism. Out of pure self-interest they created the political conditions – personal liberty, absolute security of property, the minimum of internal intervention, and adequate protection from foreign competition – best suited for generating a spontaneous industrial revolution. (1969, p. 65)

Let us look at the major factors of production as is traditionally used in economics in order to see that prior to the Industrial Revolution they had not only become 'free' from the closure of alternatives of traditional feudal society, but 'free' from the constraints of a monarchial state, 'free' from the constraints of any personal obligation, free to be subjects to the 'pure' instrumentalism of calculation.

The text will follow closely the analysis of Barrington-Moore in his superb essay on the social history of pre-industrial Britain (Barrington-Moore, 1967, pp. 3–39). (All quotations are from this source unless otherwise specified.)

Barrington-Moore suggests that from the fourteenth century there were many signs pointing to the extension of commerce in both the countryside and the towns. England had undergone a rapid displacement of feudalism and yet had, as previously mentioned, a relatively weak version of 'royal absolutism' which meant that the Crown's ability to control commerce for its own ends was always restricted in England (Perkin, 1969, p. 65). In this commercialisation the wool trade played a central role by extending international trade and linking town and country into a single commercial system. Since land is one of the major factors of production it is interesting to see that Barrington-Moore claims that during the fourteenth and fifteenth centuries radical changes were taking place by which 'The land and tenurial rights based on it had largely ceased to be the cement binding together lord and man.' Land in the feudal period had been the basis of most social relationships, the lord granted protection and land to the peasant in return for labour services and some military commitment, this tended to be hereditary and both lord and serf shared reciprocal bonds of duties and obligations, their bond was thus personalised and had the full weight of tradition behind it. The medieval conception of land saw it not only as a source of wealth, but also of personal obligation, of ties for both lord and vassal. The land and its ownership entailed a whole web of judicial and political functions. Land was thus changing from a source of social ties and mutual obligations into a commodity. The modern view of land is as an income yielding investment, where land becomes a commodity to be bought and sold solely according to the instrumental calculus. The medieval view of judging economic actions according to the contribution made to the health of the social organism was collapsing. This tendency to view land as a source of wealth independently of obligations to those who live on it, is an example of the view of 'nature' and 'society' as instruments of economic calculation unfettered by restrains other than those of expediency. The aristocracy were not only becoming increasingly percolated by new members who bought land as both an investment and a sign of status, but themselves were adapting to the new pressure of commercialism. Consequently not only was land becoming a commodity to be bought and sold but to be used according to the new criteria of impersonal investment. The enclosure movement by which estates were converted from arable farming into sheep pasture was an indication of this new calculus. Also the leasing of land for rent in increasingly large parcels, in which rent was the sole means of payment rather than payment 'in kind' or in labour services, were both trends which were to persist into the nineteenth century.

Inevitably this consolidation of landholding into 'economically viable units' free from any sense of obligation to the incumbents was a radical break with the past. Many peasants became dispossessed, or at best their lot worsened when 'common lands' were turned into enclosed pastures for profit. The logic of calculative competition is to force others to compete; it was a long-drawn-out process yet it nevertheless meant the breakdown of a system in which the peasantry enjoyed the 'rights' of their personal relationship to the lord and traditional access to the land. They became owners, or tenants, their relationship to the landowner mediated only by rent, or landless sellers of labour. Thus labour, the second factor of production, became 'free' from the bondage of traditional personal ties to the land, 'free' to sell itself on the market.

The Tudor and Stuart monarchs had done much to prevent this trend towards the displacement of the rural peasantry, fearing that such displacement could lead to unrest and civil strife through unemployment and underemployment. One of the consequences of the Civil War was a dimunition of royal power and in increase in the power of Parliament, a Parliament increasingly of wealth. Local government too was in the very hands of those who wished to promote this commercialisation of agriculture which meant the 'free' movement of labour, the right of the owner of the land to 'hire and fire', free from any other considerations than those of profit and loss. Although Parliament had to grant enclosure acts, it was an inevitable process for it was increasingly in the hands of those who most gained by the movement. The high profits and lower cost of the large unit meant an increasing decline in the amount of labour per unit of production, labour which could be 'fired' was cheaper than those who had to be maintained by right of traditional bond. Labour was becoming free from traditional bonds to respond to the call of higher wages, or just some wages; labour was becoming a commodity on the market.

The ruling class, a merger between the landed aristocracy and the emergent wealthy merchants, bankers and rural gentry ensured that the new sources of capital, from the expansion of British mercantile forces in the newly discovered parts of the world in terms of gold imports and slave trading, from the traditional wool trade and from British seapower's ability to impose favourable terms of trade, were invested in industrial ventures. This ruling class differed from its Continental counterparts in that it was not only more 'open' in that it allowed new members to be admitted, but did not share the disdain for investment and accumulation. This has two sources; first the English aristocracy was predominantly Protestant and consequently did not share the Catholic disdain and distrust for accumulating wealth for investment.* Furthermore, the fact that the aristocratic and gentry capital-

*There is an enormous literature stemming from Weber's *Protestant Ethic and the Spirit of Capitalism*, in which he links the ethical structures of extreme Protestantism to an ethical system conducive to capitalistic investment and acquisition. For the purposes of this chapter it is sufficient to say that the predominantly Protestant nature of the British upper classes would make them more receptive to the scientific and economic innovations of more radical Protestant sects than their Catholic counterparts – also more ready to adopt the inner-worldly orientations conducive to capitalism. A good summary, which is sufficient for this argument is contained in *Beliefs and Religion*, The Open University Press, 1972. 'In the case of the relationship between Protestantism and Capitalism Weber's analysis showed that the protestant ethic developed in a direction favourable to the anti-traditional spirit of capitalism. It left the capitalist free to develop whatever systematic procedures were necessary for the attainment of his goal' (p. 39).
also

See also H. Trevor-Roper, *Religion, Reformation and Social Change* for an analysis of the impact of a strong Catholic royal bureaucracy on the capacity for investment.

ists were under no compulsion to buy offices at a centralised court and thus fill the royal coffers as a means of gaining status meant that the surplus, so necessarily squandered for those who sought social elevation elsewhere, could be invested outside the royal bureaucracy and yet still gain the investor high status and the reward of a title.

In this chapter we have argued that England's peculiar history and social structure meant that prior to the advent of industrialism she had a well developed market economy. In Chapter 4 we will consider the assumptions which men held which led them to consider this unique state as 'part of nature' and to see it as in inevitable part of industrialisation. We will consider the contradictions both within the market system and between the 'reality' and the 'ideology' of the 'free market'. This will lead to an analysis of the emergence of sociology as a critique of the free market and to some key sociological concepts, such as class and state. But first in Chapter 3, we will lay out some of the central attempts of sociology to distinguish between the industrial and pre-industrial social types.

Appendix

The difficulties of building a 'single' model of a 'general' theory of industrialisation of economic growth is cogently argued by Kuznets. He lists several crucial factors which make for considerable variations in the path towards economic growth undertaken by the various states, these being:

(1) the specific historical heritage of the state;
(2) the time of entry into modern economic growth;
(3) the relations of the state with other countries, especially those who have already undergone industrialisation.

See S. Kuznets, 'Notes on the Takeoff', in G. M. Meier (ed.) *Leading Issues in Development Economics*, pp. 25–33 (New York: Oxford University Press, 1964).

The terms 'take-off' and 'sustained economical growth' are derived from the work of the economic historian W. W. Rostow. See his *Stages of Economic Growth* (Cambridge University Press, 1960).

Rostow claimed to have established a general 'analytic' theory of economic growth. Thus he claimed to have provided an explanation which was relevant to *all* cases of the process. His theory has been much criticised, nevertheless it does provide some useful guidelines for those first approaching the topic. Rostow claims that economic growth, where successfully completed, goes through five basic stages:

(1) the traditional stage;
(2) the preconditions for 'take-off';
(3) the 'take-off';
(4) the drive towards maturity;
(5) the age of high mass-consumption.

The most relevant of these stages to the purposes of this chapter is the 'preconditions for take-off', which include:

(*a*) breakthroughs in science and technology, insights of Newtonian science applied to production; this application rested upon

(*b*) expansion of world markets, the existence of a stable state, a seaboard location and an 'open class system'.

Rostow claims that the existence of these conditions in a more extreme form triggered the 'take-off' in England first. The 'take-off' occurs when, amongst other things, the proportion of net investment to national income, or net national product, rises from around 5 per cent to over 10 per cent, providing this outstrips population growth.

Suggested Further Reading

Argyle, M., Bendix, R., Flinn, M. W., and Hagen, E. E. (ed. C. Saul and T. Burns) (1967) *Social Theory and Economic Change* (London: Tavistock Publications).

Dalton, G. (1974) *Economic Systems and Society* (Harmondsworth, Middlx: Penguin Books).

Turner, B. (1975) *Industrialism* (London: Longman).

Bibliography

Aron, R. (1967) *Eighteen Lectures on Industrial Society* (London: Weidenfeld & Nicolson).

Barrington-Moore Jnr (1967) *Social Origins of Dictatorship and Democracy* (Harmondsworth, Middlx: Penguin Books).

Bloch, M. (1961) *Feudal Society* (London: Routledge & Kegan Paul).

Douglas, M. (1970) *Purity and Danger* (Harmondsworth, Middlx: Penguin Books).

Dumont, L. (1972) *Homo Hierarchius* (St. Albans, Herts: Paladin Books).

Friedmann, G. (1961) *The Anatomy of Work* (New York: Free Press).

Herskovits, M. (1952) *Economic Anthropology* (New York: Alfred A. Knopf).

Horton, R. (1970) 'African Thought and Western Science', in B. Wilson (ed.) *Rationality* (Oxford: Blackwell).

McKee, J. B. (1969) *Introduction to Sociology* (New York: Holt, Rinehart & Winston).

Martin, A. von (1963) *Sociology of the Renaissance* (New York and Evanston, Ill.: Harper & Row).

Moore, W. E. (1965) The *Impact of Industry* (Englewood Cliffs, N.J.: Prentice-Hall).

Perkin, H. (1969) *The Origins of Modern English Society* (London: Routledge & Kegan Paul).

Weber, M. (1961) *Max Weber: Essays in Sociology*, ed. H. H. Gerth and C. Wright Mills (London: Routledge & Kegan Paul).

— (1968) *Economy and Society*, ed. G. Roth and C. Wittich, vols 1 and 2 (New York: Bedminster Press).

3
Division of Labour

The sociologist seeks to make generalisations about societies. This is one of the central difficulties which preoccupies sociological methodology. Human societies and the individuals within them have a persistent tendency to vary, to be unique, to such an extent that such generalities cease to be either significant on the one hand, or indeed true on the other hand. For example, the generalisation that 'all men must eat to live' is true, but is so trivial that it lacks significance. The statement that 'all men must work and produce in order to live' is significant but unfortunately untrue since human societies produce many examples of whole classes of persons who have a positive disdain for work and the production processes yet manage to 'live' on a much higher standard than those who actually do produce. If generalisations concerned with the very crude conditions necessary for human existence are so prone to difficulty, then one can imagine the dilemmas inherent in generalising about apparently more complex social phenomena. The sociologist is faced with a dilemma concerning his function as a generaliser. Does he seek to make generalisations concerning the nature and condition of all men, to seek the essence of humanity, or does he describe the unique and individual in all its concreteness, thereby abandoning his attempts to generalise? A pioneer sociologist, Emile Durkheim, put the dilemma in the following manner: 'It seems, then, that social reality must be merely subject matter of an abstract and vague philosophy or for purely descriptive monographs' (Durkheim, 1962, p. 77).

Let us put the matter differently. Consider your family from the point of view of common sense. Let us assume that this hypothetical family consists of a father and mother and two offspring. In such a system both 'biological' mother and father share in bringing up the children. This seems quite a 'natural' type of set-up. If we look at another family in a different society, say Trobriand society, we may notice that the father, in our terms the biological father, plays a very minimal role in the upbringing of the offspring. The mother's brother plays the important male role of disciplining the children, indeed the children take on the name of the mother and her brother and the male child inherits the property of the mother's brother. The biological father has parental responsibility only for the offspring of his sister. This 'matrilineal' distribution of authority seems most 'unnatural' to our way of thinking, but, more central to the argument under consideration, it poses many problems for the sociologist who seeks to make generalisations concerning the family. Indeed, are we to suppose that the Western notion of shared responsibility for children by the biological parents is in some way more 'natural' than the customs of Trobrianders? Are we to suppose that primitive societies are in some process of transition towards the customs and institutions of the more civilised occident? Here we have the crux of Durkheim's definition of the problem of generalisation. Durkheim, in his prescriptions for a sociological method, was criticising the founding father of sociology, Auguste Comte, for assuming that all societies developed along a common path. According to Durkheim, Comte had 'thought he could represent the progress of all human societies as identical with that of a single person' (Durkheim, 1962, p. 19).

'It is the course of human progress that forms the chief subject of his [Comte] sociology. He begins with the idea that there is a continuous evolution of the human species, consisting in an ever more complete perfection of human nature; and his problem is to discover the order of this evolution.' In the same way that we would be guilty of such an assumption if we assumed that the customs of the Trobriand Islanders were but a stage of primitivism necessary for their development to our elevated notions of civilisation, Durkheim found Comte guilty of assuming that all men and all societies shared sufficient common characteristics to make all social development a similar, inevitable unilinear progression. Comte had assumed that the development of the West was the 'natural' direction to be taken by all societies, thus by generalising from the 'more advanced' societies' experiences one could know the nature of the world history that would inevitably transpire. Thus Durkheim's criticism that to generalise from some assumed universal 'human nature' in one's description of social reality would lead to an 'abstract and vague philosophy'. In the terminology of this discussion, such generalisations would lead to either statements of sociological triviality or of sociological untruth. The question that arises is how sociologists have attempted to extricate themselves from this dilemma.

It would be pretentious to describe the totality of the discipline's attempts to deal with this central problem in a few brief lines. However, the crudest response to this problem is the building of 'types' which attempt to categorise the most notable characteristics of societies in terms of gross similarities and differences. These 'type' constructs are not exhaustive descriptions of individual cases of historical reality, thus they avoid the horn of the dilemma which provides endless unique descriptions of singular and thereby non-generalisable reality. On the other hand, they are not generalisations about all different types of reality. They are merely descriptive tools which seek to categorise different aspects of societies according to certain criteria to facilitate explanation. In so far as they do not in themselves explain, they avoid the dilemma of untruth. Various authors have very different methods of arriving at these typifications, and very different views as to the status and function of these models in use. Nevertheless the ability to arrive at general characteristics of society whilst avoiding the pitfall of complete and individual description is the common function shared in spite of the methodological variations. Let us look at the construction of one of these 'typifications' in the work of one of the classic authors of sociological discourse.

Durkheim was concerned to establish a criteria of social 'normality'. He was concerned to evaluate what social patterns were 'normal' given the differences in and between societies. For instance, he recognised that crime rates varied between different societies and indeed between different groups within societies. Since all societies possessed elements of criminality he concluded that 'some' crime was a'normal' feature of the social fabric but since there were great variations in both the rates and patterns of crime, and variations in the incidence of crime over time, he was faced with the problem of the degree to which crime was 'normal' given the great difference in and between the societies he studied.

To give an example more central to the problems of industrialisation preoccupying this book: Durkheim claimed that the outstanding difference between contemporary societies and societies of the past was the nature of the social solidarity, that is the nature of the bonds that held the social fabric together. Durkheim held that the 'normal' condition of all societies was to have a high degree of coherence, of solidarity, to possess a capacity to hold together without radical disorder and conflict. Whilst this was common to all societies the basis of such an order could be radically different. Therefore what was 'normal' in an ancient society was not 'normal' in a modern society. Although all societies shared the characteristic of order and solidarity when in a state of 'normality' (Durkheim, 1964). The central preoccupation of Durkheim's seminal work on differentiation in modern society was that the all-pervasive tendency for an increasing division of labour in society was a moral phenomenon and just not an economic fact. The import of this is not immediately obvious. What Durkheim means is that the division of labour has far reaching consequences of which the economic are but a part. Division of labour involves changes in the legal and political fabric, in the individual's sense of personality and identity, in the whole moral justification for existence both individual and social. For Durkheim the world of the past has gone forever and the role of sociology is to discover the factors 'typical' of the modern division of labour that make for a state of 'normality', i.e. solidarity.

Durkheim has to build a set of categories pertaining to the most typical characteristics of non-differentiated societies that make for normality and the most typical characteristics of differentiated societies making for normality. This is necessary in order to ascertain which are the 'pathological' features that do not 'fit' with the normal social arrangements, or rather what would be normal social arrangements if the pathological elements could be eliminated. Durkheim claims that the most general characteristic of what he calls 'mechanical' types of social solidarity was the fact that 'individuals' were so much alike. The very lack of differentiation of functions meant that persons in such societies lacked individuality of personality, morality, vested interest. Society held together, cohered, because of the very similitude between the individual parts. Individuals in such societies 'mechanically' resembled and reproduced each other according to criteria of likeness. The point that is essential for the purposes of this chapter is methodological; we are concerned with the techniques Durkheim used rather than with the truth/value of his generalisations. Durkheim sought to build a typology of societies according to a single criterion, his criterion being the similarities and differences in the social arrangements which promoted social solidarity. Durkheim argues that although one cannot see or measure such a non-observable as social solidarity it is nevertheless 'real' in its consequences. Thus Durkheim sought for observable indices, indicators which were observable, of realities beneath them that were not observable. In a sense similar to our use of such instruments as thermometers as indicators of such non-observables as 'temperature'. It is the 'temperature' that is the 'reality' we seek not the 'signs' on a thermometer. 'Repressive' law was such an index of the degree to which mechanical types of solidarity existed. Repressive law, the antagonistic social reaction to individual breaches of social codes, is, he argues, much more prevalent in undifferentiated societies since the degree of repression is a sign of the collective moral outrage evoked by a transgressor. Such collective moral outrage is possible only where the individuals concerned share the common codes to such an extent that transgression evokes punitive measures. Thus punitive law is an index of the degree of collective similarity, of a social order based upon similarity. To quote Durkheim:

> there exists a social solidarity which comes from a certain number of states of conscience which are common to all members of the same society. This is what repressive law materially represents, at least in so far as it is essential. The part that it plays in the general integration of society evidently depends upon the greater or lesser extent of the social life which the common conscience embraces and regulates. (1964, p. 109)

Let us summarise. Durkheim wishes to establish a set of typical characteristics which promote social solidarity in societies of an undifferentiated nature, 'normal' societies which have a low level of division of labour. Since one cannot physically see such phenomena as 'normality' and 'social solidarity' one uses objective indices. For instance Durkheim used suicide rates as indices of the degrees of social solidarity when comparing various European nations and districts (Durkheim 1968). In order to ascertain which social orders contained the features of mechanical social solidarity Durkheim chose the relative presence of repressive law as his indicator. Commentators on Durkheim have criticised, perhaps correctly, his error in taking repressive law as an index of mechanical solidarity, especially when he anticipates its relative decline under conditions of organic solidarity. If one just considers one event from contemporary British judicial history, the Great Train Robbery, one must doubt the anticipated decline in the extent and ferocity of repressive law. Whilst one can question the wisdom of choosing repressive law as the most significant index of mechanical solidarity the methodological logic still remains. First, observations of non-observable phenomena, such as types and modes of social solidarity should seek always those external distinguishing characteristics about which there can be no doubt: which can be objectively perceived by others. Secondly, by using a single indicator, such as repressive law, as the most typical index of mechanical solidarity

Durkheim claimed that societies possessing great individual differences could be similarly categorised as typically possessing a distinct mode of solidarity. In the language of this chapter, the characteristic of mechanical solidarity, itself a function of social similarity, cross-cut all the variations which separated ancient India and Judea, classical Egypt and bygone Germany and Greece and Rome (Durkheim, 1964, p. 92). One does not have to have great knowledge of ancient history and social structure to recognise the profound nature of Durkheim's assumption, namely that in spite of all the variations in and between such societies they share the common characteristic of constituting a social type, a general mode of classification which cross-cuts and transcends their differences. This is the essential core of all such attempts to build typologies of society which attempt to distinguish that which is distinctly 'modern' as against that which is distinctly 'traditional'. It is not an exercise undertaken to ignore the great variations that existed both in time and structure amongst societies in pre-modern times but an exercise in typification, an exercise in seeking the most typical, the most general characteristics of the pre-modern *relative* to the most general characteristics of the modern world. Such typifications should never be confused with reality, they are but tools which enable us to look at reality whilst recognising that whatever is real has both general and individual features. If we turn to Durkheim's attempt to build a typology of modern society the problems and functions of this exercise may become clearer.

Durkheim's construction of a typology general to modern industrial society rests upon the assumption that 'with the emergence of the new industrial order new social needs arose and new ways of satisfying old needs were required' (Gouldner, 1967, p. 13). Durkheim thereby recognises that the institutional solutions to problems of past traditional societies are inappropriate to the problems and needs created by the new socio-industrial order. Furthermore the needs common to both types of order cannot be catered for by the institutions of the past. For instance, many of the contemporaries of Durkheim argued that their environment, of France at the end of the nineteenth century, which saw the decline of religious belief and the parallel loss of power of the Catholic Church, held these as responsible for the intense level of social and political conflict which appeared as the condition of modern France. Durkheim shared their apprehensions concerning such conflicts, but recognised that a resurgence of religious belief and church power was incompatible with the inevitable industrial division of labour and that the conformist beliefs of a universal Catholic church were not appropriate to an economy which required individuality of thought and action. In this sense Durkheim was a 'relativist'. He recognised that the truths, the beliefs and institutions of the past were appropriate to that era but only to that era in a relative sense. There were no products of any age that enjoyed the status of 'absolute' truths, of universal appropriateness independent of the context of the total relationships in which they were located. In a sense this is a restatement of the dilemma of the sociologist which dominates this chapter. Is each era, each epoch and each society so unique that no general statements can be made about them? Does this uniqueness force upon us an absolute 'relativism' by which we can describe a phenomenon only in the context in which it is found? It is in response to this problem that Durkheim built his typology of modern society, seeking the most common, the most general characteristic which is shared by industrial societies when compared to pre-industrial traditional orders. Namely, the extensive presence of the division of labour.

It is worth, at this juncture, reiterating an earlier point concerning Durkheim's sociology. In spite of his sociological relativism, his concern to recognise that the various elements that constitute society are specific and not common to all social structures, he does recognise one universal principle that is common to all societies. A society, when it is in a state of 'normality', enjoys a condition of 'solidarity'. This principle, however empirically and philosophically erroneous it may be, does enable Durkheim to have a basis for comparison between societies of very different kinds and structures. It enables him to overcome an absolute relativism.

In the same way Durkheim claims that a preponderance of emphasis upon 'repressive law' is an index of a state of solidarity (normality) based upon the similarity of parts constituting society; so he claims that the preponderance of emphasis based upon 'restitutive law' can be taken as an index of its opposite, a society whose source of solidarity is based upon the existence of differences amongst the parts. Whilst repressive law, what we would call penal or criminal law, makes a demand for suffering by the deviant, the other type, according to Durkheim, 'does not necessarily imply suffering for the agent, but consists only of *the return of things as they were*, in the re-establishment of troubled relations to their normal state' (Durkheim, 1964, p. 69).

We can see now the logic of Durkheim's exercise. Whether the category of repressive law refers to wide, ill-defined, non-specific bodies of customary morality without the benefit of a specialised legal institution, or to a set of organised specific penal laws, Durkheim claimed a society which depended upon this type of legal enforcement depended upon a low level of individuality; people must resemble each other in their sentiments and values. Moral outrage of such a force requires that individuals feel commonly outraged and therefore are extremely alike. Restitutive law, what we would call commercial law, or contract between individuals concerning specific transactions, requires a high degree of individuality and individual interest for its very existence. The basis of such individualisation of morality and of personality depends upon a high degree of division of labour. The specialisation of work roles and societal functions to such a degree that the specialisms not only require specialised productive skills but individualised social competences and psychological capacities. For Durkheim, the very existence of what he calls 'individuality', of what we consider to be of philosophy of 'freedom of the individual' was a product of the process of the division of labour. Thus division of labour was truly a moral and social being, rather than an exclusively economic production. The very 'individualised' nature of contract law made it, for Durkheim, an excellent index of social solidarity based upon the individualising tendencies of division of labour. The core of Durkheim's argument is, then, that the 'normal' form of 'organic' solidarity is achieved through the division of labour. The very fact that men differ in their functions in the occupational and social world means that they depend upon each other more and more for their individual survival. The very specialism of task and skill means that each individual can survive by contributing his own specialism, but because he is so specialised, he depends upon the production of other specialists for his survival. The butcher depends upon the candle-stick maker and vice versa, the engine driver upon the guard and both upon the passenger as a source of revenue. It is the very division of function that makes for interdependence and solidarity based upon mutual differences. The very individuality of persons which facilitates this interdependence through specialism is the ultimate source of bond between men. Solidarity is through sources of difference rather than similarity. Just as more complex physical structures depend upon the differences amongst their constitutive parts for survival, upon specialised physical functions, so the organic solidarity enjoys cohesion through the very specialised nature of the individual members and specialised groups that make up the totality. Such a solidarity is 'organic' in its living specialisation as opposed to a 'mechanical' condition where each part resembles every other in a dead, unreflective manner. Let us look at the contrast of these types of distinct social forms in more detail, before going on to consider the methodological implications of Durkheim's analysis of 'deviant' or 'pathological' forms of division of labour.

The type referring to 'mechanical solidarity' gives a profile of a society in which the individuals concerned share a common view of the world, in Durkheim's terms a common 'collective consciousness'. They feel, think and act the same, and therefore act in concert. Since they act and think in concert the world around them is reflected in the 'collective mind'. The nature of collective thoughts tends to be specific, that is limited to the immediate surroundings, the kin-group and the tribe being both the centre and limits of the social universe. Since the social structure's lack of differentiation promotes a similarity of thought and personality the very nature of thought tends towards a lack of differentiation. Not only do the individuals concerned think alike, but the very content of thought tends to focus upon the local, abstractions such as 'the individual', 'humanity' are all bounded by the specific group. Thinking tends to be basically 'religious' since all thought is 'common'. It is the very sharedness of belief and practice that promotes the traditional intensity of belief. Since the group, be it kin group, tribe or manor, constitutes the boundary of thought and since within this boundary there is little variation, then thought assumes a 'sacred' character. All actions great or small carry a collective sanction, since all actions and thoughts are collective and shared they really are more than or greater than the individual. This sense of the sacred, of actions and thought being greater than and above the individual is not only common to traditional societies, but according to Durkheim inherent in the very structure of these societies. Since there is little division of labour and individuality of personality people act in concert, the very concerted sharedness 'is' literally greater than the individual, thus religiosity, a sense of the 'sacred', is a reality inherent in the very structure of existence. Religion is a social reality. As a consequence of this the very social arrangements experienced by the individuals had a religious connotation. This perhaps is a crucial factor in so many attempts to define a social type of 'traditionalism' of which Durkheim's 'mechanical solidarity' is but one. The all-pervasive religiosity, which renders social arrangements as given, as immutable, as in the nature of things, is a major characteristic of so many analyses of the general type we call 'the traditional society'. Its very capacity to resist and oppose change, its very conservatism, can be seen to derive from this central feature, that what is, is sacred. Thus to change such arrangements is to commit an act of sacrilege. Durkheim went further than most sociologists of his time in seeing that religiosity and thus traditionalism are a product of the very homogeneity that constituted a 'reality' beyond the individual. Perhaps the differences between the distinct types of social solidarity are best summed up on the chart presented below.

Mechanical and Organic Solidarity

	Mechanical Solidarity	*Organic Solidarity*
	Based on resemblances (predominant in less advanced societies)	Based on division of labour (predominant in more advanced societies)
(1) Morphological (structural) basis	Segmental type (first clan-based, later territorial). Little interdependence (social bonds relatively weak). Relatively low volume of population. Relatively low material and moral density. Rules with repressive sanctions.	Organised type (fusion of markets and growth of cities). Much inter-dependence (social bonds relatively strong). Relatively high volume of population. Relatively high material and moral density. Rules with restitutive sanctions.
(2) Type of norms (typified by law)	Prevalence of penal law	Prevalence of cooperative law (civil, commercial, procedural, administrative and constitutional law
(3)(a) Formal features of *conscience collective*	High volume High density High determinateness Collective authority absolute	Low volume Low density Low determinateness More room for individual initiative and reflexion
(3)(b) Content of *conscience collective*	Highly religious Trans-cendental (superior to human interests and beyond discussion). Attaching supreme value to society and interests of society as a whole.	Increasingly secular Human-oriented (concerned with human interests and open to discussion). Attaching supreme value to individual dignity, equality of opportunity, work ethic and social justice.
	Concrete and specific	Abstract and general

From: S. Lukes, *Emile Durkheim, His Life and Work: a Historical and Critical Study*, p. 158.

What was uniquely Durkheimian was the recognition that under conditions of social homogeneity and consequent concerted action such beliefs were not primitive errors of an unscientific age but realistic perceptions and interpretations of a social reality which determined the conditions of individual existence. Objects, events and structures were 'really' religious in the sense that they had the total force of the community behind them, thus the religiosity is a force greater than the individual. What Durkheim's list of central characteristics of the 'traditional' shares with his contemporaries in their attempts to build similar schemes is his recognition that with the division of labour excessive individuality can and does result. It would be useful at this point to recapitulate the methodological assumptions attributed to Durkheim.

First, he attempts to build a typology of societies in which he contrasts the most general characteristics typifying traditional societies with those most common to the socio-industrial order. He recognises the great differences between traditional societies and indeed between industrial societies, but nevertheless seeks certain common characteristics which cut across these differences. Second, whilst his whole typological analysis depends upon the greater degree of relative difference between those of a traditional nature and those of an industrial nature he is able to use a language and method which enables explanation in spite of this great difference. In short, whilst recognising that the social arrangements which promote mechanical solidarity are relative to that sort of social type and not appropriate to organic modes of solidarity, they do have a basic common feature that enables a degree of generality to be applicable to all societies. Societies in so far as they are 'normal' have a degree of coherence, of solidarity. It is by the twin claim of 'normality' and 'solidarity' as the usual condition of all societies that Durkheim is able to generalise across all the differences in and between the types he constructs.

Durkheim shared with his contemporaries a sense of pessimism concerning the state of the world in which he and they live. He saw a world of disorder, of conflict and tension which was far from his image of 'normality' and 'integration'. Like his contemporaries he saw the increased division of labour as the major means of breakdown of the traditional society and with this breakdown the releasing of men from the constraints and certainties of traditionalism. Given this pessimism and doubt over the contemporary condition how is it possible that Durkheim was able to argue for the beneficial and ultimately solidaristic and hence 'normal' effects of the division of labour? Basically it was Durkheim's uneasy relativism; he recognised that the constraints upon excessive individualism inherent in the traditional society were dependent upon the lack of division of labour and that these constraints, such as universal religiosity and all-pervasive repressive law, could and would only work where there was little division of labour, where people were basically unindividual and similar. Where the division of labour does take root, then so radical and profound are its moral, legal and psychological consequences that the solutions of traditionalism are rendered totally obsolete. It is precisely because Durkheim used his method of 'typing' or categorising the most general features of social phenomena that he was able to maintain the basic postulate throughout his work, namely that '*the division of labour is essentially a source of solidarity*' (Friedmann, 1961, p. 69).

Durkheim, then, has built a model, a type, a specification of the most general characteristics of an industrial order which promote social solidarity, a state of social normality. He sees all forms of division of labour that do not promote such solidarity as abnormal forms. It is worth mentioning that because he possessed a model of the elements which constitute 'normality' he was able to specify and analyse those elements which created 'pathology'. The assumption that order and solidarity are 'normal' features of all societies has been one of the most general and telling of all criticisms of Durkheim and his disciples. Indeed it seems doubtful whether any statement about social 'normality' has much empirical credence when applied to all societies. What is of interest here is the attempt to build 'typologies' from general characteristics, even where they do not exist in reality, in order to perform two functions; first, to make statements of a general nature whilst recognising the richness of social variation, second, to evaluate reality by viewing it against a bench-mark, an intellectual device which aids analysis. This is a point worth labouring for much of the activity of sociologising depends upon the construction of such models which enable us to evaluate reality in all its complexity by abstracting out some general elements which enable us to see just what is individual, just what is particular. In Durkheim's case such a device, such a model of the most general characteristics promoting solidarity in industrial conditions, enabled him to analyse the reality around him, the conditions which detracted from the establishment of such 'normality'. It is true that Durkheim has often been criticised for ignoring the particular, the concrete, and thus being concerned with making 'universal' propositions which do not fit the facts. (see Alpert, 1939, pp. 114–19; Douglas, 1967, chap. 2). Nevertheless, central to our argument here is that the very existence of a model of the factors did enable Durkheim to give a penetrating analysis of the concrete problems associated with the division of labour. Even if he did see these specific problems as erroneously pathological and abnormal, even if he did measure these specific problems against an incorrect model of normality and solidarity, his analysis of these concrete problems has made a lasting contribution to the analysis of the contemporary socio-industrial order.

What were these 'abnormal' forms of division of labour? Abnormal because they detract from the natural state of division, namely, a natural state of solidarity, of integration. Lukes sums up these abnormal modes under three headings, first as 'anomie', second as 'inequality' and third as 'inadequate organisation'. It may have become clear that Durkheim equated solidarity with regulation of the individual, without regulation of an external nature the individual was unable to cope with existence. Unless limitations were placed upon aspirations, unless there were some clearly specified rules governing individual actions, whether of a moral or structural nature, then the individual experienced unease, disillusionment, a sense of meaninglessness, in Durkheim's own terms, 'a condition of anomie'. The anomic division of labour is precisely this, a condition in which there is an absence of rules governing the social functions which the individual has to undertake. Capitalistic modes of industrialism required the individual to sell his labour on a free labour market. It also required those who possessed capital to make decisions as to where and when to invest their capital on the basis of individual calculations as to when profitability would be maximised. The essence of this system was that 'regulation' should emerge from the 'free play' of the market. Order and regulation in such a system are the products of the rational calculations of free individuals as to where and when to sell their labour, where and when to invest their capital. In such a system there are no regulations imposed from 'outside', the only constraints are those of economic calculations of profitability. Ideally, all human relationships are subordinated to market considerations, a fact that Durkheim well recognised. He says, 'as the organised type [here he refers to the increasingly self-conscious organisation of a differentiated society] develops, the fusion of different segments draws the markets together into one which embraces almost all of society' (Durkheim, 1964, p. 369). Again Durkheim contrasts this state of affairs with that of the restricted types of markets of the 'mechanical solidarity'. Such restricted markets are limited to close relations of producers and consumers, hence they are able to anticipate each other's needs, and restrict production and consumption accordingly. Furthermore, since such markets are part of other social relationships the 'pure' economic calculations are regulated and restricted by extra-economic considerations, such as family, traditional rights and consideration of duty and need. In sharp contrast to the limited, subordinated market, the universal single market breaks down these face-to-face limitations; in such conditions, 'The producer can no longer embrace the market in a glance, nor even in thought. He can no longer see its limits, since it is, so to speak, limitless. Accordingly, production becomes unbridled and unregulated. (Durkheim, 1964, p. 370). The consequences of this lack of market regulation are the periodic crises in which individual expectations are no longer fulfilled. It creates booms in which expectations are unrealistically heightened. In short it creates a state of meaninglessness in which actions and expectations become crushed and independent of the control of the individuals concerned. The unregulated market requires the basic individuality of free decision, but crushes this very individuality by its impersonal, uncontrollable movements: thus it has potential to create an anomic form of division of labour.

This critique of the sociological consequences of the unregulated market was not exclusive to Durkheim. The reliance upon individual rational calculation as a basis of social and moral order was one of the recurrent and major themes of the reaction to industrialisation undertaken by the pioneer practitioners of sociology. What is also common to them, although they disagreed upon the causes, consequences and solutions germane to the market phenomenon, is that they evaluated the 'modernity' of this market-industrial situation against a model of the traditional society. The attempt will be made to give a synopsis of the various attempts to delineate between 'tradition' and 'modernity' later in this chapter. Suffice to say, at this juncture, that such 'types' were methodologically necessary for the classical social commentators so they could attempt to compare and contrast that which is modern and that which is traditional, despite the great variations *within* the respective types.

Whether the contrast be between mechanical and organic solidarity (Durkheim), community and association (Tonnies), status and contract (Maine) or Marx's contrast between feudal and capitalistic modes of production, the stress is on the impersonal, individualised, calculative and unregulated features of a market-orientated society as compared to the personalised, group-regulated features of the traditional order.

In a further elaboration of the anomic form of division of labour Durkheim stresses this impersonality, the separation of the worker from both his employer and from other workers, and points out that the very specialisation and subordination of the individual to the machine can exacerbate the meaninglessness of the work role. This separation from the total process of production is foremost in promoting conflict between worker and employer, the latter losing identification with needs and aspirations of the former. Since the anomic form is 'abnormal' Durkheim sees it as a function of the rapidity by which the industrial division of labour has come about. The solution to these problems must come from greater regulation of the economy and the individual enterprise by introducing modes of organisation which are appropriate to the organic nature of the division of labour. It is worth noting that Durkheim sees the main cause of abnormal forms of division of labour to be dislocation due to the rapidity of the transformation and that increased state and managerial coordination and organisation will eradicate these abnormal forms. An adjunct of this is that Durkheim sees state, managerial and professional associations regulation as being the 'normal' organisational forms appropriate to a highly differentiated society. In other words, Durkheim saw unfettered *laissez-faire* capitalism, in which the market's economic functions had ultimate control, as but a temporary aberration on the 'natural' path to a harmonious integrated division of labour.

The other modes of abnormal division of labour are products of 'inequality' and inadequate organisation. The 'forced' division of labour was a product of individuals expecting highly specialised complex roles in their work life being allocated roles inappropriate to their 'natural talents'. They are thus forced through economic necessity into occupations for which they have no affinity and no sense of identification. The very structure of differentiation which requires individualised aspiration thwarts its realisation. The second aspect of this inequality is when certain classes find that they have to offer their labour services at any price in order to live whilst others can do without them, 'thanks to the resources at their disposal'. These imperfections in the division of labour are conflict provoking because they are perceived as unjust. They are a function of the inheritance of power and property by birth rather than by merit and 'natural aptitude'. Such meritocratic standards Durkheim saw as inherent in the division of labour when in a state of normality. It is interesting to speculate as to why Durkheim did not consider the possibility that inequality of wealth, power, property and privilege through the mechanism of inheritance was no less inherent under conditions of differentiation than in a mechanical social order. Alvin Gouldner claims that had Durkheim concentrated upon the forced division of labour rather than that of the anomic forms, he could have 'examined the reasons why the hereditary transmission of wealth or position does not disappear and give way to new social arrangements more in keeping with modern division of labour' (Gouldner, 1967, p. 21).

The third form of abnormality was where the 'divided job' is of insufficient scope to employ the workers' full interests and capacities. The solution to this lay in better coordination, thus limiting the number and nature of roles not employing these capacities – more insightful management would overcome this aberration from the true division of labour.

Three basic points emerge from this résumé of Durkheim's juxtaposition of the mechanical and organic forms of the division of labour.

First, Durkheim saw that traditional society possessed a state of solidarity, of bonds between men, as a result of the similarity of the individuals and segments of society involved. He saw the division of labour as the most profound difference between the traditional and the modern types of society, but recognised that a normal state of solidarity was common to both.

Second, Durkheim defined the conflicts and tensions of modern society as abnormal deviations from the true differentiated society. This is important because much modern sociology of industrialisation has stressed that the conflicts and tensions of increasing differentiation are only consequences of the too rapid transition from traditional to modern society or are a product of 'left-overs' from the past which will be ironed out by the logic of history. These two ideas embody respectively the Durkheimian notions of the anomic division of labour and his attention to the incompatibility of inheritance and the creation of solidarity through a social division of labour.

Third, Durkheim recognised that the unregulated markets of *laissez-faire* capitalism, which perceived social order and regulation to be an 'emergent property' of the rational decisions of calculating individuals, were neither historically accurate pictures of a truly industrial society nor adequate analyses of social cohesion. Indeed the nearer a society came to approximating such an individualistic model the nearer it came to disorder.

It was mentioned earlier that Durkheim was not alone in his attempt to build typological models of the most general characteristics of pre-industrial societies and of industrial societies. One of the problems already suggested in this exercise is that the more general the features outlined the more abstract they become and less descriptive of any real, individual society. The contemporary social theorist Talcott Parsons has dealt with this problem by searching for the most general and therefore the most abstract features of *all* social systems prior to the analysis of specific societies. His 'grand theory' of social systems has given us a set of criteria which yields a very high level of generality in our exercise in distinguishing between traditional and modern types of social structures. His pattern variables are intended to represent dilemmas that confront any and all social actors in their relationships with others (Parsons, 1951, pp. 58–67). In most cases of interaction the dilemma is solved by the fact that there is a pre-existing, appropriate mode of behaviour available.

Let the demonstration of this pre-existence of appropriate behaviour be illustrated by the first dilemma or pattern variable. In Parsonian terms, there is a choice confronting any actor between *affectivity* and *affective neutrality*. If one is sitting on a bus and one is presented with the vista of a conductress's beautiful rear should one seek the immediate pleasure and grasp that vista or put off one's pleasure in favour of the calculated gains of getting to one's destination unslapped and ungaoled? Does one view the other actor in a situation as a source of immediate pleasure and gratification? In the case of affectivity the social object is treated as an immediate source of personal pleasure, in the case of affective neutrality as an object of calculation to be treated in a non-emotional way. In most situations the dilemma ceases to be a true dilemma since there are predetermined, accepted social norms already existing outlining the socially available and sanctioned responses. Since such patterns of appropriate behaviour tend to differ in different societies it is useful to build upon the differences in terms of building a typology of social 'choices'. In terms of the pattern variables, one horn of the dilemma tends to institutionalise, that is to say tends to be socially acceptable and therefore repeated. For example, in modern society we are socially expected to regard out close family relations with affection, with closeness, with no calculation as to the long-term benefits of such relationships. Close family relationships are therefore institutionalised as objects of affectivity. Relative to family relationships our employers are to be treated with cool respect with an eye to future benefits that may accrue from the relationship. We should not get emotionally involved either in love or in anger, our attitude should be one of affective neutrality. Since we can compare institutions within a single society according to the degree to which one side or the other of the pattern variable is institutionalised, so we can compare whole societies in terms of the relative weight given to these variables. The traditional type of society enjoys a predominance of face-to-face relationships, most individuals meet and remeet each other throughout the day, be it in different contexts, thus it is hardly surprising that close, personalised *affective* bonds tend to be the most typical of orientations to behaviour. How different the impersonality of the modern urban society! Here, relatively speaking, most relationships are of a calculative nature, teachers, doctors, greengrocers are all 'instruments' who perform services which are impersonal, in the sense that they are not in themselves sources of instant gratification.

Similarly with the dilemma between *diffuseness* and *specificity*. In a close, face-to-face society people tend to play roles which are multi-functional. That is to say we may meet the same individuals playing different roles, say as healer, teacher, warrior leader, consequently our attitude is one of viewing them as total persons, as diffuse non-specific persons rather than as in a specific role such as greengrocer or bus conductor. We will buy our vegetables from anyone who supplies a good service, we do not care 'who' the purveyor is. In contrast, the traditional Indian caste system defined only some persons as 'clean' enough to purchase from, thus our attitude would be a 'diffuse' concern with the whole person. We are interested in 'who' the purveyor is in terms of kinship and birth as well as adequacy of technical performance.

In the close-knit community of a traditional society the actor is concerned to place everyone according to kinship or birth, and locating all others in terms of the particularities of individual position, know the behaviour which is appropriate. Each grade, caste, kin group has its particular place and should be treated accordingly. Thus in terms of the third set of variables, *particularism* and *universalism*, the traditional order relatively applies criteria of 'particularism'. Rules are not applied on a 'universalistic' basis but according to a series of special categories. To quote from Cohen's clear and concise summary of the pattern variables: 'The most obvious example of universalism is that of the judicial procedure in most advanced, industrial societies: an officer of the court should treat every accused person or proved offender in terms of the same laws' (1968, p. 99). Such laws are universalistic criteria, of applicability to everyone without recourse to birth, race or creed. Cohen then continues his comparison with that of the feudal, traditional type of society in which 'a magnate would not apply the same laws to his peers as he applies to his serfs; legal conceptions would be particularistic' (1968, pp. 99).

The fourth dilemma of relevance here is of *quality* and *performance*, the question of whether we are concerned with what a person 'is' rather than what he can 'do'. In feudal society it was considered unfitting for a person of low birth to bear certain types of arms, no matter how competent he may have been in their use. Such an orientation can be defined in terms of 'quality', concern with the nature of the person, rather than with the abilities of the person. In our society we are concerned with the fighting prowess of the soldier rather than the nature of the person's social status, we are concerned with competence, 'performance', unless, of course, the soldier concerned is also an officer!

This last remark is more than sarcastic. It is meant as a reminder that the pattern variables are meant to be typifications of the most general patterns prevalent within a society or group relative to other societies or groups. Thus if recruitment is to an officer corps which has traditionally been based upon hereditary principles then relatively that group is using criteria of quality when compared to other groups who are concerned with sheer technical competence. In the same way the complex of affectivity, diffuseness, particularism and quality is only a summation of the most typical high level differences in traditional societies when compared with the most typical features of industrial society.

Given such a reservation here is an attempt to summarise a large number of social observations concerning the most typical differences between traditional and modern industrial societies.

It would be an error to associate Parsons's work in its totality as being an extension of the Durkheimian tradition. Elements of both of their works have been taken out of context in order to elucidate the elements concerned with building typological models of 'modern' as opposed to 'traditional' societies. The work of Durkheim is crucial in another aspect since it allows us to evaluate the condition of contemporary society in terms of his criteria of the 'normal' forms of organic solidarity resulting from the division of labour. It is this aspect of his work that has been most ignored by modern interpreters of Durkheim, yet it is perhaps the most useful. It is by evaluating the abnormal that one can, according to Durkheim, work towards practical prescriptions. That is recommending the mechanisms of social organisation appropriate to 'normal' types of society. As Giddens puts it:

Dimension	*Traditional*	*Modern*
Social Relations	Undifferentiated. Consensus based upon like-mindedness. Individual subordinated to the group. Face-to-face interaction.	Differentiated. Individuality source of solidarity through difference. Individual seen as measure of social institutions. Impersonal.
Economic Relations	Agricultural. Subsistence or for status enhancement. Lack of differentiation between economic and kinship roles.	Industrial. Production for accumulation and profit. High differentiation between economic and kinship roles.
Political Relations	Based on appeals to 'what has been'. Past the criteria of the present 'traditional domination'.	Based on appeals to individual* interest as means of achieving the 'common good'. 'Legal-rational domination'.
Belief Systems	Religious. Sacred limits to thought through device of heresy. Bounded by past.	Secular. Theoretically limitless unbounded save for limits of 'practical' expediency.
Technologies	*Ad hoc.* Unsystematically grounded in specific problems of practice. Linked to sacred ritual thus non-innovative.	Systematic. Link between theory and practice. Science source of innovation.
Social Control	Tradition. Face-to-face pressures of group. Moral and legal outrage.	Bureaucratic apparatus. Specialist agents of 'impersonal control', courts, police, mass media.
Organisation	Personalised. Control by 'status' (who you are). Inheritance criteria (particularistic).	Impersonal. Bureaucracy based on 'merit' – 'what you are'. Achievement criteria (universalistic).
Hierarchy	Superordination by 'birth'. Appeals to 'traditional' criteria – 'what has been' (ascriptive criteria).	Superordination by 'merit'. Appeals to 'public good' – 'what is best for majority' (achievement criteria).

*The political, organisational and hierarchial dimensions in this model all assume that the social arrangements on both sides of the dichotomy are accepted as 'legitimate'. That is to say that the dominated accept their subordination as 'right and proper' whether for reasons of birth or because they accept their subordination as 'being in their own interests'. The opposite of 'legitimate authority' is coercion where positions of subordination are enforced by physical violence or threat of it. Coercion is a common mode of power relation in both types of social arrangements.

> Durkheim made clear, in situations of transition or 'crisis' in society, where new forms are appearing, and others are becoming obsolete, in such circumstances, only sociological investigation can diagnose, in the flux of competing values and standards, what is of the past, and to be discarded, and what is the emergent pattern of the future. (Giddens, 1972, p. 368)

To recapitulate, Durkheim saw the unregulated market as the product of rapid industrialisation and the inheritance of property and social occupation to be 'left-overs' from a bygone past. The normal condition promoting solidarity in terms of division of labour he saw as being achieved by a higher degree of regulation by the state and by the elimination of inheritance of private property. In one sense the Durkheimian image of industrial society has considerable credibility since the agencies of government increasingly play a central role in controlling the forces of the market. The lack of regulation that Durkheim attributed to the earlier stages of industrial capitalism have indeed become superseded by the intrusions of the State. Indeed, in late nineteenth-century Britain and later in the United States – the traditional centres of 'free enterprise' – governmental apparatus came to play an increasing role in economic regulation with the growing participation of the industrial work-force in the political arena. In this sense Durkheim's prognostications concerning the 'normal' condition of industrial society appear correct.

Again, the value system of Western capitalist societies has increasingly stressed the importance of 'equality of opportunity', or, in Durkheim's terms, the centrality of individualisation of achievement. Increasingly all political parties claim to allocate opportunities and rewards according to individual merit and achievement rather than to inheritance and 'forced' occupations.

The increased regulation of the economy by the State and the promotion of policies of 'equality of opportunity' are inextricably interlaced. The State increasingly accepts responsibility for promotion of economic stability as it claims, through progressive taxation and equality of educational provision, to equalise people's chances in order to stress individual ability rather than inheritance and class position. Latter chapters will consider such phenomena as the State, the emergence of class and the autonomy from regulations by looking at developments over time rather than breaking them down into unrelated problems. The question implicit in this relies very much upon Durkheim's image of the 'normal' industrial society. For Durkheim the State would act as an independent force above and beyond the vested interests of particular classes and status groups. The following chapter on the English experience of industrialisation reveals how class relationships and the State, the political and the economic are all interrelated. The discussions on ideology and class again traverse the same problems. No definitive answers are forthcoming. What does seem to emerge through these discussions is that no simple model can capture the diversity of 'industrial' societies and by implication 'traditional' societies. Such neutral categories as the State, class and equality are charged with problems and reveal a problematic world.

Suggested Further Reading

Jesser, C. J. (1975) *Social Theory Revisited*, chap. 7 (Hinsdale, Ill.: The Dryden Press).
Parsons, T. (1966) *Societies: Evolutionary and Comparative Perspectives* (Englewood Cliffs, New Jersey: Prentice-Hall).

Bibliography

Alpert, H. (1939) *Emile Durkheim and His Sociology* (New York: Columbia University Press).
Cohen, P. (1968) Modern Social Theory (London: Heinemann).
Douglas, J. D. (1967) *The Social Meaning of Suicide* (Princeton, N.J.: Princeton University Press).
Durkheim, E. (1962) *Rules of Sociological Method*, ed. G. Catlin (Chicago: University of Chicago Press).
— (1964) *Division of Labour*, chaps 1 and 2 (New York: Free Press).
— (1968) *Suicide: A Study in Sociology* (London: Routledge & Kegan Paul).
Friedmann, G. (1961) The Anatomy of Work (New York: Free Press).
Giddens, A. (1972) 'Four Myths in the History of Social Thought', in *Economy and Society* 1, no. 4 (Nov).
Gouldner, A. (1967) *Introduction to 'Socialism'* by E. Durkheim (London: Collier-Macmillan).
Lukes, S. (1973) *Emile Durkheim, His Life and Work: a Historical and Critical Study* (Harmondsworth, Middx: Allen Lane, The Penguin Press).
Parsons, T. (1951) *The Social System* (London: Routledge & Kegan Paul).

4
Industrialisation in England

The peculiar nature of industrial society was stressed in Chapter 2. The peculiarity lies in the prevalence of a belief system which makes human and material things objects of deliberate manipulation and control, and a system of production relying on inanimate sources of power and involving increased capital accumulation, a technical division of labour, a separation of enterprise from household and initiating centralisation of production in large units. Chapter 3 demonstrates how sociology emerged as an effort to explain the common features of the transformation to industrial society. In this chapter we will consider the emergence of the 'market society' which preceded industrialisation and examine the importance of the idea of 'the market' in subsequent theories of society. The special nature of British industrialisation developed because an already developed capitalist market structure existed prior to industrialisation and because the market society in Britain developed an ideology of *laissez-faire* which explained and justified market society in such a way that state intervention was minimised. Macpherson (1962, p. 58) is insistent that there is nothing incompatible between state intervention and the development of industrialisation, and that it is the use of Britain and the United States as examples which has led to a situation in which the 'normal' pattern of development involves abstention by the State from economic activities. Macpherson defines market society in terms of the following features:

(1) There is no authoritative allocation of work.
(2) There is no authoritative definition of the rewards for work.
(3) Contracts are authoritatively defined and enforced.
(4) Individuals seek rationally to maximize their utilities.
(5) The labourer owns his own labour which he is free to sell.
(6) Land and capital are owned by individuals and can be bought and sold.
(7) Some people have greater resources than others.

He summarises:

We thus have the essential features of a modern competitive market society.

> Without any authoritative allocation of work and rewards, the market, responding to countless individual decisions, puts a price on everything, and it is with reference to prices that the individual decisions are made. The market is the mechanism through which prices are made by, and are a determining factor in making individual decisions about the disposal of energies and the choice of utilities. (1962, p. 55)

Moreover in market society all relationships are permeated by the market, *all* possessions, including men's energies, are commodities and since all men possess something, even if only their own labour, they are involved in the competitive market and continually bound up in competitive power relationships.

The emergence and development of market society in Britain was linked to a particular social theory, *laissez-faire*, which continued to exercise a powerful effect on man's understanding of his social environment long after it ceased to accurately mirror reality. In the early phases of industrialisation *laissez-faire* performed the dual ideological function of explaining why the world was developing in the ways it was and why it should develop in that way, and in these ways constituted both an explanation and a justification of the pattern. The real significance of *laissez-faire* is the ways it conditioned social thought; classical economics, classical political liberalism and basic sociological theory all are related to *laissez-faire* ideas about the nature of man and society, although sociology arose mainly as a criticism of those ideas. The central tenet of *laissez-faire* was expressed by Adam Smith in his *Wealth of Nations* (1776) in the following words:

> every individual necessarily labours to render the annual revenue of the society as great as he can. He generally, indeed, neither intends to promote the public interest, nor knows how much he is promoting it. By preferring the support of domestic to that of foreign industry, he intends only his own security; and by directing that industry in such a manner as its produce may be of the greatest value, he intends only his own gain, and he is in this, as in many other cases, led by an invisible hand to promote an end which is no part of his intention. Nor is it the worse for society that it was no part of it. By pursuing his own interest he frequently promotes that of the society more effectually than when he really intends to promote it. I have never known much good done by those who affected to trade for the public good. (1925 edition, p. 421)

Although initially an academic theory, *laissez-faire*'s significance is greatest in explaining the belief systems of practical man, even today it continues to exercise great sway in the minds of many businessmen and its influence in nineteenth-century Britain permeated all fields of economic and social policy. As Keynes says:

> the ideas of economists and political philosophers, both when they are right and when they are wrong, are more powerful than is commonly understood. Indeed, the world is ruled by little else. Practical men, who believe themselves to be quite exempt from any intellectual influences, are usually the slaves of some defunct economist. (1936, p. 383)

The assumption of the 'hidden hand' guiding the market towards some sort of societal optimum provided a rationalisation for state abstention from social and economic affairs, and by suggesting that an independent ordered society could come from the decisions of individuals pursuing their own interests provided a justification for a system of economic competition which created private wealth. *Laissez-faire*'s influence extended broader than the economic sphere, and provided a moral philosophy and social code as well and replaced the traditional beliefs which it did so much to undermine. Indeed to Smith the basic objective of economic and social policy was the maximisation of individual freedom within an orderly framework of legality. The doctrine of *laissez-faire* became part of a new secular religion, treating the historically specific developments of competition, materialism and individualism as universalistic facets of nature and ruthlessly attacking anything which sought to restrict these developments. It was this celebration of individualism which made *laissez-faire* so revolutionary, and linked the advance of commercialism based on economic freedom to the advance of social freedoms based on the destruction of paternalism and the authoritarian state.

It is central to our argument that while classical economics and political liberalism diverged on many issues, they shared the same central assumptions and these common assumptions informed all their propositions. Roll puts it thus:

> In spite of their sharp distinctions, these schools can be regarded as representative of a single trend of thought. Its essence is a reliance on what is natural as against what is contrived. It implies a belief in the existence of an inherent natural order (however that may be defined) which is superior to any order artificially created by mankind. It claims that all that wise social organisation need do is to act as nearly as possible in harmony with the dictates of the 'natural order'. (1973, pp. 143–4)

'Nature' and 'naturalness' are at rock bottom economic categories. The individual is the basic unit of analysis and it is those social arrangements that allow the individual to pursue his own natural inclinations that yield the reconciliation of the whole and its parts. By nature individuals are barterers and exchangers and those mechanisms, of which the market is the most central, which allow the expression of these individual desires become sacred. The perfectness of the competitive market became the core belief of the advocates of *laissez-faire*.

Although *laissez-faire* became a widespread and diffuse belief system Adam Smith's contribution was revolutionary because he constructed his theoretical system at the junction between a capitalist market economy and industrial capitalism. Following Dalton, capitalism is seen as:

> an economy wide or national system in which private ownership of the means of production and market transactions of labour, resources and products are not only present but also intimately linked to each other and integrated with all production processes and sectors, that is, they are the dominant or prevailing modes of ownership and transaction. In such

systems the price mechanism is the pivotal mode of allocating labour, resources, outputs and incomes. (1974, pp. 56–7)

Smith spoke for a new class in the social fabric, a group of industrialists ready and waiting to receive his message. Indeed it was the extent to which the class already existed which accounted for the receptiveness of influential groups in society to the doctrines of *laissez-faire*. This existence of a class of entrepreneurs prior to industrialisation is one of the unique factors in British industrialisation (Roll 1973, p. 151). Smith's theories were adopted because his message simultaneously linked the past with the future, explaining to those most involved in the processes of change their own condition and rendering their actions both legitimate and respectable, and identifying actions which would enhance their own wealth with a future that promised 'progress' for the common good as well. Smith identified wealth with all domestic production; this broke with the traditions of identifying wealth with trade (mercantilism) and unlike the physiocrats, who believed wealth was generated only by agricultural production, Smith argued that industrial production also generated wealth and thus strengthened the nation politically. It is in this rejection of both land and trade as the generators of wealth that Smith becomes a revolutionary: freeing production from limitation, the vision of unlimited economic growth through production is the true essence of 'modernity', the industrial vision as opposed to the traditional vision.

Much social theory has proceeded from the analysis of industrialisation in Britain and, generalised in ways which are misleading, leads to the fallacy of applying in total an historically specific explanation (Giddens, 1973). As we shall suggest in this chapter, it is the unique constellation of already existing changes in social structure linked to a new belief system, expressing those changes rather than having no links with the existing power structure, which account for the form of British industrialisation. It may well be that the conditions peculiar to Britain of a developed market capitalism were the most conducive to the development of spontaneous or 'undirected' industrialisation and that *laissez-faire* was an appropriate theory to comprehend and manipulate the changes. When imported to countries embarking on industrialisation from different pre-existing social structures *laissez-faire* has proved a misleading ideology. Despite its apparent success as the guiding belief system of the first industrialised nation, and later the most successful industrialised nation, *laissez-faire* policies require the pre-existence of free markets in land, labour and capital capable of meeting the needs of the industrial sector.

Landes argues that it is the way these pre-conditions were fostered within a system of private enterprise which is crucial. He says: 'The role of private economic enterprise in the West is perhaps unique: more than any other factor, it made the modern world. (1972, p. 15). He outlines how land, which under feudalism was caught up in a thicket of conflicting rights and usufructs, formal and informal, which were powerful obstacles to productive exploitation came to be full property in the sense that the owner could use the land in the ways he saw fit and this included disposing of it to others to use as they saw fit. Alongside this freeing of land from customary restrictions was the development of security of ownership protected, not threatened, by the political authority. Without this security of ownership incentives for long-run investment are lacking. North and Thomas describe England in 1700 thus:

> It had developed an efficient set of property rights embedded in the common law. Besides the removal of hindrances to the allocation of resources both in the factor and product markets, England had begun to protect private property in knowledge with its patent law. The stage was now set for the Industrial Revolution. (1973, p. 156)

That the arrangements which favoured capitalist market relationships and resulted in the first case of industrialism should be articulated into an all-embracing economic, political and social philosophy is not surprising since these arrangements were at variance with the totality of previous human history. *Laissez-faire* was only a highly developed case of a more general philosophy of existence, a belief system which characterised, explained and provided imagery and justification for the events of the transformation. *Laissez-faire* was part of a radical change in men's views of themselves and the societies which they were in process of transforming, it is necessary to look at both the circumstances in which particular groups of people found themselves and the content of these belief systems in order to recognise the complex interplay between conditions and beliefs in human society.

Now we will briefly look at the features that characterised the West before the revolution in production associated with the harnessing of inanimate power, in association with the emergence of the 'modern state', the expansion of commercialism and the emergence of private property and private enterprise transformed societies. Barrington-Moore claims.

> In agriculture economic modernisation means the extension of market relationships over a much wider area than before, and the replacement of subsistance farming more and more by production for the market. Secondly, in politics successful modernisation involves the establishment of peace and order over a wide area, the creation of a strong central government. *There is no universal connection between the two processes:* Rome and China both established powerful and far flung governments for their time without generating impetus towards a modern society. (1967, p. 468, our italics)

How did the unique balance of state centralisation of power and extensive commercialisation of agriculture come to provide sufficient impetus to revolutionise the English economic system? In the Middle Ages, the monarchy of England was probably in most respects the most powerful centralised monarch in Western Europe but paradoxically, as Anderson says, 'the strongest mediaeval monarchy in the West eventually produced the weakest and shortest Absolutism (1974*a*, p. 113). It is crucial to recognise the degree to which relationships which constituted the State and its controlling echelons had profound effects upon tendencies and paths to industrialism. Indeed, it is the peculiar 'weakness' of central powers in England and the consequences of this weakness that accounts for the commercialisation of agriculture which promoted a spontaneous industrialisation in the hands of private or free enterprise. The British monarchy achieved early a degree of strength greater that its Continental counterparts because the forces of disorder and competition between rival power groups were less difficult to contain than in the broader stretches of continental Europe; but because the power needed to provide internal order was less, the control exercised over the activities of the people was not so thorough. Subjects could be allowed a degree of freedom without jeopardising the basic position of the monarchy; in particular these freedoms created new social groups whose economic welfare depended on the order provided by central government which guaranteed their property rights. Thus England was the first to break with feudalism and did so largely without the agency of a government exercising total or absolute control.

Following the breakdown of the Roman Empire in Europe, feudalism was a response to a series of invasions from without, the system of feudalism linked a mode of production to a way of providing military protection against outsiders. As North and Thomas say, 'Feudalism provided a measure of stability and order in this fragmented world. Where security prevailed, population began once more to increase. If growing numbers threatened to crowd a manor uncomfortably, there was always new land to be cleared and cultivated within the protection of a new lord (1973, p. 11)'. Thus feudalism was a system of political domination in which the aristocracy extracted the surplus from the peasantry through labour services, embodied in the institutions of serfdom, in return for providing protection from the devastation of crops and destruction of homes which accompanied the raids by outsiders. As the nobility successfully asserted themselves the areas of chaos and uncertainty declined and the self-sufficiency of the siege economy began to give way to systems of trade which exploited the comparative geographic advantages of different areas. As the stability of the feudal system increased a measure of specialisation occurred within town and country, the nobility creating towns to supply their expanding needs both for military equipment and for consumption goods. Indeed it is important to stress that feudal Europe was not a subsistence economy, and while during crop failures people died of starvation, there was for the most part a surplus which could be extracted by the privileged class, the nobility. Feudalism thus created systems of trade and a division of labour that later provided the seed-bed for the entrepreneurial classes who nurtured industrial capitalism; initially however the traders and manufacturers floundered under the patronage of the state and nobility and formed an extension of the feudal mode of extraction of surplus, rather than a contradiction. Indeed initially the trading and merchant group were supporters of the *status quo*; since its fortunes will tend to be bound up with the existing mode of production it is more likely to be under an inducement to preserve that mode of production rather than transform it. 'It is likely to struggle to 'muscle in' upon an existing form of appropriating surplus labour; but it is unlikely to try to change this form' (Dobb, 1972, pp. 17–18).

Serfdom or the system of direct labour service was not flexible enough to cope with the needs of the expanding feudal mode of production. But as Anderson stresses, 'the end of serfdom did not thereby mean the disappearance of feudal relationships from the countryside' (1974*a*, p. 17). Basically, the substitution of money rent did not lead to the abolition of feudal agrarian relations. Coercion of an extra economic nature continued and the peasantry retained certain instruments of production in their hands, livestock and common grazing rights for example. As long as the aristocratic nobility prevented a free market in land and labour by various 'personalised' devices and as long as the peasant labourer was able to subsist, that is re-create himself via his entitlement to land, common pasture and ownership of animals and implements, then capitalistic relations of the 'free market' could not prevail. The demise of feudalism based on serfdom thus gave rise to the new absolutist state with power and economic control now concentrated in the central authority, an authority which in the words of Anderson (1974*a*, p. 17) 'introduced standing armies, a permanent bureaucracy, national taxation, a codified law and the beginnings of a unified market'. These necessary preconditions for capitalist development were, however, not accompanied by a freeing of economic activity from the traditional class structure which operated to extract the rural surplus for a privileged aristocracy, and was based on personal patronage. While the aristocracy lost autonomy and were subject to the authority of the absolutist state, rather than seeing the changes as a loss of power it would be more appropriate to see the new system as a consolidation of the basic economic and social privileges of the aristocracy in the changed environment resulting from feudalism's success in re-establishing social order and allowing trade to flourish.

The sponsorship of certain groups, the use of a money economy, the creation of internal peace, the extension of the division of labour and the emergence of towns and cities all created tensions within society that became more and more difficult to contain, and the pattern the tensions took in the West, of rural modernisation and the commercialisation of agriculture on the one hand and centralised government on the other, that determined the path to industrialism. Now we must try to refine the analysis of the English transition from feudalism to capitalism, and to locate the patterns of this development within a context of the interplay of classes and their precursors. This requires some clarification of the relationship between industrialism and capitalism.

Giddens contrasts Marx's and Weber's treatments of capitalism:

> The basic difference between the two thinkers is that, whereas for Weber the rationalisation of technique expressed in the machine epitomises the intrinsic character of modern capitalism both as an economic and social structure, for Marx this rationalisation of technique is, in a highly important sense, secondary and subordinate to the core attribute of capitalism as a class system. (1973, p. 140)

Marx sees the process of industrialisation as being secondary and subordinate to capitalism, being merely the logical expression of the class character of the mode of production. Technique and the relationships determined by technique are subordinate to the class system (See Chapter 8, 'Convergence Theories'.) Defining capitalism as where production is primarily oriented to profit accruing to privately owned capital and where the processes of production are organised in terms of a market in which commodities including labour are bought and sold according to standards of monetary exchange,

Giddens distinguishes 'capitalism' from 'capitalist society'. This is a crucial distinction because by confining capitalism to these features it is possible to locate enclaves of the capitalist mode of production in pre-capitalist societies. Giddens suggests that 'capitalist society' refers to the situation in which the standards of the capitalist mode of production become the dominant standards of the whole of social life, that is where all action revolves around market considerations of the prices of factors of production and the private appropriation of surplus by property owners. Moreover once capitalism becomes linked with industrialism the elimination of mixed societal types is inevitable, Marx argues, as the superiority of the capitalist mode of production sweeps away the remnants of pre-existing forms. Giddens argues (1973, p. 146) that Marx's failure to realise the extent to which the aristocracy played a part in British capitalism has led much historical and sociological analysis to underplay the importance of rural developments. It is not only the staying power of the landed aristocracy that has been underestimated but also the role of the peasantry. As Giddens says, 'Even prior to the twentieth century revolutions, the peasantry have played a major role in shaping the form taken by the advanced societies – and, again, the early "disappearance" of both the bonded and independent peasantry has proved more the exception than the rule' (1973, p. 147). It is the balance between rural relationships and the outcome of their interactions with centralised state power which needs clarifying. Indeed the development of non-feudal modes of production is governed by the extent of surplus that can be extracted from the peasantry and the developments of the coercive state apparatus which are necessary to protect the extraction of surplus from the peasantry for use elsewhere.

Man is distinguished from other animals by this ability to create a surplus, and once created this surplus creates a need for organisation to distribute the surplus. In the various solutions to distributing surplus exploitation may occur. Some groups may use positions of advantage to exploit those less advantageously placed. Since men are able to transform both nature and their own conditions of existence and impute meanings of a symbolic nature to their relationships with their environments the limits on both meanings and relationships are infinite. In any specific case they are limited by the productive and distributive situation. As men operate in the symbolic sphere they can generate needs, aspirations and motivations in their social interaction, and consequently in order to reproduce themselves the productive and distributive systems create and sustain aspirations and norms which are contingent to existing relationships. When the social system can no longer generate appropriate motivations to re-create itself it must cease to exist or change its character. This is what happened to feudalism in Britain between 1500 and 1800.

Feudalism was basically an agrarian mode of production, but unlike other 'traditional' socio-economic systems was not a static unchanging system. From 1100 onwards there were dramatic increases in agricultural productivity linked to technical innovation. 'The technical instruments which were the material instruments of this advance were, essentially the use of the iron plough for tilling, the stiff-harness for equine traction, the watermill for mechanical power, marling for soil improvement and the three field system for crop rotation' (Anderson, 1974*b*, p. 113). Parallel with the technical changes came the changes in the legal status of land ownership which made land absolute private property and allowed the break from feudal systems of obligation based on 'conditional' land ownership in which the aristocracy were stewards of the land rather than owners. The heritage of Roman law in Europe made possible this shift in the definition of property which did not occur elsewhere, and in Britain, influenced by Roman law but not tied to it was continental Europe, the needs of the privileged groups were reflected even more rapidly. As Hartwell says, 'In England by the eighteenth century the concept of property – politically, socially and legally – was not confined, as on the continent, to the ownership of real things, but extended to the ownership of non-tangible claims to property, like copyrights and company shares' (1971, p. 251). This extension of 'property' rights to cover non-tangible property was crucial, and in part reflects the different systems of legal patronage in Britain where the property owners rather than the centralised state were the patrons of the lawyers.

The complex evolution of the law can be seen if we take the example of law regulating labour services. Here it might be assumed that it was in the economic interest of the nobility to ensure the continuance of labour services; however the changing legal regulation of labour reflected a much more complex reality. Feudalism expanded by reproducing itself on virgin land, so the expansive energies led to the development of marginal lands where the basic structure of society was set up as a replica of existing manorial units. Moreover the limitations of the agricultural technology and the extension of trade, which destroyed self-sufficiency, combined with the population expansion and associated territorial expansion to produce a society in which marginal productivity declined. Put simply, the new population produced less per head than the existing population because they were working less fertile land. The inherent weakness was brought to a head by a series of bad harvests in the early fourteenth century which initially raised agricultural prices but then brought famine and a decline in the birth rate; these, when combined with the ravages of the Black Death, radically reduced the rural labour force. According to North and Thomas:

> The significant and prolonged decline in population induced three parameter shifts which account for the observed changes in the institutional arrangements and property rights of the period. These changes were: (1) the alteration in relative factor prices with rents falling relative to the value of labour, and the consequent decline in feudal revenues heavily dependent upon land rents; (2) the relative increase in the minimum level of government expenditure; and (3) the rise of the costs (transaction costs) of using the market to organise economic activity. (1973, p. 73)

The decline in agricultural prices and consequently rents made the aristocracy's position somewhat desperate and led them to rely on military activities to sustain their revenues. These military activities compounded the basic problem of living beyond their means and led the nobility further into debt, creating simultaneously inflation which further reduced the value of rents, and towns which, relatively independent of the nobility, thrived on provisioning their military activities. Moreover the attempts to reaffirm the old models of labour service were met with strong opposition among the peasantry, who staged series of revolts against the oppressive measures used to keep them to their station. Although the revolts were suppressed they had their effects on productive relationships, especially where the towns provided peasants a real opportunity to escape. The aristocracy reacted in this context of labour scarcity by what Anderson described as 'a slow but steady commutation of dues into money rents in the West, and an increasing leasing out of the demesne to peasant tenants (1974*a*, p. 206). This process was most pronounced in England, where the labour shortage was so great that it also provided the incentive for the first enclosures and the shift to wool production, which further reduced the independence of the aristocracy from the rest of society. This was the beginning of the emergence of the tenant farmer who became so important as a source of expansive energy in agriculture in the seventeenth and eighteenth centuries.

Giddens (1973, pp. 82–3) suggests that feudalism is characterised by (1) an authoritative allocation of work, that is there is a belief in a 'divine' schema which restricts men to particular vocations by virtue of their station at birth, (2) distinct legal categories separating different estates, and defining the duties and privileges of members of each estate, (3) an economy only geared to meet the needs known to exist in the local community, (4) a personalised system of domination and subordination, (5) agricultural production the basic fabric of the system, (6) the fusion of economic and political power. A distinctive feature of capitalism is the separation of economic and political power. Serfdom meant that this unity of economic and political was focused at the local level; the serf owing allegiance to 'his' lord and his lord in turn to the liege lord who granted him the lands in return for military service. The introduction of money rents weakened the unity of political and economic power and the 'personalised' coercion of the lord became inappropriate. 'The result was a displacement of politico-legal coercion upwards towards a centralised, militarised summit – the Absolutist State' (Anderson, 1974*a*, p. 19). The depersonalised authority involved in the growth of central government guaranteed property rights and freed property from the obligations operating in personal systems of domination. Landes stresses the importance of assurance in the security of property as being essential for the conversion of property into productive investment and points out: 'This security had two dimensions: the relationship of the individual owner of property to the ruler and the relationship of the members of society to one another' (1972, p. 16). In terms of the first, Landes's analysis highlights the special nature of the Western nation states, in which rulers increasingly depended on, and recognised, the advantages of routine methods of appropriating rural surplus over the methods of confiscation and seizure. The absolutist state also was involved in balancing the demands between the needs of the states and the needs of individuals and in balancing the competing claims of other power groups in society. It is in this latter function that the uniqueness of Western governmental developments lies. As North and Thomas put the matter: 'The King, by the end of the Middle Ages, was in a position to enforce exclusive rights to markets within his Kingdom. Voluntary associations of artisans and merchants organised in guilds were willing to pay for the exclusive privileges that only the King could now provide' (1973, p. 88).

We will now attempt to summarise the main points so far covered, as they provide the framework for the rest of the chapter. First, full-scale capitalist society requires a developed free market in land, capital and especially labour. Labour is critical because surplus is extracted by the employment of wage labour to produce goods which are sold not according to the cost of production but according to what the market will bear. The surplus generated in this way is appropriated by the owners of capital. Second, capitalism brings capitalist society only when it harnesses industrial technology; until production is revolutionised in this way there is insufficient surplus to support a full market system. Third, in early industrialisation commercialised agriculture and the nation state occurred simultaneously with the emergence of clear-cut private property. Fourth, the transition from feudalism depended on the emergence of an 'autonomous' economy, reacting primarily to market rather than political forces. The shift from the 'conditional property' of feudalism where property rights were really only rights to the revenues derived from the land, to 'absolute property', which could be disposed of in any way the owner saw fit, was an essential pre-condition for this autonomy. Moreover the establishment of those property rights acted as a check on the development of the total control which emergenced in the Orient and stifled spontaneous economic development.

To elaborate this point about the independence of the economy Macpherson says: 'There is a change in the rationale or justification of private property: before capitalism, various ethical and theological grounds had been offered; with the rise of capitalism, the rationale came to be mainly that property was a necessary incentive to labour required by society' (1975, p. 106). The distinguishing feature of the capitalist orientation to property is the basically egalitarian nature of property, that is to say, in a strictly formal sense *all* men were being brought into the valuations of market relationships and *all* men were being made free to contract in the market. Exclusive rights to property could no longer be legally confined to special groups by virtue of birth, which practice had been the foundation of the feudal social system. The estate system, which categorised people according to birth and allocated rights, and privileges on the basis of this classification, provided a justification for the extraction of surplus from the peasantry in terms of their inherent inferiority. The emergence of market capitalism meant that property was now no longer defined in terms of customary rights to revenues, but in terms of the thing itself, and the legitimation of unequal property distribution could no longer rest on beliefs in God-given differences because the market stressed the equality of all to enter exchange freely and benefit as much as possible from their efforts in the market. The justification of property shifted and property was justified in terms of securing the fruits of one's labour, and the chance to acquire property was seen as a necessary incentive for labour which is socially useful. Property thus becomes the index of a man's usefulness, because society bestows property in proportion to the services rendered. Usefulness or worth in capitalist society is defined by free operation of supply and demand in the market, and the economic sphere claims an independence from the political. The political system is left to provide the necessary security for the smooth functioning of the economy but not to determine social priorities.

It is within this transition from feudal relationships to the full market relationships of capitalist society that we much locate the specific forces of change that made England the first industrial nation. It is against this common background that we can understand the different responses within European nations that made the English experience so untypical. The common elements which distinguish Europe are the emergence of a system of market relationships within the context of an absolutist state. The differences between the classes and groups within the states account for the unique divergence of Britain from other countries as they moved from a common feudal heritage.

Population

Sweden and Ireland experienced similar population growth to England prior to the mid-eighteenth century, but neither experienced growth of industrial production until much later. This highlights the way in which it was the interaction of a series of changes that accounts for the British industrialisation, and while the same changes were occurring elsewhere, they did not produce similar inter-actions. Population in Britain had only reached about nine million by 1801, then by 1851 it had doubled, and one of the problems is discovering the extent to which population growth was as much a consequence as a cause of economic growth. Perkin says, 'Between population growth and economic growth the relationship is never a simple, one-way, causal link but a sensitive, two-way servo-mechanism, which transmits from one to the other the shock of every change in momentum' (1969, p. 101). Although there is debate about whether population growth came from a fall in the death rate or rise in the birth rate and whatever are the initial cause and effect relationships between population growth and economic growth, the expansion of the industrial labour force required by full industrialisation involved the commercialisation of agriculture and the associated increases in agricultural productivity.

Musgrave (1964, pp. 58–85) provides a nice example of the delicate interplay of population and economic changes in his analysis of the breakdown of the apprenticeship system. 'As the traditional system of apprenticeship broke down because of irrelevance to the eighteenth century, and the legal requirements to serve an apprenticeship to a trade were repeated in 1814, the young were liberated to their true level on the changing economy' (p. 42). The finding of their true level involved both earlier marriage and larger families as peak earnings were no longer deferred by training and the family income depended on the number of child workers as it was the quantity of labour not the quality that determined earnings.

Differences in the property system also partly accounted for the differences in population growth between European countries. The processes of freeing the rural young were further advanced in Britain than elsewhere because the shift towards absolute property ownership and the destruction of traditional use rights in the land had proceeded further, and the chance of inheriting these rights no longer provided a disincentive to early marriage for the British young.

Population growth was necessary for economic growth, but cannot adequately be explained simply in terms of a Malthusian type of argument that saw population expanding constantly, subject only to the checks imposed by food shortages, which the revolution in agricultural technology had temporarily removed. The process of industrialisation changes family structures and alters the economics of child rearing. This is a continuing process and is at the centre of the argument about economic growth and birth control (see Holloway, 1973). It is necessary to look at the unique characteristics of English society to explain why it was in Britain that this European-wide population explosion should trigger industrial expansion and why the response to growing demands for industrial products was met by a system of capitalistic enterprise and led to the first fully capitalist society. Part of the answer lies in the degree to which market society had already created social groups in England who generated an effective demand for industrial goods. The commercialisation of agriculture and growth of trade in the towns had created sizable groups with incomes which allowed and encouraged them to look to new ways of spending their money. Moreover Perkin stresses the fine balance between industrialisation and population growth in which Britain nurtured economic growth

> For the Industrial Revolution required, in addition to all the ancillary and economic factors brought into operation by the peculiar structure of English society, a very delicate adjustmenc of population growth: not too fast, for that would cheapen labour to the point of deadening demand and suppressing the need for labour saving machinery; nor too slow, for that too would discourage demand while making labour expensive and fractious. (1973, pp. 101–2)

This is a very important factor in the growth of British industrialisation; if labour had been too plentiful there would have been no incentive to continually substitute capital for labour, and it was in this continual search for labour-saving devices that the major innovational efforts were concentrated.

If population growth is to provide for economic growth it must create two conditions: First, an available work-force providing the labour power willing to enter the new occupations opened by industrial production; second, an increase in consumer demand necessary to provide a system of incentive that made it worthwhile to invest in a production system based on large-scale demand and incorporating increased division of labour and machines. Population growth in itself provides neither a willing work-force, if alternative more conducive work opportunities exist, in traditional economic activities, nor a structure of effective demand, if the increased population is too poor or by custom unwilling to buy the goods produced by industrial methods.

The emergence of a potential industrial labour force

As we have seen, England, in comparison with her Continental competitors, had taken the process of severance of traditional rural relationships based on personalised bonds between master and servant a long way, although nineteenth-century labour law, despite the influence of *laissez-faire*, continued to use the language of master and servant to curtail the rights of the working class to organise. Although serfdom had disappeared in western Europe by 1800, it was only in Britain that it had been replaced predominantly by pure contractual market relationships in the country; even the processes of poor relief had been put on a bureaucratic basis. As Kemp concludes, 'if one overriding reason can be given for the slower transformation of the Continent, despite the fact that in the West there were many signs of growth and change in the eighteenth century, it must be the continued prevalence of the traditional agrarian structures' (1969, p. 8). It was only in England, then, that there was, by the eighteenth century, no important peasant class, still tied to subsistence farming and providing a bulwark against change. The Continent had not produced a landless labour force compelled by necessity to seek employment off the land. As Shanin suggests, the peasantry create cohesive, family-based units of production and consumption, bound from a self-sustaining unity to a specific geographical location, which leads to a very restrictive orientation to economic activity. He says, 'The economic action is closely interwoven with family relations, and the motive of profit maximisation in money terms seldom appears in its explicit form' (1971, p. 15). The elimination of the peasantry from the English countryside is thus a key variable in explaining the malleability and early responsiveness of the English work-force to the demands of factory employment. The pervasiveness of the 'domestic' and 'putting' out systems of rural manufacture provided a half-way house in the transition and began to accustom the work-force to the rigours of factory discipline. In France, the bourgeoisie's reliance on the peasantry in their revolution against the absolutist state radically restricted the availability of the necessary labour force. As Kemp puts it, 'In historical perspective the peasantry exacted a heavy price from the bourgoisie for supporting them in the Revolution' (p. 59). That price was the continuance of the peasantry, which stood in the way of a free labour system responding to market forces. In England the system of inheritance by the first-born son encouraged economic improvement of landholdings and provided the incentive to make the agricultural innovations that preceded industrialisation; elsewhere in Europe land was distributed among all the children and this disrupted continuity and acted against the consolidation of holdings and the introduction of new methods, as well as discouraging labour mobility from the land. Again to quote Kemp, 'The continued predominance of agriculture in the economy and the weight of the peasantry in the agrarian sector acted as a brake on industrialisation. Purchasing power and incomes were kept down, thus limiting the market and discouraging investment in industry' (p. 60).

The more pronounced decline of guild control of manufacture in England is another important distinguishing feature of the English case of industrialisation. Weber's definition of the guild is 'an organisation of craft workers specialised in accordance with the type of occupation. Its functions through two things, namely internal regulation of work and monopolisation against outsiders. It achieves its objectives if everyone joins the Guild who practices the craft in the location in question' (1961, p. 110). This makes clear, on two scores, the incompatibility of guild control of production with free market conditions. First, guilds restrict the free market for labour and second, they deliberately stifle demand for goods, the production of which would undermine their monopoly of supply. In England the erosion of the guild monopolies occurred early. The early growth of trade fostered the division of labour and growth of scale and increased the capital needed to produce goods. These developments destroyed the uniform status of the craftsman on which guild control rested, and created a new class of town 'masters' who owned the raw materials and machines used to process those materials. These developments eroded the independence of the town worker and began to create an urban working class with nothing to sell but their labour power. In Britain, according to Rudé, 'The guilds had of course changed as society had changed: they had lost a great deal of their own vigour and relevance and their regulations were seen increasingly as a restraint on trade rather than as a protection' (Rudé, p. 44). The changes in the town labour markets were accompanied by a more significant development: rural manufacture. The new town merchants evaded the remnants of guild control by the system of 'putting out' and 'cottage labour', which allowed them to exploit the unorganised landless rural labour force. It is the peculiar nature of the market society to overcome rural/urban distinctions, since the particular logic of the market is to avoid centres of resistance and thereby render them, in turn, obsolescent. Indeed, when industrialisation returned to a new urban environment it did so by creating new towns and cities where the guilds had never existed.

It is important to recognise that labour supply was most available where traditional regulations were least effective, namely in the villages and countryside. The history of English rural relationships had resulted in a situation in which the increased population was most amenable to the call of the labour market. With the destruction of their traditional protections, the guild, and rights to use the land, the rural working class were 'free' to enter wage employment and there was an inbuilt tendency to accept economic development as the alternative, quite clearly, was starvation. English agrarian developments meant that a land-free group were available to move to the opportunities for wage labour, and industrialisation was not stifled by labour's unwillingness to move to the areas where factory construction was most favoured by climatic factors or access to raw materials.

The creation of effective demand for industrial goods

Capitalist industrialisation required a rapid expansion of demand for mass consumption goods. It was this demand that called forth the changes in production methods which led from market society to industrial society. 'Most of the economically important inventions of the Industrial Revolution period can more plausibly be ascribed to the pressure of increasing demand rather than to the random operation of the human instinct of contrivance, changes in factor prices, or some Schumpeterian innovator (who became an important agent of advance only at a relatively late stage)' (Habakkuk, 1968, p. 31).

Although later the Colonies were to prove crucial to the development of British capitalism it is doubtful whether the colonial activities of Europe prior to the Industrial Revolution contributed to the emergence of the demand which nurtured industrialism except where they reinforced patterns of trade already occurring within Europe. Where, as in Spain's case, colonialisation involved straightforward annexation, or theft of gold and silver, it did not foster the new order, but rather bolstered the old order. Colonisation and trade imperialism reflected beliefs about the nature of wealth which were inimical to the growth of rational capitalist accumulation.

A very brief excursion into the role of religious belief systems and religious institutions suggests that the peculiar developments of British religion played a part in freeing economic activities from traditional orientations to economic actions. The break with Rome and the Civil War had reduced the grip of the Church over men's minds. Reflecting the changes in economic activities in society the Church and religious sects did not oppose this world economic activity. In the more centralised monarchies of Europe religion remained essentially part of the restraining apparatus of the traditional order, in Britain the Church reflected the greater independence of social groups from the monarchy, and although confirming traditional authority structures did not oppose economic change. In Britain religion did nothing to prevent the emergence of the new social groups whose life styles provided the demands for industrial goods.

The aristocracy and economic change

What is unique to England is the degree to which the aristocracy itself had undergone commercialisation. The greater changes in concepts of property are an index of this commercialisation and to the degree that England had become a market society prior to industrialisation and largely at the behest of the aristocracy. The aristocracy had been involved in the commercialisation of agriculture, not primarily through their own innovations, but largely through their encouragement of the innovations of their tenants, which they saw would make it possible for tenants to pay higher rents and still make a good return for themselves. This process whereby the aristocracy saw its own interests being served by economic change was critical, because it was still the aristocracy who called the tune and it ensured, in Barrington-Moore's words, that 'there was no very solid phalanx of aristocratic opposition to the advance of industry itself' (1967, p. 30). Not only were the aristocracy not resistant to commercialisation, but their ranks were relatively open to anyone who succeeded in making fortunes in trade and manufacture. As land could be sold, the self-made man could buy the necessary adjuncts for admission to the aristocracy, and this openness to new entrants from trade was something peculiar to English development. Stone describes the situation thus:

> The peerage in 1640 was a landed aristocracy increasingly devoted to money making, infiltrated partly by capitalist bourgoisie obsessed with aristocratic pretensions, and partly by jumped-up lesser gentry who owed their elevation to political favour but some of whom had failed to extract from the Crown the favour of a great landed estate with which to endow their success. (1965, p. 22)

The peculiar nature of English history had resulted in a landowning aristocracy which had, after the Civil War, re-established a limited monarchy over which it was able to exert control through Parliament. In economic terms the central apparatus exerted power only over external trade through its control of customs and excise. Local government was firmly entrenched in the hands of the landowners, and Parliament, controlled by the same interests, ensured that internal trade remained unimpeded by requirements of the Crown. The lack of formal requirements to reside at the court of the Crown meant that the aristocracy lived on and maintained control over their estates and were actively involved in the commercial overseeing of their affairs. Land, labour and capital were thus regulated in the interests of the commercially minded aristocracy and Parliament, controlled by those interests, functioned to remove any barriers to the exploitation of commercial opportunities. It was to this receptive audience that the doctrine of *laissez-faire* was so appealing as a justification for what they had already begun to do, namely replace traditional relationships by market relationships.

What was unique to England was the degree to which the separation of the political and economic had proceeded and the self regulating market had become a reality (see Polanyi, 1963, p. 67). More important still was the acceptance of the belief that the self-regulating market was 'natural'. The markets at this point moreover were to a very large extent beyond the control of any one producer or any one power group. In particular the State was restricted simply to a role of providing a framework of law and order within which the directions of social life were decided by other forces. *Laissez-faire* was adopted by the aristocracy because it allowed them to justify the breaches with traditionalism and simultaneously defend as 'natural and just' the existing distribution of property and power. Who better than the propertied to govern since they could be relied on to ensure the 'free play' of the market and thus ensure the achievement of the 'common good'? And while codified widely held public beliefs in *laissez-faire* were much more prevalent by the nineteenth century, already during the late eighteenth century, the period of the birth of industrialisation, many groups were trying to establish new understandings of the relationships between God, Society and Nature.

John Stuart Mill has characterised the traditional authority relations of pre-industrial society thus: 'The relation between rich and poor should be only partially authoritative; it should be amiable, moral and sentimental; affectionate tutelage on the one side, respectful and grateful deference on the other. The rich should be *in loco parentis* to the poor, guiding and restraining them like children' (1848, vol. 2, pp. 319–20). It was this belief in the duty of the upper orders to care for the poor that was eroded and replaced by a belief that each individual was equal in the market. Continued poverty came to be seen as an indication of lack of personal endeavour or as an inability to contribute to the social welfare of the community; either of which absolved the successful from any moral obligation to help the less successful and served to justify the individual consumption of the material benefits of success. Moreover the belief spread that the market was the best allocation of societal resources and that any interference which stopped the working out of the 'hidden hand', actually was counter productive and lessened social welfare. Bendix stresses this point when he comments on the finality of the Poor Law Amendment Act of 1834 (1963, p. 94):

> 'These legislative deliberations and enactments made the theory of self dependence for the first time the centre of widespread public attention, and eventually implemented the Malthusian view that poverty was the fault of the poor, not the responsibility of the rich.

This replacement of traditional moral tutelage by the belief in self-responsibility is a critical element of the development of moral beliefs to ensure that there were no blocks placed in the way of economic change by the associated social conditions of factories and working-class towns and the living conditions of the labouring classes in general.

The pioneer case of industrialisation, created in the context of the first full market, was unique in the degree to which factors coalesced to enable an independence of 'economic' from 'political' factors. The commercialisation of agriculture, the weakening of the guilds and a property-owning aristocracy meant that there was a hostility to centralised interference in economic affairs unprecedented elsewhere. Unlike the aristocracy and landowners of the rest of Europe, the British landowners did not rely for the protection of their privileged stakes on the physical suppression of the subordinate classes by an absolutist state. Already in Britain the dominant groups had found new alliances to protect their privileges and new ideologies to persuade the subordinate groups of the rightness of the social order which favoured the privileged.

Britain was distinguished from the rest of Europe by the larger numbers of middling groups in terms of wealth and social status in England and by the possibility that existed for members of these middle groups to turn economic success into a base for upward mobility and entry into the aristocracy. This openness of social structure is important both to the explanation of the emergence of the supply of entrepreneurial talent and to the explanation of the emergence of a demand for the goods that industrial manufacture could provide. Kemp, contrasting the British and French experience, argues that in France industrialisation was much slower than in England, partly because in France 'Much industrial production was geared to satisfy the exigent tastes of wealthier consumers: the emphasis was on quality not low cost, on skilled craftsmen rather than on machine technology' (1969, p. 61). In England the social structure provided a sufficient number of people both willing and able to consume on a mass scale. Indeed, one of the distinctive features of the British social structure was the desires of the middle orders to emulate their social superiors. This created demand for the cheaper substitutes for luxury goods which mass manufacture allowed, the first demands were for cheap cotton cloth to replace the more expensive hand-woven cloths and for pottery to replace the sparse kitchenware of wood or pewter. Later demand expanded to an ever-widening range of goods and the building of railways and machines created demands for coal and steel which led to the development of industrial production techniques in these industries as well.

Cotton provided the key to British industrialisation and British access to the colonies and cheap raw materials was an important inter-acting factor with the growth of internal demand (see Foster, 1974). Perkin, however, brings into perspective the importance of internal demand for sustaining industrial growth, when he draws attention to the role of exports in the growth of the cotton industry and comments on the theory that colonial consumption was critical to the emergence of industrialisation. 'Even in cotton, the trade upon which this argument heavily leans since an extra ordinarily large proportion of total production was exported, the ratio of exports to production was scarcely more than a third at the beginning and about half towards the end of the Industrial Revolution, in spite of a 75 fold increase in the consumption of raw cotton' (1969, p. 10).

Thus, unlike most other European countries, England lacked the formal barriers to consumption. The tendency of all levels of English society to 'ape' each other was of crucial importance, because when allied to the size of the middle groups, it meant that demand was not fragmented, with small groups using consumption to distinguish themselves from one another, but rather aggregated so that most groups found the same standardised product perfectly acceptable. Perkin says that foreign visitors to England were prone to comment that 'the common people, at work and especially at leisure, wore a conscious imitation of the dress of their superiors' (p. 94). This was because in Europe the feudal restraints on consumption styles appropriate to particular groups were still powerful influences, disrupting the establishment of the mass demand required to justify mass production techniques and the harnessing of inanimate power to production. Perkin argues that the revolution in tastes extended to food and drink and in England emulation of the privileged classes accelerated the decline of localised tastes in food and encouraged the standardisation which all but destroyed the independent baker and brewer by the middle of the twentieth century.

The growth in demand for industrial goods is not only to be explained by desire to emulate the better off. In England there existed a large and growing class who had no alternative to resort to the market for the satisfaction of their consumption needs, as indeed they had similarly no alternative but to resort to the market to sell their labour power. The landless class was larger and grew more quickly in Britain than elsewhere in Europe. The operation of the market made the landless labourer one of the major sources of the demand which allowed the entrepreneurs to create a factory system and property system which ensured both the continual growth of industrial production and the maintenance of the new structures of social privilege.

Cotton, class and entrepreneurship

There is no doubt that Britain's industrialisation was as much influenced by the centrality of cotton goods as by the development of the social structure which allowed the growth of demand and entrepreneurship. We will now very briefly look at the issue of where the impetus to industrial production came from, and the degree to which an ideology of the 'self-made man', or 'industry bringing its just rewards' is compatible with the facts.

There is disagreement among historians about the source of initial capital in the cotton industry. Bendix stresses the relatively small sums of money involved in setting up in business, and the degree to which it was thus possible for the middle orders to use this route to improve their social position. 'Since the major developments of industry in the second half of the eighteenth century occurred in the textile industry and since capital requirements in the industry were modest at the time, it is probable that a proportion of the early cotton manufacturers in particular did come from families of workers, craftsmen and peasants' (1963, p. 23). Bendix thus supports the idea that the development of market forces allowed people to rise freely from humble origins. This belief is central to the justification of the market as the right allocative mechanism, unless individual effort is rewarded and individuals confront the market with equal chances there can be no guarantee that 'the hidden hand' will maximise social welfare. Foster, however, casts doubt on Bendix's conclusions on the basis of his findings for Oldham: he found 'Of the first forty-two cotton mills built in the Oldham area between 1796 and 1811, the overwhelming majority were built by men who started out with capital. And most by men with a good deal: coal owners, bankers, merchant hatters, wholesale tradesmen, yeoman manufacturers. Only two are known to have been built by men originating from worker families' (1974, p. 9).

However, whatever the extent of the opportunity for upward mobility, it is clear that the small capital required in the early stages made it possible for the advocates of industrialisation under *laissez-faire* conditions to weave elaborate systems of justifications, celebrating entrepreneurship, making the market the 'sacred' method of establishing social welfare, resisting state intervention in the affairs of the wealthy, and making poverty the fault of the poor. These justifications became important as political weapons in the early nineteenth century, when the sectors of the aristocracy who still basically relied on agricultural production desired a continuance of restrictions on trade, but were forced to capitulate to the demands of the new groups. These new groups, however, were not devoid of aristocratic support, because many English aristocrats had become involved in industrial production, either through the leasing of mineral rights or their estates and through their ownership of the land, now greatly enhanced in value, on which the factories and factory towns were built.

The cotton industry, labour discipline and the social organisation of work

The development of the cotton industry was not a smooth process of transition. The various technical processes were 'modernised' at different times and in the uneven process certain groups of workers experienced periods of high earnings followed by periods of very low earnings as the relative demands for spinners and weavers varied. E. P. Thompson (1963) has drawn attention to the revolutionary change in work experience that accompanied the growth of the factory system, stressing the way that the machines demanded a work discipline previously not required. The harnessing of inanimate power to the machines meant that workers had to learn to serve the machines and employers had to devise schemes to ensure that discipline. The market provided one discipline and the industrialists encouraged the migration of labour to the towns to ensure there was not a labour shortage which would give labour some bargaining power. The cotton industry illustrates many of the techniques used by the employers to ensure that the working class was not able to sustain a united opposition to them. The use of female and child labour in the early phases of factory production is one example, the use of immigrant Irish labour another.

The development of the management function

The large-scale factory with its demand for large-scale capital investment and continuous oversight of labour marked the start of the true industrial revolution. The revolutionary nature of the factory cannot be overstressed in terms of pace of work, development of industrial centres of production and the degree to which work organisation became dictated by machines. However, as Weber says: 'The real distinguishing characteristic of the modern factory is in general, however, not the implements of work applied, but the concentration of ownership of the work place, means of work, source of power and raw material in one and the same hand, that of the entrepreneur. This combination was only exceptionally met before the eighteenth century' (1961, p. 224).

It was this concentration of ownership and control over the means of production that allowed the full implementation of the ethic of rational calculation (see Chapters 6 and 7) that Weber identified as the central developmental tendency of capitalism. This calculation involved the extension of rational accounting procedures as well as the extension of rational technique and as Perkin stresses, 'The entrepreneur, the active working capitalist who both owned and managed his own enterprise was the key figure in the revolution in organisation' (1969, p. 112). The English industrial revolution was founded on the owner-managed factory; moreover it was distinguished by its relative independence from the dominance of the financial institutions. In Britain, industrial development fostered the growth of two distinct economic interests in British capitalism. The owner-managers of early industrialisation did not rely on the banking institutions to finance production but relied on reinvesting their accumulated profits. This tended to accelerate development in the early phases but later led to a tendency for over-investment in established and declining industries. The banking institutions created by the colonial trade expanded as world trade grew, and their role as central mediating bodies grew as British capitalism began to expand by exporting capital to invest in North and South America as well as in the countries of the Empire. This pattern of the relatively independent development of industrial and finance capital is another unique feature of British industrialism.

It has been suggested that the entrepreneurs of the cotton industry were great technical innovators and the pioneers of new organisational forms. This view forms a central part of the justification of *laissez-faire* economic policies, because innovation becomes linked to market freedom and individual creativity and becomes seen as an unquestionable social good. Pollard (1968) has suggested that far from most of the early entrepreneurs being risk-taking innovators, for the greater part they were simply adopting the methods proven to be more effective for the pursuit of profit. Perkin (1969) however stresses that not all the merchant classes of pre-industrial market society were prepared to assume the duties involved by the continuous pursuit of profit through industrial production, and that it needed a group with the willingness to undertake the rigid supervision of labour and monitoring the costs before industrial organisations could be created. This difference in emphasis reflects the basic tension both in history and sociology between explanations which rest on the assumption that the presence of opportunities for economic exploitation is sufficient to explain the growth of the continuous pursuit of profit and explanations that believe that it is necessary to explain why the opportunities were exploited in some but not other cases. E. J. Hobsbawm observes that 'What strikes us retrospectively about the first half of the nineteenth century is the contrast between the enormous and rapidly growing productive potential of capitalist industrialisation and its inability, as it were, to broaden its base, to break the shackles which fettered it' (1975, p. 33). This suggests that English industrialism's character was not, nor should it be, the model for any society consciously trying to industrialise.

Summary and conclusion

Britain was distinguished from Europe by the development of a market society while there was still a basically agrarian and commercial economic system. Prior to industrialisation the aristocracy had taken part in a transformation of social relationships which had removed all but the last vestiges of personal dependence and generalised reciprocity from the relationship between master and servant. Moreover, in Britain, to a degree not matched elsewhere, the central state authority was subordinate to the aristocracy. In Europe, the aristocracy depended on the repressive power of the central authority to maintain their privileges, in Britain the aristocracy had made sufficient concessions to new middle groups not to need to rely for their privileges on repression by a strong central monarchy. As Landes says, 'The concern of the British gentleman for the accretion of his fortune made him a participant in society rather than a parasite upon it – whatever judgement one may pass on the character of this participation. Business interests promoted a degree of intercourse between people of different stations and walks of life that had no parallel on the Continent' (1972, p. 70). In Britain the privileged groups of previous social systems were thus actually actively involved in transforming themselves and throughout the nineteenth and twentieth centuries the descendants of the aristocracy have maintained a great deal of political power.

The uniqueness of the pre-existing conditions in Britain account for the fertility of *laissez-faire* policies of economic growth. These conditions can be summarised, at the risk of some oversimplification, as:

(1) The emergence of a stable political system in which the aristocracy through a series of strategic alliances with the new middle groups had established a degree of independence from the central monarchy.

(2) The creation of new legal concepts of property which allowed the aristocracy to use their lands for new purposes and in new ways without the fetters of traditional obligations to rural labour.

(3) The involvement of the British aristocracy in the economic manage-

ment of their estates, which was made easier by the lack of any need to take part in court activities in the capital city. The rights of the British landowners to the mineral deposits on their land became an important factor in explaining why the aristocracy was not uniformly opposed to industrialisation and why some aristocrats promoted the legal changes required to facilitate the new production system.

(4) The existence of landless rural and town labour forces compelled to accept wage labour on the terms of the new capitalist entrepreneurs.

(5) The existence of an extensive Empire from which cheap raw materials could be obtained.

(6) The existence of sufficient surplus agricultural produce over a prolonged period to create a complex structure of social groups with enough spending power to warrant revolutionising production techniques.

(7) The ability of the new capitalist class to adopt an ideology which explained and justified the economic transformations which were occurring, and allowed employers to successfully adapt to the challenge from the working classes and divide the working class by creating groups of workers whose privileged status made them supporters rather than opponents of the system.

Finally, it is important to remember that the nineteenth century was not a century of smooth economic progress. Industrial development was uneven and progressed by fits and starts, and the alliance between the dominant groups of the new and old orders was not continuous. During the expansive phases it tended to be possible for compromise in policy to be reached which left both groups satisfied. In the downturns and when the agricultural sector suffered poor harvests there was a tendency for the two groups to come into conflict. The history of the Corn Laws and the various Poor Laws illustrates how the different interests ebbed and flowed as conditions changed.

Suggested Further Reading

Barrington-Moore Jr (1967) *Social Origins of Dictatorship and Democracy*, chap. 1 (Harmondsworth, Middx: Allen Lane, The Penguin Press).

Kemp, T. (1969) *Industrialisation in Nineteenth-Century Europe* (London: Longman).

Bibliography

Anderson, P. (1974*a*) *Lineages of the Absolutist State* (London: New Left Review Editions).

— (1974*b*) *Passages from Antiquity to Feudalism* (London: New Left Review Editions).

Barrington-Moore Jr (1967) *Social Origins of Dictatorship and Democracy* (Harmondsworth, Middx: Allen Lane, The Penguin Press).

Bendix, R. (1963) *Work and Authority in Industry* (New York and Evanston, Ill.: Harper Torch Books).

Dalton, G. (1974) *Economic Systems and Society* (Harmondsworth, Middx: Penguin Books).

Dobb, M. (1972) *Studies in the Development of Capitalism* (London: Routledge & Kegan Paul).

Foster, J. (1974) *Class Struggle and Industrial Revolution* (London: Weidenfeld & Nicolson).

Giddens, A. (1973) *The Class Structure of the Advanced Societies* (London: Hutchinson).

Habakkuk, H. J. (1968) 'The Historical Experience of the Basic Conditions of Economic Progress', in S. N. Eisenstadt (ed.) *Comparative Perspectives on Social Change* (Boston: Little, Brown & Co.).

Hartwell, R. M. (1971) *The Industrial Revolution and Economic Growth* (London: Methuen).

Hobsbawm, E. J. (1975) *The Age of Capital 1848–1875* (London: Weidenfeld & Nicolson).

Holloway, S. (1973) *Human Societies: An Introduction to Sociology*, chap. 5, 'Population' (London: Routledge & Kegan Paul).

Kemp, T. (1969) *Industrialisation in Nineteenth Century Europe* (London: Longmans).

Keynes, J. M. (1936) *The General Theory of Employment, Interest and Money* (New York: Harcourt Brace Jovanovich).

Landes, D. S. (1972) *The Unbound Prometheus* (Cambridge: Cambridge University Press).

MacPherson, C. B. (1962) *The Political Theory of Possessive Individualism* (London: Oxford University Press).

— (1975) 'Capitalism and the Changing Concept of Property', in E. Kamenka and R. S. Neale (eds.) *Feudalism, Capitalism and Beyond* (London: Edward Arnold).

Mill, J. S. (1848) Principles of Political Economy, vol. 2 (London: People's Edition, Longmans).

Musgrave, F. (1970) 'Population Changes and the Status of the Young, in P. W. Musgrave (ed.) *Sociology, History and Education:* A Reader (London: Methuen).

North, D. C., and Thomas, R. P. (1973) *The Rise of the Western World* (Cambridge: Cambridge University Press).

Perkin, H. (1969) *The Origins of Modern English Society 1780–1880* (London: Routledge & Kegan Paul).

Polanyi, K. (1963) *The Great Transformation* (Boston: Beacon Press).

Pollard, S. (1968) *The Genesis of Modern Management* (Harmondsworth, Middx: Penguin Books).

Roll, E. (1973) *A History of Economic Thought*, 4th ed. (London: Faber & Faber).

Rudé, G. (1972) *Europe in the Eighteenth Century* (London: Weidenfeld & Nicolson),

Shanin, T., ed. (1973) *Peasants and Peasant Societies* (Harmondsworth, Middx: Penguin Books).

Smith, A. (1925) *An Enquiry into the Nature and Causes of the Wealth of Nations*, ed. E. Cannan (London: Methuen).

Stone, L. (1965) 'Class Divisions in England, 1540–1640', in B. Barber and E. G. Barber (eds.) *European Social Class: Stability and Change* (New York: Macmillan).

Thompson, E. P. (1968) *The Making of the English Working Class* (Harmondsworth, Middx: Penguin Books).

Weber, M. (1961) *General Economic History*, trans. F. H. Knight (New York: Collier Books).

5
The Family and Industrialisation

In pre-industrial societies there was no sharp division between the world of work and the world of bed and board. Economic activities took place within the organisation of the family and usually involved all the adult members of the family household. The family was controlled by a patriarchal figure who maintained his authority by his control of the economic resources of the group and was legitimated by a religious ideology which emphasised the woman's duty to obey and the husband's duty to provide. The family comprised a large number of kin, usually spanning three or more generations. It was organised with established roles for the young and the old as well as clearly defined roles for the adult men and women. The centre of the family was the marital pair, but adult unmarried brothers and sisters of the married couple, as well as their parents and their children, were present. The family provided a total form of security for its members, with an ordered accepted progression from one status to the next. The fusion of economic and familial activities and the close relationship to the land tended to combat feelings of alienation from work because they led to a natural harmony between individuals and their environments. The pre-industrial family, thus, comprised an ordered society in which the problems of the various age groups were catered for and the uncertainties of life were minimised. The large size of the family and the large number of economically active adults provided a measure of insurance against the economic uncertainties of the day. In sum the family was a total institution which served as the individual's welfare state as well as his or her arena for the satisfaction of emotional needs.

The preceding picture of the pre-industrial family continues to exercise a strong grip on the imaginations of many people, not least sociologists and those concerned with social problems of family organisation. We offer it, however, only as a starting point for an attack on the problems of establishing what effects industrialism has had on the family and how pre-existing family forms have altered the impact of industrialisation in particular societies. The portrait of the pre-industrial family just offered highlights two very important distinctions which must be born in mind when the family is being investigated. First, it highlights the need to distinguish between the ideology of what family life should be like and the reality of what family life actually is like. It is important to make this distinction because otherwise we may end up arguing that changes in the ideology reflect changes in the reality without any evidence to demonstrate changes in the actual forms of family life. The ideology of the family is the set of 'ideals' or 'norms' about familial organisation to which people who accept that ideology strive to conform. When the ideology of the family is the object of study, the question is; how has the ideal or sought-after organisation of the family changed? Another problem with the ideology of the family is that of distinguishing between the ideological construction placed on the family by contemporaries and the ideological construction placed on it by people at a later date. Many accounts of the present family are concerned not only with analysis but also with prescription, i.e. what the family should be like. These analyses often contain an ideology of the family which involves an ideological construction of the family in history. That is to say the present organisation of the family and the new problems identified depend upon the author's picture of past familial organisation, and this picture is constructed without reference either to the actual reality of past family life or indeed even to the ideology of the family actually present in earlier periods, but with reference solely to its usefulness in sustaining a given line of argument.

The second problem our picture of the pre-industrial family raises is the problem of generalisability. There is a tendency to assume that in a society there is only one mode of familial organisation at any point of time. That is, one form of family is 'approved' as the ideal and is also the dominant mode of familial organisation. When we study the impact of industrialisation it is crucial to avoid this simplistic assumption because industrialisation had varying effects on different strata of society and even if we do move from one dominant mode of organisation to another, one dimension of critical interest is which groups altered their patterns or ideology ahead of the general trend and which groups afterwards. Moreover when we consider theories of the fit between family forms and economic organisation it may be that economic organisation makes different demands of family organisation depending on the level of an individual's participation in the economic organisation. This is a complex way of saying that class is a critical variable in the study of the relationship between industrialisation and the family and any study which does not explicitly consider the problem is not likely to deal adequately either with the problem of generalisability or with the separation of ideology and reality.

There is no justification for splitting off the effects of industrialism on the family from the effects of the family on industrialisation, except the purely practical one that in systems of reciprocal causation one has to start somewhere. In practice, the dominant tendency has been to treat the family as the dependent variable and show the ways that industrialisation has affected the family. Without accepting that industry has necessarily had more influence on the family than vice versa, we will adopt the strategy of first examining the arguments about the way in which industry has influenced the family. We will then appraise these theories in the light of the growing body of historical and empirical data on the structure and organisation of the family in pre-industrial nineteenth and twentieth century society. Then we will consider some ideas about the ways in which family form may have been an important factor in determining the acceptance of industrialisation and the speed of adoption of values and behaviours consistent with an industrial economic system. Finally we will examine how far the family and economic organisation may both have been reacting to the spread of the twin concepts of rationality and individual responsibility.

The impact of the process of industrialisation on the family

We will concentrate here first on the notion of fit between the needs of industry and the potential of familial forms to supply those needs. Kerr *et al.* (1973) have presented explicitly a theory of the position of the family in industrialisation and the transition of family organisation implied in the process of industrialisation. They argue that the culture of industrialisation is characterised by a nuclear family system which tends to accentuate individual incentives to work, save and invest; and is impeded or slowed down in so far as there is an extended family system which reserves key managerial positions for family members regardless of competence. The extended family stands in the way of industrialisation because it carried over into the industrial sphere sets of obligations based on family ties and therefore interferes with the rationality of economic enterprise. Less competent members of the family hold positions of strategic control not by virtue of their technical abilities but by virtue of kinship connections. Nepotism, instead of the exception, tends to become the rule, and leads to a poor allocation of the scarce resources of human talent and consequently prevents the rapid spread of industry via growth. The extended family is thought not to encourage saving or investment because the group saving and the group investing are made up of different people, and the group of savers cannot see sufficient return to themselves to justify their foregone consumption. The nuclear family promotes saving and entrepreneurship because the unit of benefit is directly tied to the person sacrificing current consumption to invest in the future.

Kerr *et al.* suggest that the 'overall ideology' of industrialism and its associated individualism tends to create forces which lead to the overthrow and replacement of social institutions which stand in the way of economic growth. The implication of Kerr's study must be that the extended family of pre-industrial society gives way to a nuclear family structure at a fairly early stage in industrialisation. This is not an appropriate place to outline all the criticisms of the Kerr theories but two points must be made; first, in many countries at the initial stages the only units capable of supplying sufficient capital to undertake industrial enterprise were extended families which could expropriate the surplus earnings of more than one male and one female and thus increase the size of their savings; second, Kerr assumes that all pre-industrial societies had extended family systems: this assumption is empirically unjustified as we shall see later. One strength of their analysis is that they do explicitly realise the 'ideological' aspect of family organisation and devote some time to discussing the strategy of the group which is introducing industrialisation with respect to family organisation.

Kerr *et al.* borrow very heavily from Parsons's conceptualisation of the place of the family in modern industrial society. Parsons (1955) is concerned with the fit between the family forms and the occupational system of society. He argues that all social action is infused with sets of values which guide the appropriateness and inappropriateness of certain behaviours. He claims that these sets of values can be described in terms of four principles. Parsons conceptualised the problems facing actors in orientating their action in everyday life in terms of four choices that they had to make. These choices become institutionalised and the individual finds himself in a social structure which assumes certain choices have been made in terms of these four principles.

What are these four choices that have to be made and solutions to which are embodied in the existing social structure?

(1) Achievement – ascription

The actor has to decide whether his activities towards others are going to depend on evaluative response from others based on what he has achieved or upon who he is by virtue of some unalterable social characteristic. Government by elders is a governmental structure which embodies ascriptive choices about who should govern, i.e. the old are chosen to rule on the basis of their long lives.

(2) Functional specificity – diffuseness

The actor has to decide whether particular actions are limited in purpose or are designed to serve multiple functions. Is activity to be tailor-made to a single purpose or fashioned to satisfy a wider range of purposes? The dinner jacket is functionally specific, but the dark lounge suit is functionally diffuse; when we buy a dinner jacket we do so with one particular type of usage in mind, but our lounge suit is expected to see us through the wedding, the evening out and the interview, or in other words, is bought with a variety of usages in mind.

(3) Universalism – particularism

The actor has to decide whether his action towards others should be the same towards all others or whether there are particular groups of others to whom he should respond differently from others. The actor also has to appraise whether he will be treated in the same way as everybody else by the people he interacts with or whether they will treat him in special ways because he is who he is. The election returning officer who ensures the rule of one man one vote is acting universalistically towards voters: they are all receiving the same treatment from him. The bus conductor who lets his friends ride on his bus free is acting particularistically: his friends are receiving a special privilege denied to others.

(4) Affective neutrality – affectivity

The actor has to decide whether particular activities are significant in themselves or whether their significance is purely in terms of their instrumentality for the achievement of certain ends. Membership of Leeds United Supporters' Club may be a satisfying pursuit in itself, taking part in the collectivity may be intrinsically satisfying: in this case the orientation is affective. If, however, we joined Leeds Supporters' Club solely because we wanted tickets to the Cup Final and knew that one way to get them was to join the Supporters' Club our orientation to the club would be predominently affective-neutral.

Parsons argues that the modern industrial economic system is organised around the assumption that people in their economic activities will be orientating their actions guided by the principles of achievement, specificity, universalism and affective neutrality or instrumentality. The economic system is organised on the assumption that these are the basic values of the participants; the parts of the economic system articulate together because they can count on certain patterns of responses in other parts of the system. If the values of the economic system are those of achievement, specificity, universalism and instrumentality, Parsons argues that the values of the family system even in industrial society are the polar opposites, namely, ascription, diffuseness, particularism and affectivity. The family, however, remains the source of labour resources for the economy and there has to be some form of articulation between the family and the economy. Given the incompatibility of the competing values systems of the two institutional spheres, what structural arrangements minimise the clash?

First, Parsons argues that although the family is dominated by ascriptive, particularistic, diffuse and affective values, it lives in industrial society in a society in which the values of the economic sphere are paramount. In the general case Parsons argues that the values embodied in the economic sphere come to dominate all social activities. The conflict between family values and economic values is partially resolved thus by the subordination of the family to the economic. This seems to be unproblematic for Parsons; however, there seems to be little reason to assume this ordering *a priori*. Dore, in his study of Japanese industry (1974), suggests that the family value system in Japan has not been totally dominated by the economic value system, and that firms like Hitachi have to trim their recruitment patterns according to the expectations of the family system: witness their practice of sacking women at marriage.

The next stage in Parsons's argument, however, is to show how one particular structure of the family, namely, the nuclear family, can serve to reduce the value conflict between the economic and familial system. Parsons argues that the nuclear family, with the husband the sole or dominant labour market participant, is the appropriate familial form for industrial society. The first reason advanced is that modern industry is based on achievement values and requires the mobilisation of human resources to their most advantageous economic employment regardless of their initial status. Modern industry requires 'free labour', that is labour which is free of ties to given localities or particular groups of kin. The structurally isolated nuclear family is well suited to the mobility needs of industry, as it is a family structure which emphasises responsibility to the children of the marital pair above all other ties and economic advancement via social and geographical mobility can be argued to enhance the opportunities of the children. On the level of geographical mobility it seems logical that it is easier for a single nuclear family to move rather than an extended family: only one economically active male has to find a suitable job rather than a group. On the social mobility level the extended family tends to make demands on its most successful members which prevent them undertaking the investments necessary for further mobility; thus the nuclear family facilitates the upward passage of the talented to the jobs where their talents can best be utilised. We will return later to show that social mobility is relatively unimportant to the explanation of the advent of industrialism, and that geographical mobility is not necessarily hindered by the extended family.

Secondly, Parsons argues that the nuclear family with the male as the dominant point of articulation with the economic system solves the potentially conflicting career demands of the larger kin group with multiple males all pursuing careers. There are two caveats here; first, the notion of careers should alert us to the problem of the class relevance of Parsons's argument, and second, a point we will return to, there is the problem of the growing involvement of women in the labour force.

The third point Parsons makes is that the family provides an enclave which is proof against the instrumentality of the economic system; it provides the individual with a chance to satisfy his emotional needs in a structurally separate and contained sphere of activity. The family, therefore, provides an antidote to the alienation of modern industrial employment, an opportunity for the individual to enjoy authentic relationships untinged by the instrumentality of economic activity. Without such an efficient antidote the economic system would be unable to push its rationality as far, and industrialisation would be slowed down. The family is the expressive safety valve of a society dominated by instrumental values.

To summarise the position, then, a high incidence of certain types of pattern is essential to our occupational system and to the institutional complex in such fields as property and exchange which more immediately surround this system. In relatively commonsense terms it requires scope for the valuation of personal achievement, for equality of opportunity, for mobility in response to technical requirements, for devotion to occupational goals and interests relatively unhampered by 'personal considerations'. The family structure which allows this is the structurally isolated nuclear family. By structural isolation Parsons means that there are no institutional supports for family relationships which extend beyond the nuclear family; if they exist they are discretionary rather than mandatory under the norms of the system. We cannot yet escape the influence of Parsons's thought. Our next task is to consider the argument that the functions of the family have changed over time.

Viola Klein has put it thus:

> Shorn of a substantial part of its economic and educational functions; reduced, moreover in size, both by the virtual exclusion from the normal household of members of the wider family – such as grand-parents, maiden aunts, etc. – and by the spreading practice of voluntary limitation of births, the modern family is left with two basic functions intact: first, the raising of children, including the care of infants and the socialisation of the young; secondly, acting as a generator and focal point of all the strongest and most lasting affections. (1963, p. 26)

The industrialisation process thus reduces the family from an institution with many functions to an institution with rather few functions. It is all too easy to interpret the loss of functions as evidence of the loss of importance of the family; very few of the sociologists who argue that the family has lost functions would argue that it is any less central to the social structure as a result.

Smelser (1959), drawing heavily on Parsonian concepts, argues that the family is caught in a process of structural differentiation as industrialisation makes the extended family archaic and unable to cope with the needs of the economic system. The theory of structural differentiation states that an existing structure differentiates itself by definite and specific sequences of events into two or more roles or organisations which function more effectively in the new historical circumstances. Smelser takes the Lancashire cotton industry between 1770 and 1840 as a locale in which to test his thesis, and devotes considerable energy to attempting to illustrate the process with respect to the family.

> The family may become, under specific pressures, inadequate for performing its defined functions. Dissatisfaction occurs when it is felt either that performance of roles or utilisation of resources falls short of expectations. The symptoms of disturbance resulting from these pressures are first handled by mechanisms of social control. Gradually as the energy is harnessed, it is directed to the more positive tasks of legitimising and specifying ideas for social action, and transforming these ideas into social experiments. If successful, these experiments produce one or more new social units. (p. 3)

Smelser demonstrates the ways in which the shared and multifaceted activities of the family give way to the situation of specialisation, in particular the separation of child rearing from production. He also considers the ways in which internal family organisation was influenced by the opportunities for employment provided by the nascent industry. The first consequence of the process of industrialisation was the discovery, after the initial period of putting out, that women and children were cheaper and more suitable forms of labour than men, and although the man might obtain a job in the employ of the same employer it was likely to be outside the room where his wife and children worked; thus physical separation destroyed the possibility of the extension of child rearing into the factory situation. Smelser seeks to explain the attitudes of operatives to the Ten Hour Bills in terms of their desire to preserve family working units and to preserve parental control of their children.

This separation of male and female work, allied to high male unemployment and the demise of the male economic hegemony that had prevailed in the domestic consumption unit, threatened the patriarchal basis of the family. The early periods of industrialisation provided women with their first taste of independence from the male dominance of the family sphere. The shift in power towards the women, however, was a temporary phenomenon and by the middle of the nineteenth century a new ideology was growing, that women should not work at all: women's leisure was the first comsumption good of the rising affluence of the working classes.

Smelser thus shows how the economic and educational functions of the family were altered by the strains of industrialisation. The family loses its responsibility for the production of goods and for the education and training of its children, these functions devolve to new institutions: the factory and the school. The economic functions of the family are now specialised: 'The goal of the family economy is to generate motivation appropriate to occupational performance through the mechanisms of socialisation of the child and the management of tensions of the family members' (1959, p. 158).

Berger and Kellner (1970), following Durkheim, suggest that the family has become increasingly important as industrialisation has destroyed the intermediary groups which previously linked the family to the central structures of society. The family is one of the main bastions against anomie, or a sense of confusion about the organisation and purpose of life. The economic sphere confronts the individual as an omnipotent and hostile world, incomprehensible and totally alien to the human character. In such a world the only sphere in which the individual can try to work out a meaningful construction of reality is the family. In the family sphere the individual negotiates typifications or categorisations of reality with his or her spouse and attempts to establish some individually meaningful pattern of existence. The high incidence of divorce is, when allied with the high rate of re-marriage, indicative of the crucial nature of the family for self-expression in twentieth century society. The family is the arena in industrial society where individuals try out behaviour and confirm their pictures of themselves as individuals.

The nuclear family and industrialisation – fact or fiction?

The time has come to begin to demolish stereotypes of the theories of the fit between the nuclear family and modern industrial society. The first notion that will be examined will be that the modern family is significantly more nuclear than the pre-industrial family. This will involve a consideration of the size and composition of the household since the seventeenth century. The second area to be re-examined is the notion that the nuclear family promotes mobility. Third, we will examine how far the problem of the value clash between family and industrial system was solved by male dominance, and how far it is actually an unresolved structural contradiction in modern industrial society.

Marion J. Levy has hypothesised that 'Despite variations in the ideal patterns the vast majority of all human beings have been reared in a family context that involved or involves a total of five or fewer members. The probability was and is overwhelming that those five members will include representatives of no more than two generations, of one marital spouse pair, and will contain representatives of each sex' (1972, p. 17).

The evidence accumulating for Britain tends to very much confirm this. Laslett (1965) made an estimate at the beginning of the 1960s that the mean family size has been 4.75 for the entire history of the last four hundred years. Actually if we examine Table 5.1 we find that it is only since 1891 or 1911 that there has been any appreciable tendency for the family unit to become smaller in number. Figure 5.1 demonstrates the changing proportions of family units of different sizes, and confirms the demise of the large family. The evidence accumulated by the Cambridge group and others now suggest

Table 5.1 Mean household size in England 1564–1821
Mean household size in England and Wales 1801–1961

Parish Samples	*Mean Household Size*
1564–1649	5.07
1650–1749	4.70
Kent 1705	4.43
1770–1821	4.78
Westmorland 1787	4.61
Census data	
1801	4.60
1811	4.64
1821	4.72
1831	4.68
1841	Not available
1851	4.73
1861	4.38
1871	4.40
1881	4.54
1891	4.60
1901	4.79
1911	4 36
1921	4.14
1931	3.72
1941	No census
1951	3.19
1961	3.04

Adapted from P. Laslett (1972), table 4.4, p. 138. 'Mean Household size in England since the Sixteenth Century', in P. Laslett (ed.) *Household and Family in Time Past* (Cambridge: Cambridge University Press).

that if anything the figure of 4.75 is too high and average family size should be adjusted downwards a little.

What Laslett's (1972) and Anderson's (1972) studies have demonstrated without doubt is that industrialisation did not destroy an extant three-generational extended family system. If one bears in mind that expectation of life was 39.9 years at birth in 1838–45, and this represented little change on the eighteenth century and was not to change radically until the twentieth century, this finding is not particularly amazing. Death was a remarkably important phenomenon in the pre-twentieth-century world, as it still is in many underdeveloped countries. It is extremely important to remember that high birth rates and high numbers of children per marriage do not necessarily mean that most people grew up in large family units, although obviously the mean family size will tend to be less than the size of family in which most people were raised. Using Anderson's data for women married at age 25–9 in 1851–61 as a proxy for the total group, and utilising the 1911 Fertility Census and the death figures in Anderson articles, and, if we exclude children who died before they were two years old, the average size of family was considerably less than six. Thus the early years of industrialism did not lead to any appreciable change in the size of the family nor its composition;

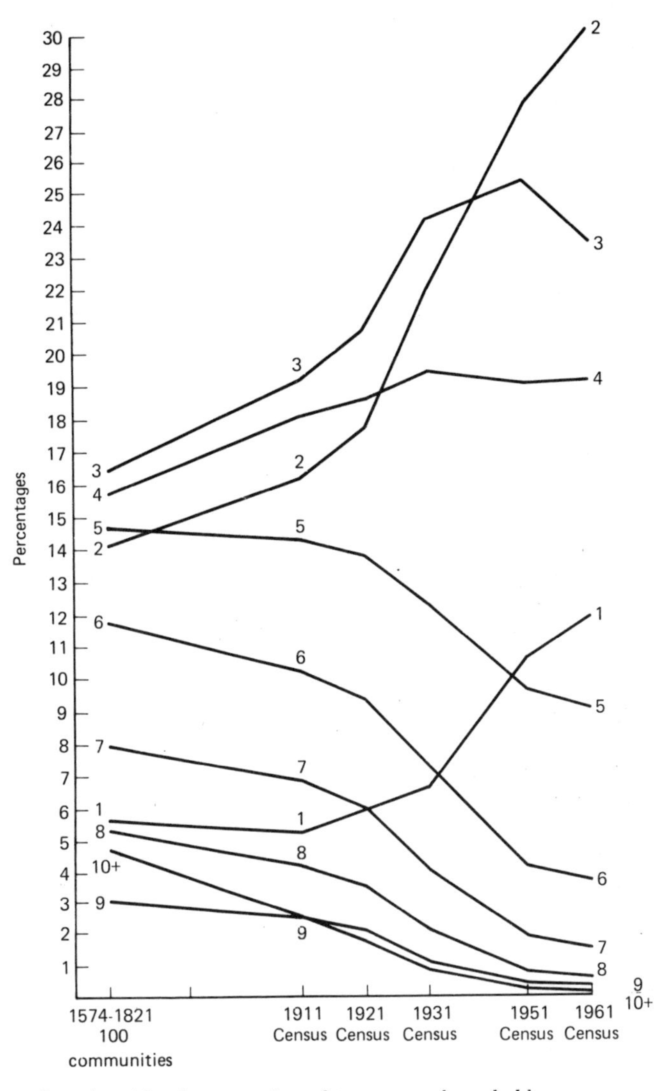

The figures from 1 to 10 refer to number of persons per household.

Figure 5.1 Distribution of households by size (percentages)

Adapted from P. Laslett (1972), fig. 4.4, p. 143, 'Mean Household size in England since the Sixteenth Century', in P. Laslett (ed.) *Household and Family in Time Past* (Cambridge: Cambridge University Press).

it continued to be predominantly a nuclear family system made up of small units of parents and their offspring. Three exceptions to the straightforward nuclear family were important in understanding nineteenth-century Lancashire, the cradle of British industrialisation. First, the very high number of orphans associated with the short expectancies of life, second, the much higher numbers of people who were unmarried but of adult status and third, the prevalence of servants in all but the household of the working classes.

The adoption of orphans by other members of the extended kinship network was the most common cause of variation from the nuclear family pattern. The advent of birth control and advances in public health and medicine have revolutionised the structure of the family since the turn of the century. Life expectancy has nearly doubled and the birth rate has more than halved. We no longer live in a society which is dominated by large numbers of young children. But we do now live in a world where the old form a significant part of the population, and this raises the problem of the context within which they should pass their old age. A common myth is that in the past they would have been cared for within the nuclear family of one of their married offspring; Anderson, however, provides evidence which suggests that this is part of a current ideological construction of reality. Anderson (1972) shows that while 80 per cent of old people in nineteenth-century Preston, with children alive, lived with one of these children, three out of four of them lived with unmarried rather than married children. Industrialisation has created the problem of the old not by destroying an existing extended family, but by destroying the group of unmarried children, by allowing them to become economically capable of sustaining a marriage, and by much enlarging the numbers of the old.

The spread of industry has thus not had the straightforward effects that some would have us believe. The extended family did not give way to the nuclear family. There have been changes in the family in Britain since the advent of industry: urban crowding has actually increased the amount of co-residence among kin although it remains both normatively and really the exception to the rule. For the bulk of the population family experience has changed; marital partners can now look forward to a long period in which they will live as an isolated pair after their children have left home.

The evidence so far has been aggregated data, and while it is most probably safe to use it as a description of the effects of the Industrial Revolution on the families in the lower strata it may be unwise to extend it to the upper and middle strata. We have little data which allows statements to be made about these groups but it does seem that in the early industrial period the extended family played a more important role. The rules of inheritance and then the lack of limited liability made the family particularly important in economic affairs. Crozier (1965) has provided evidence on the importance of kin in certain nineteenth-century companies, and while Lupton and Wilson (1959) and Nichols (1969) suggest that family ties are still important in managerial success, the nature of their importance has probably changed. In the earlier period joint family ventures provide the necessary element of trust which is lacking in purely instrumental relationships, but which is necessary for a division of labour which allows the benefits of specialisation to be reaped.

With the separation of ownership from control, the family loses its importance as a mechanism of control, although it retains its importance for the transmission of economic advantages.

Parsons suggests that industrial society's economic system depends on high social and economic mobility. There is relatively little evidence to suggest that industrialisation necessarily brings any real long-range social mobility. There is no reason why existing privileged classes cannot control the rate of industrial expansion in such a way that only their offspring are qualified for the new privileged and powerful positions. There is, indeed, much evidence that suggests that industrialisation does not bring downward social mobility for the sons of the existing privileged classes (Blau and Duncan, 1967).

The total amount of social mobility needed may be small compared with the potential mobility. It is important to distinguish an 'ideological element' from a 'descriptive statement'. Part of the ideology which supports modern industrial societies is the notion of the 'career open to talents' or the 'myth of opportunity'. Modern capitalist societies may depend upon a belief that they foster social mobility; they do not seem to depend upon any widespread and long range mobility: Britain and France share low long-range mobility profiles while the United States and Russia share higher long-range mobility profiles.

The evidence on geographical mobility, however, is even more problematic. A most important agency in geographical mobility seems to be the family: very far from kin ties forming barriers to mobility, for the working classes they provide the channel of mobility. Anderson (1971) has suggested that the nineteenth century family was very important in channelling immigration from the country to the town; there was a leader–follower pattern: once one member of a family went to an urban location information about the facilities and a source of job introductions were available to those who had remained. This led to large numbers of wider kin groups emigrating to the towns. Once they got there they were more likely to share households with relatives than ever before. Indeed Anderson shows how the tendency for relatives to co-reside is now higher than ever before. He compares his figures for co-residence for Preston in 1851 with his figures for the Lancashire countryside and Rosser and Harris's (1965) figures for Swansea in 1960, and finds most co-residence in Swansea. The evidence on residence on new estates reported by Wilmott for Dagenham (Wilmott, 1958) and Greenleigh (Young and Wilmott, 1957) suggests further the role of the extended family in geographical mobility.

Another way in which the family helps rather than hinders the mobility of labour has been thrown up by studies of the process of labour mobility (Sheppard and Belitsky, 1966). The assumptions of perfect knowledge in which everyone knows about all job opportunities is obviously an unreal assumption. When we examine the studies of occupational choice we find that for the working class the family network remains very important for the transmission of information about job opportunities. The working-class kin network distributes knowledge mainly about vacancies. 'Joe's uncle who delivers oil heard they were taking on new lads in the machine shop of X, so Joe applied and got the job,' is an example of the way this mechanism works. Watson (1964) and Bell (1968) have explored ways that the wider kin network help middle-class children to become established. If the role of the family with respect to mobility changes, it changes from a situation where the family has sanctions it can apply to prevent mobility to one in which if the individual wishes to move there is little the family can do to prevent it, but much to facilitate it.

We will now turn to woman's position in the family and how it has changed with the development of industrialisation. Prior to the factory, economic activities took place in the home and the women had important though subordinate roles to play in the production process. The early factories destroyed the family units of production and, drawing the women into the factories with their children, temporarily reversed the power of men over women that stems from economic superiority. The nineteenth century, however, witnessed the creation of the 'ideology' of the lady of leisure, the wife whose place was at home, whose very inactivity reflected the success of her husband. By 1919 women's participation in the labour force had declined considerably, and the era of the family articulated to the economy via the man was well established. Two World Wars, declining birth rates, and continually growing needs for consumption goods liberated the servant group to serve the needs of industry and now these same forces threaten to liberate women and destroy the articulation of family and economy. The last twenty years has seen a resurgence of women's employment and has changed the balance of power within the family once again. If the stability of society does depend upon the separation of family and industry, and industrial values are predominant, the drawing of women into the world of work must threaten to destroy the affective enclave of the family. The contradiction between industry's needs for more labour and its need for a safety valve is currently becoming more and more obvious. We must, however, guard against too easily accepting that the women's movement is the revolutionary vanguard. First, the number of women reaching the top may actually have declined since the 1930's (Klein, 1966), second, the women who succeed share similar class backgrounds to the men who succeed. The most important feature of woman's employment is the control it gives her over the discretionary spending of her family; the increasing employment of women does seem to be altering the relative power of the marital partners and supporting a more egalitarian ethos in the home (Blood and Wolfe, 1960).

The time has come to try to assess how far the family system influences the form of industrialisation. Industrialisation depends upon the flows of labour and capital to the economic sub-system of the society. Prior to industrialisation labour and capital both lived essentially in the family. What forms of family allow for the most advantageous transfer of these resources? There is no easy answer; indeed it may be that at one historical period one form is advantageous while at another the same form is disadvantageous.

If we take 'capital accumulation' as an example, Habakkuk (1955) has shown that single inheritance systems, i.e. where one child inherits all, are associated with early industrialisation. They help to provide capital in sufficiently large amounts to promote the risk taking necessary for entrepreneurial activities. They also allow a single man to operate without dependence on others. At an early stage this was important, because there was no limited liability and this made the isolation of business ventures from personal wealth impossible. Once capital markets have emerged and the notion of limited liability is adopted widely, the dangers of extra-familial economic activity declines. Once capital markets exist the small inheritances of the many offspring from many different families can be aggregated with the savings of many other familial units, and the need for large pre-existing capitals declines. The capital market has taken over the task of assembling the large capitals now needed. Indeed no family system could provide the volume of capital needed for modern industrial investment on the basis of one family one venture. The countries industrialising in an industrial world thus face different problems in raising capital from those of early 19th-century English entrepreneurs.

If the family form does influence capital accumulation it does so by altering the 'marginal propensity to consume.* Some argue that the nuclear family has a lower marginal propensity to consume than the extended family and thus promotes the growth of savings. There is no evidence to support or refute this, but it rests on a psychological premise which is unproven, namely that man is selfish and works better for himself than for any larger grouping.

Turning now to labour resources, it is argued that the nuclear family is more flexible and that the extended family stands in the way of the transfer of labour from the agricultural to industrial sectors. Again there is no evidence to support this contention, although it appears logical enough.

There is considerable evidence, on the contrary (Wolpe, 1972), that certain forms of industrialisation are possible only where there is an extended family system. The wages paid by the industrial sector are so low that they do not allow for the reproduction of the labour force; workers in the mines and factories do not receive enough wages to support and raise a family. The extended family, basically grounded in agriculture, sends certain members to work in the industrial sector, when there is a surplus of labour which cannot usefully be employed on the family agricultural holding. However, it supports the raising of a family by these members, either directly by sending food or indirectly by only sending those members of the family not involved in child raising to the industrial sector. The industrial labour force in these systems is replenished because the industrial workers supplement their earnings by drawing on the agricultural surplus generated by their extended family. In a subsistence agriculture it is an efficient method of extracting the agricultural surplus and using it to subsidise industrial expansion.

The form of the family makes different policies appropriate but in general the extended family does not form a barrier to industrialisation, although it may temporarily have more power to resist the demands of particular strategies of industrialisation.

Most industrial expansion involves the simultaneous taking on of considerable amounts of virtually undifferentiated wage labour; for the mass of the

*The marginal propensity to consume refers to the proportions of extra earnings which will be spent on goods and services rather than saved.

population there is no reason why whole extended families cannot be taken on together.

Finally, it has been suggested that certain forms of family organisation promote entrepreneurship. Habakkuk's findings (1955) on inheritance systems suggest that single inheritance systems may favour growth because they allow for anticipatory socialisation, or more simply they allow people to prepare for their later positions in life. In particular the infusion of the third and subsequent sons of the aristocracy into commerce is seen as a distinctive feature of British industrialisation. The second suggestion is that the nuclear family, with the dominant male head, promotes *N* achievement, the need to succeed, more than the extended family, where responsibility for child rearing is diffused, and that the need for achievement is the crucial variable in the explanation of industrial growth. McClelland's idea (1961) remains highly speculative, but it seems unlikely that the key to growth is as simple as the inculcation of the need for achievement.

We will conclude by suggesting that the idea that the nuclear family is most appropriate to industrial society stems from the ideologies which are advanced to justify them both. Goode (1963) has stressed that the ideology of the nuclear family stresses the individual's right to choose and the individual's right to be evaluated as an individual. The core of the ideology is some form of democratic individualism; the supreme values are those of individual freedom to choose rather than loyalty to some wider grouping. The industrial system is supported by an ideology which similarly stresses the individual: success in the system follows individual effort and is a reward for individual merit. Individual rewards draw out the best performances and increase society's wealth as well. Both ideologies owe a great deal to the Weberian thesis concerning the role of the 'Protestant Ethic' in the generation of the 'Spirit of Capitalism'. It has been a need for ideological compatibility which has led to the prominence of the notion that the nuclear family fits the needs of the industrial system, and its usefulness as a justification of the *status quo* which partly explains its persistence, in the face of accumulating evidence that industry can coexist with a variety of family forms and can even prosper where familial rather than industrial values dominate.

Suggested Further Reading

Anderson, M., ed. (1971) *Sociology of the Family* (Harmondsworth, Middx: Penguin Books).

Goode, W. J. (1963) *World Revolution and Family Patterns* (Glencoe, Ill.: Free Press).

Harris, C. C. (1969) *The Family* (London: Allen & Unwin).

Laslett, P., ed. (1972) *Household and Family in Past Time* (Cambridge: Cambridge University Press).

Bibliography

Anderson, M. (1971) *Family Structure in Nineteenth Century Lancashire* (Cambridge: Cambridge University Press).

— (1972) 'Household Structure and the Industrial Revolution: Mid-Nineteenth Century Preston in Comparative Perspective', in P. Laslett (ed.) *Household and Family in Past Time* (Cambridge: Cambridge University Press).

Bell, C. (1968) *Middle Class Families* (London: Routledge & Kegan Paul).

Berger, P. L., and Kellner, H. (1970) 'Marriage and the Construction of Reality', in H. P. Dreitzel (ed.) *Recent Sociology* 2 (London: Collier-Macmillan).

Blau, P., and Duncan, O. D. (1967) *The American Occupational Structure* (New York: John Wiley & Sons).

Blood, R., and Wolfe, D. M. (1960) *Husbands and Wives* (New York: Free Press).

Crozier, D. (1965) 'Kinship and Occupational Succession', *Sociological Review* 3, no. 13, pp. 15–43.

Dore, R. (1974) *British Factory – Japanese Factory* (London: Allen & Unwin).

Goode, W. J. (1963) *World Revolution and Family Patterns* (Glencoe, Ill.: Free Press).

Habakkuk, H. J. (1955) 'Family Structure and Economic Change in Nineteenth Century Europe', *Journal of Economic History* 15, pp. 1–12.

Kerr, C., Dunlop, J. T., Harbison, F., and Myers, C. A. (1973) *Industrialism and Industrial Man* (Harmondsworth, Middx: Penguin Books).

Klein, V. (1963) 'Industrialisation and the Changing Role of Women', *Current Sociology* 12, no. 1, pp. 24–34.

— (1966) The Demand for Professional Woman Power', *British Journal of Sociology* 17, pp. 183–97.

Laslett, P. (1965) *The World We Have Lost* (London: Methuen).

— (1972) 'Mean Household Size in England since the Sixteenth Century', in P. Laslett (ed.) *Household and Family in Past Time* (Cambridge: Cambridge University Press).

Levy, M. J. (1972) 'Some Hypotheses about the Family', in N. P. Dreitzel (ed.) *Recent Sociology* 4 (London: Collier-Macmillan).

Lupton, T., and Wilson, C. S. (1959) 'The Social Background and Connections of Top Decision Makers', in J. Urry and J. Wakeford (eds.) *Power in Britain* (London: Heinemann).

McClelland, D. C. (1953) The Achievement Motive (New York: Appleton Century Crofts).

Nichols, T. (1969) *Ownership, Ideology and Control* (London: Allen & Unwin).

Parsons, T., and Bales, R. (1955) *Family, Socialisation, and Interaction Process* (London: Routledge & Kegan Paul).

Rosser, C., and Harris, C. C. (1965) *The Family and Social Change* (London: Routledge & Kegan Paul).

Sheppard, H. L., and Belitsky, A. H. (1966) *The Job Hunt* (Baltimore: Johns Hopkins University Press).

Smelser, N. J. (1959) *Social Change in the Industrial Revolution* (London: Routledge & Kegan Paul).

Watson, N. (1957) 'Social Mobility and Social Class in Industrial Communities', in M. Gluckman (ed.) *Closed Systems and Open Minds* (Edinburgh: Oliver & Boyd, 1964).

Wilmott, P. (1963) *The Evolution of a Community* (London: Routledge & Kegan Paul).

Wolpe, H. (1972) 'Capitalism and Cheap Labour Power in South Africa from Segregation to Apartheid', *Economy and Society* 1, no. 4, pp. 425–56.

Young, M., and Wilmott, P. (1957) *Family and Kinship in East London* (London: Routledge & Kegan Paul).

6
Weber, Rationalisation and Western Industrialisation

This chapter will focus attention on Max Weber's treatment of the development of modern industrial society in Western Europe. Weber's treatment of rationality and the increasing rationalisation of the everyday world lies at the centre of his analysis of the development of industrial capitalism, which has been considered by many sociologists to constitute an alternative explanation to that advanced by Marx. Marx stresses the centrality of ownership of property and the way this is reflected in the relations of production, with the wage labourer selling his labour power to the bourgeois owner of capital. This opposition to Marx is an over-simplification of Weber's position and in this chapter it should become clear that on many issues Marx and Weber agreed. None the less part of Weber's importance is that his ideas have influenced the growth of theories of industrial development, especially those theories which have attributed only minor importance to the distribution of ownership of property. Weber's scepticism about the possibilities of socialism reversing the tendencies within industrialism, which he thought might form an 'iron cage' for the individual, made Weber's thought an ideologically compatible starting point for many Western sociologists, certainly up to the 1970s.

The core of Weber's treatment is his contention that industrialisation is a concomitant of the process of rationalisation, or the application of reasoned and logical thought to problems of everyday life. What then is rationality and what constitutes the process of rationalisation? Initially a simplified definition of each will be considered and then it will be shown how Weber used the concept, rationalisation, to form a bridge linking together a series of developments which he saw as leading to the emergence during the seventeenth century to nineteenth century of the new and distinctively different type of society, industrial capitalism. Nisbet has tackled the problem of defining rationality by contrasting it with tradition: rationalisation, he argues, is accompanied by the conversion of social values and relationships from the primary, communal, and traditional shapes they once held to the larger, impersonal, and bureaucratised shapes of modern life (Nisbet 1966). While impersonality and bureaucracy are linked to rationalisation they do not constitute its essential features. For the present rationality will be assumed to involve social behaviour, which is deliberately and consciously enacted by the individual with the intention of achieving certain ends, or which conforms to a strongly held system of values. As Weber himself puts it, 'One of the most important aspects of the process of rationalisation of action is the substitution for the unthinking acceptance of ancient custom, of deliberate adaption to situations in terms of self interest' (1968, p. 30). The process of rationalisation is the extension of the principle of rationality to wider and wider areas of social life; more and more activities are subject to scrutiny and assessed according to their relationship to the ends of the individual actor. The idea of rationality, however, implies more than a simple emphasis on self-interest; it involves a belief that human reason can understand the relationship of various behaviours to one another and, as a result of this understanding, manipulate events to ensure desired outcomes. Action which is rational is action which is based on the understanding of the reasons for and consequences of that action. Rationalisation therefore involves a spread of systematic bodies of thought which allow the attribution of meaning to broader ranges of situations. The most obvious development of this nature has been the growth of natural science: ever-increasing numbers of events in the physical environment are shown to be interrelated and this expands the scope of actions whose results can be explained and predicted in advance.

The emphasis of rationality is therefore on conscious and deliberate mastery of the social environment. Action is based on the appraisal of alternatives and the selection of behaviour patterns based on a systematic representation of social reality. Rational action requires that the relationships between events are symbolically represented in systematic bodies of knowledge which allow the actor to evaluate his potential actions against general rules which set out the relationships between the most important factors influencing the area of decision and thus allow him to predict the outcome of his behaviours in advance.

Weber clearly distinguishes two types of rationality: the first type involves a separation of the means from the ends of action. The means to a given end are rational when they represent the most probably successful strategy for the achievement of the chosen end. This is what Weber calls 'formal rationality'. Formal rationality has a close relationship to technical efficiency; it is used to describe methods of decision making and implementation which are based on logical generalisation and application of abstract interpretations of activities to concrete events. Formal rationality, therefore, applies to the processes of implementation of action designed to achieve predetermined goals. A trivial example of formal rationality might be the decision processes of the businessman confronted with two alternative routes to the office: on the one hand, the train from the local station, on the other the car in the garage. The problem is which method will get him to the office quicker, or which means to this limited end is most efficient. The decision will involve predicting the likely traffic density at the particular time of day and the associated traffic hold-ups and computing the most likely journey time using the various road routes and comparing these with the likely travel time by train, taking into account the frequency of service, the punctuality of the service, and the problems of getting to the station. The businessman's decision will be formally rational with respect to minimising the time to get to his office in so far as he bases it solely on information which allows him to predict relative journey times. When he starts letting other considerations enter in unintentionally, formal rationality diminishes: if for five years he has driven to work every day, and this week they have dug up the street to his office leading to a half-hour delay which makes the train quicker, but, despite knowing this, our businessman continues to drive, he is no longer acting in a formally rational manner with respect to his original goal of minimising travel time.

Weber clearly distinguishes this type of rationality from substantive rationality. Substantive rationality involves much more than the assessment of the logical correctness of action: it involves a consideration of the relationship of particular actions and the ends they are designed to achieve to the overall interests of the individual actor. Substantive rationality requires a conscious inspection of the relationship between action and the system of values which the actor espouses. The actions must be consistent with the actor's belief system and represent attempts to actualise the ends of this belief system. As Weber puts it, analyses which are distinguished by their substantive rationality differ from those characterised by formal rationality because they 'apply certain criteria of ultimate ends, whether they be ethical, political, utilitarian, hedonistic, feudal, egalitarian, or whatever, and measure the results of the economic action, however "formally rational" in the sense of correct calculation they may be, against these scales of "value rationality" or "substantive goal rationality" ' (1968, pp. 85–6).

While Weber argued that Western development had involved the extension of both substantive and formal rationality, he was at great pains to make clear constantly that the two were not necessarily mutually compatible and that the extension of 'formal rationality' often endangered 'substantive rationality'. We will return to this when we consider Weber's fears about the fate of man in modern industrial society. For the moment the important thing is to be clear that Weber constructed these two abstract concepts – ideal types: one-sided accentuations of reality – to help in the process of understanding the processes of change which had occurred and were occurring in the West. Both 'formal rationality' and 'substantive rationality' are constructions to help analyse reality: they are ideal in the sense that they exist only as ideas. There is no suggestion in the 'ideal type' method that the type is something which should be striven for, which represents an ideal or perfect state of affairs.

Finally, before looking at Weber's uses of the terms 'rationality' and 'rationalisation' it must be made clear that Weber did not believe in a single unilinear developmental process in which all actions become more and more integrated and guided by a single 'rational' process of decision making. For Weber 'rationality' manifested itself in various places and led to a variety of developments which were not always compatible with one another. Indeed one of the central tasks Weber set himself was to see how far the different spheres of culture, for example, economic, scientific, technological, legal and political authority, had been infused with rationality and how dependent particular developments were on the concurrent development of rationality in these spheres. Weber framed the problem thus.

> Hence rationalisations of the most varied character have existed in various departments of life and in all areas of culture. To characterise their differences from the viewpoint of cultural history it is necessary to know what departments are rationalised, and in what direction. It is hence our first concern to work out and to explain genetically the special peculiarity of Occidental [Western] rationality and within this field that of the modern Occidental form. (1930, p. 26)

Let us now focus attention on the processes of development which Weber claimed were essential pre-conditions for the emergence of industrial capitalism. Each of these developments serve in a variety of ways to increase the formal calculability of action, the control of reason over action, and planning over spontaneity. Weber's distinctive contribution to the analysis of the emergence of industrial capitalism was his attempt to answer the question of where the impetus came from which transformed the basis of European society and led to the spread of rational conduct. This is not to suggest that Weber ignored or underplayed the role of economic factors in the transformation, certain economic developments were necessary but not sufficient reasons for the emergence of industrial capitalism. Weber was clear that economic avarice had existed at all times and that pursuit of private gain could not be the distinguishing characteristic of modern industrial capitalism.

> The impulse to acquisition, pursuit of gain, of money, of the greatest possible amount of money, has in itself nothing to do with capitalism. One may say that it has been common to all sorts and conditions of men at all times and in all countries of the earth, wherever the objective possibility of it is or has been given. It should be taught in the kindergarten of cultural history that this naive idea of capitalism must be given up once and for all. (1930, p. 17)

What Weber sought to establish was what had led to the situation in which economic activity came to be characterised by three major principles: first, expectation of profit stemming from the utilisation of opportunities for exchange involving peaceful chances of profit; second, continuous production by enterprises seeking to exploit a market situation; and, third, the omnipresent calculation of appropriate economic action in terms of its effects on capital. All three of these developments are intimately related to the spread of rationality.

As Weber says,

> In the last resort the factors which produced capitalism are the rational permanent enterprise, rational accounting, rational technology and rational law, but again not these alone. Necessary complementary factors were the rational spirit, the rationalisation of the conduct of life in general, and a rationalistic economic ethic. (Eldridge, 1971*a*, p, 278)

There are, in this way, two sides to the development of capitalism as the dominant mode of economic production: on the one hand the emergence of the conditions which permit the rational organisation of resources in the pursuit of profit, on the other the emergence of sets of ethics which provide the motivation for entrepreneurial activity and simultaneously the discipline which ensures the willing compliance of the working classes.

Before we consider Weber's treatment of the Spirit of Capitalism we must examine changes in the form of society. The most critical pre-condition for the spread of capitalism was the emergence of a rational system of calculating the consequences of economic actions. Double-entry bookkeeping, with its emphasis on the balance, forms the necessary calculus for the penetration of rationality to every economic activity. The emergence of the double-entry system depended upon certain changes in the environment which minimised unpredictability and made future-oriented, this worldly activity rational. The first of the necessary changes was the establishment of clear legal rights in property, or the appropriation of all physical means of production as the disposable property of autonomous private industrial enterprises. This was essential because it reduced the risks of expropriation or of conflicting claims, which would make the investment of capital unattractive to its owners. The second change needed was the emergence of markets and the absence of irrational barriers to trade in the market either in the markets for finished goods or in the markets for labour. This involved a movement away from situations in which particular status groups monopolised the consumption or production of particular items, away from feudal restrictions on the types of consumption permitted commoners and away from the guild restrictions on the supply of labour. Third, rational accounting assumes rational technique and rational techniques involves a high degree of mechanisation, as mechanisation reduces the unpredictability inherent in human performance of mechanical tasks. This mechanisation occurred in both the production and distribution of goods and services. The fourth factor, and one we will return to after our consideration of the Spirit of Capitalism, is the need for a stable and calculable legal system in which the adjudication and administration of the law is highly predictable and can thus be taken into account in the planning of economic action.

The fifth and absolutely critical factor is the existence of free labour. Labour, that is, which is free from all the residual ties of feudalism, free in the sense of no longer having rights or obligations. The existence of free labour is essential for calculability. As Weber puts it, 'Rational capitalistic calculation is possible only on the basis of free labour; only where in consequence of the existence of workers who in the formal sense voluntarily, but actually under the compulsion of the whip of hunger, offer themselves, may the costs of products be unambiguously determined by agreement in advance' (Eldridge, 1971*a* p. 277).

The final factor Weber considered necessary for the forms of capitalism to emerge is the commercialisation of activities, in particular the separation of the enterprises finances from household finances. Without the evolution or discovery of new methods of financing and coordinating industrial investment and the trade in commodities, it would be impossible to calculate accurately. So once again commercialisation is related to rationality as it is a necessary condition for calculability (Weber, 1968, pp. 161–4).

These six factors can be related back to the treatment of British industrialisation in earlier chapters and it should be possible to see that in the treatment of the necessary conditions for the emergence of industrial capitalism there is a large measure of agreement between Marx and Weber. They differ, however, in some respects, notably in that Marx argues that the bourgeoisie, when they gain ascendancy, create a stable state, further commercialisation of the economy and extend free markets, rather than that they gain ascendancy because these developments occur for autonomous reasons.

Not only, does the new system of beliefs provide an impetus to entrepreneurial activities, however, it also provides an ideological justification for their consequences. It allows the fortunate to believe that they 'deserved' their fortune and that those less fortunate are also merely experiencing their dues. In this way the transformed system of ideas simultaneously enjoined capitalistic enterprise and justified the unequal distribution of wealth which followed.

This new spirit, allied to the individualism and anti-mystical nature of the original doctrine, transformed the nature of economic activity and it came to be rationally oriented to opportunities for continuous profit making via the method of the enterprise. For Weber it is the new set of ethical beliefs enjoining rational pursuit of this-worldly activity in one's calling, allied to an ethical imperative to avoid wanton luxury, which is the catalyst that sets off the reaction among the causes and foments the original expansion of capitalist activity. Once capitalistic activities are underway imitation becomes important in explaining their continual expansion: people copy the successful innovations of those imbued with the capitalist ethic for pragmatic reasons of self-interest, no longer because they espouse a system of beliefs which make such innovations substantively rational.

Now we must turn our attention to the developments that led to the exploitation of these opportunities for the peaceful pursuit of profit. This involves trying to explain how beliefs about this worldly activity and particularly about economically productive activities come to compel individuals to adopt patterns of behaviour which involve the exploitation of these opportunities for profit in a systematic and ongoing manner.

The first important factor was the Renaissance and the rediscovery of classical knowledge and its extension to new fields. It is the Renaissance and its associated patterns of expanding the boundaries of rational knowledge which allows the birth of the rational technique which formed one of the bases of the growth of capitalism, both in providing the base for mechanisation and in providing the base for increased calculability. Weber says,

> Now the peculiar modern Western form of capitalism has been, at first sight, strongly influenced by the development of technical possibilities. Its rationality is today essentially dependent on the calculability of the most important technical factors. But this means fundamentally that it is dependent on the peculiarities of modern science, especially the natural sciences based on mathematics and exact and rational experiment. 1930, p. 24)

The Renaissance and the spread of science is not, however, directly related to the expansion of the Capitalist Spirit. The Catholic Church was capable of sustaining the expansion of scientific interest and the extension of rational explanation, while it was inimical to the Capitalist Spirit. For Weber it was the change in ethical outlook occasioned by the Reformation that was critical for the expansion of the Capitalist Spirit, because the new systems of ethical imperatives broke down barriers between the religious ideal of monastic life and the conduct of everyday life, and replaced a church which mediated between the individual and his salvation by a system of beliefs which stressed the individual's direct responsibility to God for his behaviour in this world. Thus the immanent individualism of the emergence of markets, the breaking of feudal ties of personal bondage and the emergence of free labour were reinforced by a system of religious ethics which enjoined individual responsibility, and the essential accompaniment of rationality emerged, namely the individual decision taker, who acts on the basis of his own interests. In his essay *The Protestant Ethic and the Spirit of Capitalism* Weber set out to establish the role that the ascetic Protestant Reformation played in the spread of rationality and thus the growth of industrial capitalism. Essentially Weber argued that it was possible to establish, by careful analysis of the writings of the leading spokesmen of Calvinism and the writings of such prototypical capitalists as Franklin, that the two systems of beliefs represented by these writers could be related to one another meaningfully. Or put another way, it is comprehensible how the one set of ideas, ascetic Protestantism, gave rise through a series of transformations to the other, the Spirit of Capitalism. Weber described the Spirit of Capitalism as present when there are people who accept as a guide to their own conduct the idea of increasing one's capital as an end in itself and out of a sense of duty. The pursuit of profit for its own sake and a belief in the rightness of such a pursuit are the critical elements.

There are four elements in ascetic Protestantism which are important in the transformation of people's attitudes to work from those of traditional society, where all economic activity was personalised and subject to the ethical control of a church which excluded higgling, overpricing and free competition as unethical, and instead adhered to the notion of the just price and the notion of assurance of the survival of all. Prior to the Reformation the role of economic activity was such that while it might be possible to avoid sin and still conduct business, economic activity could not in itself be pleasing to God. The appropriate method of serving the greater glory of God was via a monastic life devoted to other-worldly activities and regulated by other-worldly time schedules. The clock, later to become a symbolic representation of the tyranny of employment, was set not to the rhythms of commercial activity but to the rhythms of prayer and meditation.

The first element was the doctrine of predestination. This was the central idea of Calvinism, which stated that man's destiny with regard to salvation was determined from birth and there was no course open to the individual to change his election or non-election. The idea was that some people were chosen by God to be saved, for eternal life, while others were not so chosen and therefore could never enter life eternal. The second idea is the notion of the calling; here the stress is placed upon the fact that it is the ethical duty of everybody to pursue God's will in a particular station in life or in a particular occupation, i.e. people were called by God to perform certain work on earth so that earth might be transformed in his image. At first these two ideas were unrelated: non-election to salvation did not excuse the individual from the obligation of his calling. The third feature was the asceticism of the new religions; the injunctions against idleness, luxury or the consumption of wealth generated in economic activity. Asceticism thus involved the eschewing of conspicuous consumption, but it also enjoined the utilisation of the fruits of economic endeavour in the expansion of these activities. In this it is obviously significantly related to the doctrine of the calling. The fruits of success in the calling must be reinvested for greater success still in pursuit of these activities to which the individual had been called by God.

The fourth feature of Calvinism we have already touched on briefly, and this is its hostility to magic manifest in its rejection of such devices as absolution of sins and the confessional. Man's relationship to his God was an individual relationship, and everyday activity in the world was governed by rational principles in pursuit or satisfaction of this individual duty to God.

These four elements are the critical dimensions of Calvinist thought if we are to understand Weber's treatment of its transformation and adoption by the new emerging entrepreneurial élites who were the catalysts of capitalism. While the doctrinal purity of Calvinism was guaranteed by elders who were capable of ensuring ideological rectitude, Calvinism did not promote the growth of capitalism. So in Geneva and Scotland, where the religious control of the ideas of ascetic Protestantism was strongest, capitalism, or the Spirit of Capitalism especially, had difficulty emerging because it essentially involved the debasement of some of the basic doctrines. In particular it involved an emergence of a belief in a link between predestination or salvation and the pursuit of the calling. Weber argued that the doctrine of predestination was psychologically stressful, it left people uncertain as to their election or non-election and this was uncomfortable, so they began to look for signs of election. Once this process of looking for signs of election occurred it became inevitable that success in the calling would come to be seen as a sign of election; after all, if God does favour the activities engaged in in the calling this must be an indication of his satisfaction and vice versa.

Thus the psychological tension set up a predisposition to amend the system of beliefs to accept this worldly success as a sign of satisfactory performance of one's duty. This new belief allied to the asceticism formed the basis of the capitalist spirit. Profit became the sign of satisfactory performance, asceticism guaranteed its reinvestment in pursuit of further profit.

The remaining task of this chapter is to show how these developments are related to the development of bureaucracy, because if it is possible to express the central feature of industrial capitalism at a structural level it is, according to Weber, the ever-growing importance of bureaucracy. Before we can tackle bureaucracy we must briefly consider Weber's treatment of domination and this will involve picking up and developing the idea that stable and predictable law is one precondition for the emergence of capitalism. It is important to remember that Weber's treatment of the growth of bureaucracy is part of an attempt to explain the development of the nation state during the nineteenth century, and only in passing does he draw parallels between the growth of state bureaucracy and the growth of bureaucracy in industrial enterprises.

Weber stressed that coordination of individual action was effected via systems of domination. Certain groups acquired the ability to coerce or convince other people that their particular commands should be obeyed. Weber was clear that one basis of such domination was power; the monopoly of physical violence being the most obvious source but economic power was equally important.

Weber however believed that power-based systems of domination were inherently unstable and that the strains involved in the continuous use of force made them relatively inefficient. Slavery and serfdom disappeared at least partly because they were replaced by forms of domination which were more effective. Because of this inherent instability Weber believed that there was a built-in incentive for the dominant group in any society to try to change its basis of domination from one based on physical or economic force to one based on an acceptance by the dominated groups of the rights of the dominant group to issue orders of particular kinds and with particular contents. So Weber argued that attention should be focused on the ways that the claims of dominant groups to the rightness of their dominance were made and how far the advance of industrialism depended upon changes in the bases of the claims of the dominant group to legitimacy.

Weber identified three bases which he argued could be used to justify or legitimate the dominance of the ruling group. The important facet of legitimation, however, is not just the claim to the right to issue orders made by the dominant group but also the acceptance of that right by those who are subject to the orders. Weber described the three types of authority in terms of the behaviour and beliefs of the dominated, not in terms of the claims of the dominators. The three pure types (established for analytic purposes, not as descriptions of actual systems of domination, which usually involve elements of all three) are traditional, charismatic and rational-legal.

Traditional authority involves obedience which rests on established beliefs in the 'sanctity of immemorial traditions' and beliefs in the legitimacy or rightful claims of those occupying certain statuses to be the guardians of those traditions and issue orders in accordance with the precedents of past practice. People essentially obey the dominant group because they can see no alternative to the established ways, one of which is a way of distributing power in society. Traditional authority is basically hostile to change and to the extension of rational enquiry which might undermine the bases of traditional behaviour. As such, traditional authority systems were unsuited for the task of providing an environment conducive to the spread of industrial capitalism. Although a simplification of Weber's position, it could be said that he saw a transition from systems of domination based on traditional authority as inevitably linked to the transition to industrial capitalism.

Rational-legal authority involves obedience resting on beliefs in the 'legality of patterns of normative rules and the rights of those elevated to authority under such rules to issue commands. Actually there are the two distinct elements within rational legality. One is the emphasis on 'legality', which amounts to a belief that authority is exercised within patterns of rules which have been established in a manner acceptable to both the dominated and the dominant group. Democracy is one obvious device for the creation of these legal rules, although one of the enduring problems for Weber was the relationship between democracy and rational-legal authority, because democracy threatened the 'rational' element of rational legality. The other element, then, is rationality, the idea that the rules and regulations imposed by the dominant group can be seen to relate in a meaningful way to the normative rules which are believed to be legitimate. This involves a distinction between means and ends and the rational element of rational legality stresses that the means are related to the ends in a systematic manner and moreover there is a conscious and systematic endeavour to relate the various ends and ensure that inconsistencies are minimised.

Albrow (1970) argues that legal authority rests on five related beliefs.

(1) A legal code can be established which successfully claims obedience from members of the group.

(2) That legal code is a system of abstract rules applied to particular cases, and administration looks after the group within the limits of that law.

(3) The man exercising authority is also subject to the control of this legal code.

(4) The member of the group obeys the 'legal code' as member of the group. Or negatively the individual is only bound by the legal codes of groups to which he belongs.

(5) Obedience is not owed to the individuals who wield power and authority but to the positions of authority which have been created by the legal code and whose occupants are empowered as occupants of those positions to issue orders of specific form and content.

It is 'rational-legality' which replaces 'tradition' as the main basis of authority systems in modern industrial societies.

The third type of authority is charismatic authority. Charismatic authority rests in the belief in and devotion to the 'specific and exceptional sanctity, or exemplary character' of a particular individual and the belief in legitimacy of the normative patterns or order revealed or ordained by this individual. In contrast to the other forms charismatic authority inheres in the individual, not in the position. Very briefly we will consider some well-known leaders or groups of leaders and see how the Weberian ideal types can illuminate the bases of their authority. The main purpose however, of the illustrations is to make clear what the types mean. The Christ of the Bible, real or mythical, is the obvious example of a charismatic leader. Christians obviously believe in his sanctity and possession of peculiarly gifts by virtue of his status as Son of God, and they have obviously felt bound by the system of normative rules which are attributed to his teachings.

The feudal system of medieval Europe represents a system based largely on the sanctity of immemorial tradition or traditional authority. Authority inhered in the nobility not in the individual, indeed the lord's authority was severely curtailed by traditional constraints upon his activities, the most obvious of which was his inability to alienate or sell his estates freely. He was obeyed as landowner and caught in a web of traditional expectations about what orders he could issue appropriately.

The British prime minister, since the Second World War, has been typical of the leader relying on rational-legal authority. The British did not obey Wilson or Heath; neither did they obey Macmillan. They obey the occupant of the office of prime minister and they obey him only so far as he is carrying out the duties legally affixed to the role of prime minister. In practice mixed bases of authority are common and perhaps Churchill's wartime leadership, relying on an amalgam of rational legality, tradition and charisma, will serve as an example. Churchill was elevated to leadership constitutionally: he therefore enjoyed rational-legal authority. He also undoubtedly enjoyed a personal authority stemming from many people's belief in his exceptional talents, and finally he probably derived further authority because he stood for certain normative values held dear by many in British society: he was a personification of 'Bulldog Britain'.

Now we must draw the threads together and try to establish a relationship between the spread of rationality, authority systems, economic systems and systems of administration; or expressed differently the relationship of bureaucracy to rational legality and to industrial capitalism. Albrow's treatment of rational-legal authority system points the way. Industrial capitalism and rational-legal authority systems both involve the application of rational knowledge to the task of finding ways to achieve clearly established goals. Both create the need for an administrative mechanism to translate goals into tangible programmes of practical endeavours. Bureaucracy is important because, according to Weber, it forms the most formally rational way of administering the authority of the dominant group.

What Weber had done is to separate two aspects of authority systems; he has distinguished administration, or the means to the achieving of ends, from the process of deciding what ends are to be pursued. Bureaucracy is the ideal type of administration that maximises the formal rationality of the quest for ends. Bureaucracy becomes simply a means, and like all means, one criteria for judging it is the extent to which it formally promotes rationality. One of the major problems with work on organisations since Weber which start with his ideal type is a failure to realise the limitations of 'administration'. Administration is one phase of organisational processes and is not synonymous with organisation.

Bureaucracy is the mode of administration which is most compatible with rational-legality and which fosters the growth of industrialism. It is compatible because of the particular combination of rationality and legality it represents. Weber essentially identifies three major facets of the ideal-type bureaucracy: first, it is administration based upon knowledge; second, it is administration based on separation of the individual from ownership interests, or administration in which the individuals occupying positions do not bring personal interests into consideration; and finally, it is based on a hierarchical authority structure characterised by discipline, in which administration is carried out by officials bound by clearly defined rules which delimit their authority. It is important to remember that bureaucracy is the administrative arm of a rational-legal authority system, and depends upon the presence of some other structure for the creation of the legality which makes the administration acceptable. Child *et al.* (1973) have made quite clear this distinction in their discussion of rationality and trade union government, where they distinguish between administrative rationality and representative rationality. They clearly point out the limitations of abstracting administration as a process which can be treated in isolation from consideration of substantive as well as formal rationality.

Bureaucracy, therefore, fits into the process of rationalisation as a method by which systematic reason is applied to practical problems. It helps promote industrial capitalism by increasing the stability of political regimes; it enhances their ability to manage their environments and thus increases the predictability of the environment within which entrepreneurs operate, and this in turn fosters the growth of industrial capitalism.

'Today, it is primarily the capitalist market economy which demands that the official business of administration be discharged precisely, unambiguously, continuously, and with as much speed as possible' (Weber, 1948, p. 215). Indeed it is the technical advantages of bureaucracy which gives rise to its growth. Weber is quite clear that as the development of organisations increases the size of the units to be coordinated, so do the advantages of bureaucracy increase.

> The decisive reason for the advance of bureaucratic organisation has always been its purely technical superiority over any other form of organisation. The fully developed bureaucratic mechanism compares with other organisations exactly as does the machine with the non mechanical modes of production. Precision, speed, unambiguity, knowledge of the files, continuity, discretion, unity, strict subordination, reduction of friction and of material and personal costs – these are raised to the optimum point in the strictly bureaucratic administration. (Weber, 1968, p. 973)

Weber's treatments of bureaucracy, rational-legal authority systems and industrial capitalism are thus all related to the spread of a peculiar form of rationalisation in the West. As Nisbet (1966) points out, initially the spread of rationality broke down the barriers and constraints of traditional society and allowed a quantitatively great leap forward in the economic capacity of industrialised countries. However, Weber was not a believer in the benign consequences of the spread of rationality in the forms he saw it taking. This takes us full circle back to the distinction between formal and substantive rationality. Weber saw rationalisation as a process in which formal rationality was driving out substantive rationality, or, as Giddens (1971) remarks, Weber perceived a fundamental irrationality within capitalism.

The irrationality comes from the way that the power of formal rationality expands and technical questions of the efficiency of means come to assume a dominant position in the conduct of life. The means come to usurp the ends. Wrong argues that 'Rationalisation does not indicate an increased and general knowledge of the conditions under which one lives' (1970, p. 26). 'For while formal sets of rules, systematic technologies, and rationally planned enterprises clearly embody rationality, their very efficiency and reliability eliminate the need for wide knowledge and rational understanding' (p. 26). In other words the bodies of knowledge on which bureaucratic administration is based become so specialised and lead to such a fragmented division of labour that a total picture of the activities of the bureaucracy eludes its members and with this they become alienated from the organisation.

> The formal rationality of bureaucracy, while it makes possible the technical implementation of large scale administrative tasks, substantively contravenes some of the most distinctive values of western civilisation, subordinating individuality and spontaneity. (Giddens, 1971, p. 216)

It is an ineluctable consequence of the development of industrial capitalism and rational-legal authority systems that bureaucracy escapes control and tends to impose a close-knit network of rules and regulations closely specifying the formally correct behaviour and leaving no scope for individually oriented creative action. For Weber 'capitalism' and particularly the development of large-scale industrial enterprises seeking to regulate their environments leads to a situation in which life loses its meaning: since it appears outside the control of individuals it seems futile.

In summary Eldridge has identified four strands in Weber's treatment of the development of capitalism which culminate in the de-mystification of life and the spread of purely instrumental action. These are:

> (a) the life renunciating character of a spirituality whose goal is profit making to God's glory.
>
> (b) the secular replacement of the puritan work ethic by the utiliarian work ethic. Moral values are themselves judged against their usefulness in promoting economic success.
>
> (c) more and more the emphasis placed upon techniques which may be correctly understood and employed for increasing wealth.
>
> (d) The eventual divorce of this emphasis upon techniques from moral valuations, which leads to a barrenness of life of which the participants may or may not be conscious. (Eldridge, 1971*b*, p. 174)

Moreover Weber saw socialism as an irrelevance which could not reverse these tendencies because all it offered was the more systematic application of formal rationality to economic life, a replacement of the creative forces of the market by a further dead hand of formal rationality. Socialism merely threatened to expand the scope of technical rationality without allowing any compensating reassertion of substantive rationality.

It is appropriate to leave Weber's treatment of rationality by quoting from his conclusions to *The Protestant Ethic and the Spirit of Capitalism*.

> No one knows who will live in this cage in the future, or whether at the end of this tremendous development entirely new prophets will arise, or there will be a great rebirth of old ideas and ideals, or, if neither, mechanised petrification, embellished will a sort of convulsive self importance. For of the last stages of this cultural development, it might well be truly said:

'Specialists without spirit, sensualists without heart; this nullity imagines that it has attained a level of civilisation never before achieved'. (1930, p. 182)

Suggested Further Reading

Albrow, M. (1970) *Bureaucracy* (London: Macmillan).

Bendix, R. (1960) *Max Weber: An Intellectual Portrait* (Garden City, N.Y.: Doubleday & Co.).

Thompson, K. (1972) *Religion and Economy* (The Open University, D283 Unit 13).

Bibliography

Albrow, M. (1970) *Bureaucracy* (London: Macmillan).

Child, J., Loveridge, R., and Warner, M. (1973) 'Towards an Organisational Study of Trade Unions', *Sociology* 7, no. 1, pp. 71–92.

Eldridge, J. E. T. (1971*a*) *Max Weber: The Interpretation of Social Reality* (London: Nelson University Paperbacks).

— (1971*b*) *Sociology and Industrial Life* (London: Nelson University Paperbacks).

Giddens, A. (1971) *Capitalism and Modern Social Theory* (Cambridge: Cambridge University Press).

Nisbet, R. A. (1966) *The Sociological Tradition* (New York: Basic Books).

Weber, M. (1930) *The Protestant Ethic and the Spirit of Capitalism*, trans. T. Parsons (London: Unwin University Books).

— (1948) 'Bureaucracy', in H. H. Gerth and C. W. Mills (trans. and eds.) *From Max Weber* (London: Routledge & Kegan Paul).

— (1968) *Economy and Society*, ed. G. Roth and C. Wittich (New York: Bedminster Press).

Wrong, D. H., ed. (1970) *Max Weber*, introduction (Englewood Cliffs, N.J.: Prentice-Hall).

7
Class and Ideology

The highly developed pre-existing trade and agricultural market relationships enabled England 'spontaneously' to become an industrial market society and the smoothness of the transition reinforced a system of beliefs which saw the unfettered or free market as the only route for economic progress and as the sole guardian of social welfare. Whatever the ultimate causes of the vast changes in the West that preceded and made possible the ultimate take-off into industrialisation, there can be little doubt that the fundamental changes in belief systems and in productive systems were related. Science's attempt to understand the physical universe as a natural phenomenon, at least theoretically amenable to human control, united rational habits of the mind with empirical practice and encouraged experimentation and threatened the intuitive and mystical explanations of traditional belief systems. Technology, at first the apparent product of the inspired hunches of practical men, became part of a systematic interchange betweeh theory and practice and it is this coalescence of science and technology that typifies the common productive measures of advanced industrial societies whatever their political system. The growth of science and technology was accompanied by a decline in the belief in the divine right of kings, or the belief that kings were agents of God, and this led to a new age of political discourse in which authority could no longer be justified in terms of appeals to the 'sanctity of immemorable tradition' but had to be rendered legitimate in terms of public utility of an observable nature. Order and control were no longer viewed as part of a total, integrated mystical cosmology in which the political hierarchy was but a continuation of the governance of God's will, but became part of a man-made order. This is not to say that actual social relationships became, in fact, in any sense more equalitarian but that the inequalities had to be justified in terms of theoretical and practical criteria which could be demonstrated to be socially necessary or useful. Legitimation of political control and of inequality had to be rendered meaningful in terms of a language of relevance of this world. Scientific secular discourse and political secularism were part of a singular and unique symbolic code. Whilst both were concerned with control, the latter was concerned with the control of man over man rather than the conquest of nature. Social science was part of this language, since its primary objective initially was to explain the contemporary condition in terms of external and objective laws which could be discerned with the same certainty as those of natural science laws, and therefore could determine the rational course of action.

Science and political legitimation through appeals to reason and human necessity are part of the same anti-traditional intellectual framework. In this sense political policies based on appeals to human necessity are couched in terms either of 'natural rights' accruing to all individuals by virtue of their membership of the human race or in terms of the inevitability of revealed laws of social development. Authority in the traditional order of feudal society was bestowed upon estates, guilds and associations rather than upon individuals; this authority was based upon the belief that qualities of leadership and moral superiority were God-given privileges and should form the basis of rank in society and led to a system in which political domination accounted for the distribution of economic resources rather than vice versa. It was the political arrangements, and the traditional beliefs that sustained them, that determined the allocation of landowning privilege and the corporate monopolies of the guilds and trading companies. The beliefs in an unchangeable hierarchy based on God-given qualities narrowly circumscribed the range of economic activities people could embark on and the individual was bounded by the legal rights and obligations attached to the specific social group into which he was born. Individual rights and obligations were bounded by the collective privileges of ascribed estates. 'Each jurisdiction accords positive public rights which entitle particularly privileged persons and corporate groups to exercise a specific authority and to levy fees or tolls for that exercise' (Bendix, 1964, p. 38).

It is important to recognise the revolutionary nature of the change from feudalism. Each group in the traditional order had been viewed as having a place within a totality which integrated both natural and moral phenomena. The social order and the moral order had been seen as this-worldly aspects of a God-given universe which because of its divine origins was unchangeable. Hence moral changes were equally sacrilegious and heretical as changes to the religious fabric and therefore opposed as equally dangerous. It was this unbroken link between the sacred and the social fabric that allowed the supremacy of the political over the economic, as it was clear that unrestrained economic action would undermine hierarchical arrangements which reflected the sacred distribution of rights and obligation. Unger sums up the revolutionary nature of the transition thus: 'The traditional view of a continuity between the natural and the moral order was overthrown and replaced either by the reduction of the moral world to the natural one or by the idea of a complete separation between the two realms' (Unger, 1976, p. 38).

Power is the capacity that individuals or groups have to command from others compliance to their requirements. Physical violence and coercion are one basis for ensuring such compliance, but domination based on physical violence is inherently unstable and requires the constant surveillance of those in the subordinate situation. None the less monopolies over the means of violence are often justified in terms of promoting the common good. For example in the Roman Empire the use of force to suppress the slaves and extract their labour was justified in terms of the benefits it brought the citizens. The slaves were defined as non-persons and as such the use of force to coerce them was easy to justify. Additional monopolies over violence are justified in terms of promoting civil order and preventing disorder and anarchy. Since in everyday life the maintenance of livelihood depends upon routine, people are by and large willing to accept order rather than run the risk of disorder which threatens the degree of predictability necessary for routine activities.

Weber distinguished between tratitional forms of domination, in which political authority was justified in terms of appeals to the past, and legal-rational forms of domination, which appealed to some abstract or formal principles which are impersonally argued. Unlike a traditional order which claims subordination as part of a handed-down pattern of divine ordination the legal order claims procedures are derived from a consciously articulated pattern, a plan in which subordination is justified according to demonstrable norms which impersonally limit and prescribe the action of both subordinate and superior.

'Those subject to legal authority owe no personal allegiance to a subordinate, and follow his commands only within the restricted sphere in which his jurisdiction is clearly specified' (Giddens, 1971, p. 158). This concern with the routine as a primary aspect of social life is essential for the understanding of Weber's approach. Individuals bestow meaning upon objects and persons and it is only when these meanings have a degree of constancy and consistency that routine social life is possible. Whilst rulers have an interest in securing compliance through non-violent means the ruled also require a degree of stability in order to pursue their diverse goals of everyday living. Thus the attempt to render the social order as legitimate is an activity in which both the subordinate and superordinate have interests. The mechanisms used to create and sustain legitimacy are various. Legal-rational bases of legitimacy depend on qualitatively different types of beliefs from those of traditional orders.

While traditional legitimation can rest on the symbolic language of religion, the secularisation of society which was part of the political and industrial revolutions of the eighteenth and nineteenth centuries meant a rapid break in the language of political domination and the engineering of legitimacy. Under rational-legal systems even the defence of tradition has to be justified in terms of rational discourse. The meanings of the past have to be translated into a contemporary language of justification in terms of contemporary usefulness. Tradition had been a language of ritual repetition, in which ceremonial derived from its very embeddedness in the 'nature of things'. Justifications of tradition had become articulated in external, that is to say reasoned, even planned, opportunities for the promotion of order, now with rational legality order was no longer God-given but something that had to be consciously strived for. Gouldner quotes from Mannheim, who states that 'tradition was being transformed in Conservatism via this self-awareness and via the justification of rational discussion. Tradition was, in short, being modernised into ideology' (Gouldner, 1976, p. 26).

From a sociological viewpoint the beliefs of the medieval period can be seen to function as an ideology. The beliefs cloaked and justified powers and privileges and led people to accept their positions willingly and with good grace. Indeed the very 'traditionalism' of the social arrangements meant that control was not viewed as an instrumental manipulation but as part of an ordained scheme in which both subordinate and superior were acting out their roles in accordance with God's will. So ingrained and oft repeated were these arrangements that they were unselfconsciously 'acted out' by the recipients. The age of explicit ideology and of social class are inseparable, for ideological alternatives are only possible where class divisions create separate social worlds in which distinct life styles emerge and within which social reality poses distinctly different problems. Only when contrasting views of the world are available are ideological debates possible; only when alternatives are thought to be available does the order of things become problematic.

Class relationships in market society are inherently equalitarian in one sense. A person's class is determined by objective forces of the market and the ability to control a sector of that market. Since all people are equally likely to experience joy or despair from the market, and since there are no formal barriers to participation in the market, class is inequality determined by formal equality. That is, all are equal to participate in the race even if some by virtue of their superiority are prone to win.

In this sense class relations have a degree of equalitarianism historically unprecedented, the estate system of stratification in feudal society denied any norm of equality since inequality was immutably given in the ordained nature of things. The class system derives from the market in which all equally participate. Since inequalities do derive from this formal equality they have to be justified and justified in terms of man-made rather than religiously ordained schema. For example, inequalities are attributed to the hard work, the shrewdness or the risk-taking of the investor–entrepreneur.

Competing ideologies are only possible where alternatives in everyday life become recognised as needing explanation. The rural life of the medieval peasantry was such that it discouraged the emergence of new patterns of thought or behaviour, and the extreme inward lookingness of village life hampered the spread of the few innovations that did emerge. This uniformity of outlook is reinforced by the central role of a universal church carrying a single religious interpretation of life's meaning. When control over nature becomes a possibility and the authority of the Church is successfully questioned, when printing and literacy break the stranglehold of lack of alternatives, then the age of ideology has dawned. Ideological justification appeals to tenets of reason and conscious rational argument rather than to mystical beliefs and ritualistic observances of past behaviours. Whether bemoaning or applauding the changes, the eighteenth-century 'enlightenment' appealed to rational criteria.

> Its champions believed firmly (and correctly) that human history was an ascent rather than a decline or an undulating movement about a level trend. They could observe that man's scientific knowledge and technical control over nature increased daily. They believed that human society and

individual man could be perfected by the same application of reason, and were destined to be so perfected by history. (Hobsbawn, 1973, p. 286)

The rigid application of principles of materialism and empiricism to scientific matters led to the belief that similar applications were leading to the perfectability of the individual and society. The age of ideology sought to control and divert man's energies to the quest for this state of perfection. Even the conservative branch of the ideological enterprise recognised that the control of man's affairs could not be left but had to be engineered, even if it was retrogressive engineering towards a bygone age of perfection. Gouldner sums up the radical break between the age of religion and the age of ideology well when he says:

> Religions are concerned with the sacred and thus those powers within whose limits, or under whose governance, men act. Religions thus see men as limited, created, or other-grounded beings and foster a sense of men's limitedness; ideologies, by contrast, focus on men as sources of authority and as sites of energy and power. (1976, p. 26)

In this sense the age of ideology and the age of class are synonymous in so far as both stress man the actor, the source of power, at the centre of the stage. Political domination thus has to be couched in terms of impersonal norms which stress the project, the plan of societal welfare, as the justifying source of asymmetrical power rather than appealing to traditions of sacred order which stress the divine will and the ascribed and therefore inactive or passive aspects of human life. 'In a word, the Enlightenment postulated the human, as opposed to a divine construction of the ideal' (Dawe, 1970, p. 212).

Rather than there being, as Dawe suggests, two distinct sociologies deriving from this period and its central intellectual concerns there are a series of sociological and philosophical schools which respectively stress the importance of the 'meaning' of action as opposed to external determination of human action, and which emphasise differently the degree of self-assertion over events and the degree to which natural and social phenomena differ both in kind and in method. Giddens (1976*a*) stresses the myth of the problem of order as a central concern of the classical authorities of sociology. This myth is largely a result of the tendency to associate sociology with the pervasive nineteenth-century ideology of utilitarianism and *laissez-faire*. Durkheim, however, was concerned to establish the social as a distinct level of explanation, not to replace the individualistic assumptions of *laissez-faire* with equally ahistorically social assumptions. For Durkheim the problems of the late nineteenth-century crisis in social order were not abstract ahistorical problems of 'lack of control', or indeed lack of constraint, but an historical problem in which social arrangements which were conducive to regulating the individualised market forms of relationship had not developed. Thus sociology in both Marxist and non-Marxist forms developed as a critique of nineteenth-century utilitarianism and *laissez-faire* economics. While it is true that some early sociologists, for example Spencer, were favourably disposed towards the contemporary economic system, it is not true to say that they were conservatively impressed with a model of man which stressed the need for constraint and the need both to lessen the demand for man-centred control and to place limitations on that control. Durkheim was concerned to analyse social institutions in order to establish what arrangements were appropriate for self-determined control in an 'individualised' society. To quote Giddens (1976*a*, p. 707), 'at a relatively early stage of his intellectual development, Durkheim specifically, though rather casually, dismissed the "Hobbesian problem" as being of no interest to sociology, saying that it depends upon a hypothetical state of affairs (man in a state of nature) which is of no interest to social theory, because it is wrongly posed in the first place.'

This attribution of a central concern with order illustrates the degree to which ideological considerations have distorted the image of sociology. The functional theory of stratification, for example, which explains inequality in terms of society's need to ensure the optimum allocation of human resources to positions within the division of labour by rewarding certain positions more highly than others, owes far more to the utilitarian individualism of nineteenth-century economics than it does to the key problems of classical sociological theory. Although both economics and sociology are equally prone to ideological influences it is as well to recognise that the historical antecedents of these influences are radically different, if often interpenetrating, and this is of more than passing importance to the history of sociological theory.

The radical break with tradition effected by the change in the system of production meant a break with the traditional system of symbolic constraint upon purposive action and has deep significance. It is necessary to spell this point out, and Habermas's distinction between *work* and *interaction* derived from Weber's concept of rationalisation is helpful (Habermas, 1971, pp. 91–4). The category of *work* is confined to the area of 'instrumental action or rational choice of their conjunction', and such instrumental action is governed by technical rules based upon knowledge. The criterion of empirical provability is the key to this concept. The expediency of such action and its pragmatic base means that it can be changed, given up altogether or continued according to its success in achieving the actor's goals. Such action is evaluated in terms of calculative criteria, and strategies are derived according to evaluations of possible alternatives. On the other hand, *interaction* belongs to the realm of communicative action, and is symbolically derived and conducted according to consensual norms which must be shared and understood by the actors in such an interaction. Action is sanctioned by mutuality of expectation rather than by purely pragmatic success. As Habermas himself puts it, 'While the validity of technical rules and strategies depends on that of empirically true or analytically correct propositions, the validity of social norms is grounded only in the intersubjectivity of the mutual understanding of intentions and secured by the general recognition of obligations' (1971, p. 92).

Whereas incompetent behaviour results from violations of technical rules and is sanctioned by lack of success of the act itself, deviant behaviour resulting from violation of norms is punished by conventional sanction. Skills are the learnt patterns of purposive rational behaviour, whereas norms internalised into the self constitute personality. As Habermas puts it: 'Skills put us in a position to solve problems; motivations allow us to follow norms.' According to Habermas, and following Parsons, we can distinguish between the parts of society in which certain types of action predominate: the economic system and the state apparatus are predominantly purposive-rational, the family and kinship systems predominantly interactional-normative.

Using this framework Habermas attempts a reformulation of Weber's approach to the concept of 'rationalisation'. Traditional civilisations, such as feudal society, had a system of distribution and production which, while allowing both the creation of surplus and the distribution of that surplus according to criteria other than kinship alone, placed severe limits on the extent of technical and organisational improvement. The institutional order of pre-capitalist cultural systems prevented developments that would come into contradiction with their self-justifying 'sacred' systems of political domination. Feudal society took on an absolutist form to the extent that the absolute monarch could protect best the interests and thus the political dominance of the aristocracy. The limits set by the monarchical-aristocratic state on economic action, such as usury, monopolies and charters meant that economic, technical or purposive rational action were limited in order to preserve the traditional fabric of 'divine' ordinance. To quote Habermas again, 'The expression "traditional society" refers to the circumstance that the institutional framework is grounded in the unquestionable legitimation constituted by mythical, religious or metaphysical interpretations of reality – cosmic as well as social – as a whole' (1971, p. 95).

It is the domination of shared meaning which prevents the extension of purposive rational behaviour and marks out the traditional society. The force of the market system with its stimuli to invention and organisational innovation has an inherent logic which undermines this shared traditionalism since it exposes all relationships to questioning. The unification of the market and industrialisation which is first seen with capitalism means that self-sustained growth is possible. The extension of self-generating change to all walks of life is the true nature of the political and economic revolution associated with the advent of capitalism. In these terms the very success of capitalism renders the capacity of traditionally defended norms to sustain themselves problematic at first and unsustainable in the end.

'Only with the emergence of the capitalist mode of production can the legitimation of the institutional framework be linked immediately with the system of social labour' (Habermas, 1971, p. 97). And it is precisely because the productive system of capitalism provides its own criterion of justice, that is of equivalence, that it can both undermine the cultural order of tradition and yet provide its own mode of legitimation. It is through private property that all relationships are measured, since all start equal in the market place and inequalities are the product of this impersonal market which promotes social welfare and therefore justifies the emergent pattern of inequality. Market rationality replaces appeals to traditional political beliefs. Law, justice and politics must inexorably conform to the basic equality of the market. Political domination can only be justified, as indeed can legal rules and all other social relationships, in so far as they aid the working of the market mechanism. Ideologies are a product of this selfsame movement of social transition and, appealing to objective reason rather than to the status of the proponents, they claim empirical credibility in this world, and indicate that man controls the institutional order and that it is not merely one aspect of the divine order. According to Gouldner:

> Ideology and social science are both responses to the newly problematic nature of social reality in post-traditional society. It deserves remembering that social sciences, like outright ideology, also sought in its beginnings to live by the doctrine of the unity of theory and practice and to impose certain obligations for public action upon its adherents. (1976, p. 33)

Adam Smith's work provides an excellent example of this simultaneous emergence of ideology and social science organised around the unity of theory and practice. Wealth creation was seen as part of a social process of natural law unfolding in the guise of laws of economic determination. Morality was inherent in the operation of the market since, in spite of individual suffering, these law-like principles enhanced the common good. Thus the autonomy of economics and its principles was no longer merely a neutral statement of fact but also a moral enjoinder to practices of a socially beneficial nature. As an ideology, Smith's notions can be seen as urging upon men a respect for the virtues of the industrious middle class against the decadent rentiers of the aristocracy, nevertheless the ideological expression was linked to a social science analysis which was a search for the law-like principles governing economic activity.

To say that ideology and social science are never far apart is not to suggest that they are the same thing. Indeed the constant mutual criticism between ideology and social science is the best and probably only safeguard against totalistic views of reality which preclude innovatory thinking and prevent actions designed to introduce change. For students of business, it is important to recognise two related things. First, the most apparently objective statements about the nature of the social world contain ideological elements, that is, one-sided distortions of reality that serve to maintain and reinforce the interests of particular interest groups. Second and conversely, ideological statements usually contain approximations to social reality, which, no matter how unpalatable, can through their analysis reveal important features of the social reality which they also serve to mystify. For example, however much his celebrations of the free enterprise market might have provided a one-sided justification for the actions of the emergent entrepreneurial classes against the landed aristocracy, who sought where possible to preserve their interests by appeals to tradition customs, and however much his ruthless individualism may have justified the free movement of capital without concern for the victims, the landless labourers, Smith's system of thought did provide a rational core of truth that enabled the apprehension and understanding of many of the changes that were pushed forward by the capitalist mode of production. Indeed the very autonomy of the economic principles he advocated partially described the reality of the increasing independence of market forces, or in other words the emergence of purposive rational actions from the mire of traditional obligation and interactive control. The very image of the individualistic entrepreneur enjoying control over his own destiny within the constraints of the market encapsulates the emergent rationalism and expediency of the epoch. Whilst rational action, to a degree never considered respectable in traditional circumstances, results in self-determination, it is always within the limits set by the market, that is by certain inviolable laws which command a higher, extra individual, purpose.

It is this very ambivalence or contradiction that the analysis of Smith's ideologically biased social science reveals. The individual was free from traditional constraints to pursue his own interests in a rational purposive manner in the realm of workmanlike endeavour – yet the very product of collective actions, the laws of the market, impersonally set limits to self's control of self's own destiny. The nineteenth century saw the further development of capitalism and the increasing separation of the economic and economics from social and moral contexts. The autonomy of economics and its protestation that it had freed itself from ideology is indicative of this development. Both sociological and ideological criticisms of the consequences of this profound change in the nature of the world are indicative, however distorted, of the real interests that these movements of history challenged and overturned.

Ideology, then, is a modern product striving for the increase of men's control over their natural and social environment through the application of knowledge. It is modern in the sense that it appeals to this-worldly change and modification and to rational purposive action. Both social science and ideology share the same percentage of rational justification and accountability and thus their destinies are inextricably intertwined.

The ideology of the emerging bourgeoisie claimed that the ownership of property was a necessary and just reward for endeavour in an open and equal market. The denial of historical dimensions in this analysis is evidence of its ideological distortion. If inequality is held to be a product of competitive virtue in a market and property and wealth are both reward and incentive then it is necessary to adopt a 'timeless' frame of meaning, since to go back to the past, to put flesh on this abstract model, would indicate a system of interests, would draw attention to the unfairness of various groups' starting points in the competitive race. If it is shown that certain individuals are successful because of inherited position, then it indicates that far from enjoying real equality at the start of the race this privilege gives the owner a start on the rest. If personalised favour is revealed to have brought good fortune for the winner, for example position through family connections, then it is difficult to sustain the objective formal equality of the impersonal mechanism.

It is this emphasis upon the substantive as opposed to the formal nature of equality that suggests the interwoven modernity of both ideology and class. While human beings sustained themselves through collective action and collective beliefs in pre-modern society, and while inequality was systematically sustained in such societies; these inequalities were of a qualitatively distinct nature to those of the era of purposive instrumental action. Inequality was held to be a product of personalised forces which reflected the capacity of certain cateories of persons to perform the will of God and to be agencies of supernatural forces; thus the justification system was enmeshed in the web of traditional sentiment. The market breaks down this personalisation of inequality as scientific thought breaks down the mystery of an enchanted world interpenetrated by divine will and spirit.

Thus conservative respect for the order of things as they are is part of a justificatory network based on a veneration for 'what is' as functional, that is, necessary for the social good in utilitarian terms; for the existing worldly order is justified in terms of practical consequences for this world. Class is both an objective and subjective factor when individual position is defined as a product of impersonal forces ultimately grounded in this world. That is, it is the product of man-made institutions. The market, even in its most celebratory exponent's hands, is a product of man and of his natural inclinations, not some immutable divine will; although there may be a happy coincidence between the two. Class is thus a product of impersonal mechanisms of market society; whether it is considered legitimate or not depends upon the degree of moral righteousness that men are willing to bestow upon impersonality and its mechanism or the degree to which the forces are perceived to be purely impersonal and unmediated by man-made institutions which prejudice the outcomes of the competitive system. Put another way, the application of formal equality will aid those who are substantively unequal; ideology and class are twin-born products of the mechanism of social distribution which results from the freeing of purposive rational action from the web of traditional and customary interactive relationships. Socialistic ideologies which criticise the market for its competitive impersonality seek to prevent its excesses by planned economic growth and planned redistribution of income, wealth and ownership of the means of production. While they may define the substantive situation as one in which the inequalities are a product of systematic unfairness in terms of historically derived inequalities of power, control and ownership of the means of production, their solutions are the planned extension of purposive rational action over a much wider social base. In this sense ideologies of socialism and capitalism are truly modern beliefs resulting from class inequalities which can only arise when purposive rational action is freed from the constraints of tradition.

The rise of the Welfare State in the nineteenth century is partly a product of the free market need to contain the social consequences of the total impersonality of market mechanisms. It is also the response of the various classes interacting together in a qualitatively distinct world, a world in which men believed that control over nature and society is possible, even if such control involves the choice to leave social outcomes to impersonal forces in the belief that the outcomes will be beneficial.

Although classes existed in an 'analytical' sense, as did the 'economy' prior to industrial capitalism, so intermeshed were relationships in the customary hierarchy and traditional obligation that such objective forces as class were explicable only within models that fully expressed this interpenetration.

Bendix states that 'If "modernity" is shorthand for the separation of class, status and authority, then "tradition" stands for their fusion. Until the early modern period, economic activities were an aspect of the household. Status depended more upon the individual's family ties than it does where modernising tendencies prevail' (1976, p. 83). Thus, if one accepts this analysis, the analytical abstraction of the 'economic' from the totality of status and belief that typified the pre-industrial household with all its personalised dependency is to commit the 'fallacy of misplaced concreteness', that is, confuse an analytic device with the reality it seeks to explain. Furthermore, some analytic devices are more useful than others; to impose the exclusively modern categories of 'economy' and the correlates of class and ideology is to distort and impede explanation as well as to disguise the revolutionary nature of modernity.

Polanyi sums up this crucial distinction between the traditional and modern when he states that in the modern system, 'Instead of economy being embedded in social relations, social relations are embedded in the economic system' (1963, p. 57). The separation of class, status and authority is an entirely modern product and this means that the economy may play a more or less determining relationship with each and all of these aspects of social life depending upon the particular circumstances. Indeed a major problem of both sociological and ideological explanation is the degree to which the form of the economy determines the form of the class system, the political system and the status system. Put another way, the degree of autonomy these areas of social life have from the economy is one of the key problems of contemporary social thought. What is certain is that such questions could not be posed where belief and status are embedded in interactive custom of the traditional society. It is only where purposive rational thought and action are freed from the constraints of traditional interactions that we can recognise a world of alternatives both in theory and practice that can be implemented by man. It is thus possible to talk about class, ideology and economy in a substantive sense, rather than as analytical categories, only when the innovation of purposive rational action becomes a distinct mover of the social fabric. Indeed the very autonomy of the economy and its capacity to 'cause' the changes in other social spheres is another way of expressing this profound essence of modernity.

Discussions as to the nature of class accompany this radical split with the past. It is only when there is a divergence from tradition that political legitimacy and social distribution become problematic. In traditional society political legitimacy is questioned only when the actions of either subordinate or superordinate are seen to diverge from traditional prescriptions. Peasant revolts were, by and large, protests against authorities defined as having failed to maintain their traditional obligations rather than basic questionings of the distribution of political power and social inequality on a fundamental level.

One of the pioneer sociologists and founders of the analysis of social class was Saint-Simon. His writings were very much a response to the changes of the French Revolution. For Saint-Simon the state of knowledge was the major force of change in society. The stability of the preceding medieval order was viewed in terms of the consensus surrounding the nature of society, that is, it was seen as an extension of the natural order which involved a hierarchy in which everyone played his part as an extension of the divine pattern. Ascribed status was thus inherent in this transcendental pattern and by 'acting out' one's given role one was subscribing to the will of God. The educated élite of the Middle Ages had expressed this unity of ideas in the form of theology and metaphysics and the landowning warrior classes had disguised their power based on force through these beliefs. However for centuries the nature of material progress had changed only under the impact of new views of natural phenomena. But these changes increased the visibility of man's control over nature. The temporal order of landowning, militaristic control thus became increasingly out of harmony with the real facts of material and social life. The political system of self-justification through the divine will of God ceased to be in harmony with a world in which nature could be controlled by critical knowledge and wealth was increasingly produced by bankers, industrial entrepreneurs and factory workers. Political power had remained in the hands of an increasingly irrelevant landowning aristocracy and justified by an out-of-date priesthood. According to Saint-Simon, the French Revolution was merely the result of the developing inequality in which the real source of material welfare became scientists and industrialists (both owners and workers) and the aristocracy and priesthood were unable to provide for the needs of this new order of industrialism and became totally parasitical. However he is critical of the assumption that the free market enables the achievement of the collective good through the unbridled pursuit of individual self-interest. He claimed that a science of man which would bring to individual consciousness a sense of societal need, and welfare should replace religion since its scientific status would yield in men's minds a feeling of accordance with 'natural' order. He recognised that there were divergences of interest between those in the new industrial order but felt that such interests could be overcome if the economic and social fabric were controlled by those scientists who understood the true nature of social needs in the industrial society. Saint-Simon epitomised the equation of reason and progress, he typifies the optimistic nineteenth-century view of the new entrepreneurial classes and provides a justification for these classes expressed in terms of their social utility.

Second, Saint-Simon provided a critique of the aristocratic order based upon its social redundancy and stressed the utility of inequality in terms of contribution to collective wealth. That is to say, inequality becomes justifiable only in terms of its contributions towards productivity: he thus groups bankers, industrialists, manual workers and scientists as producers as against others who are idlers. Inequalities amongst the producers were acceptable since scientists and industrialists and bankers contributed towards the organisation of the social totality by providing a consensual set of beliefs and values about how the world should be organised. It is this scientific view and its application which cuts across class interests and reconciles men to inequalities which are accepted as legitimate because of their planned and rational nature.

Third, his scheme is of interest since it proclaims the virtues of a planned industrial order as opposed to the free play of the market. Private property would no longer be the ultimate reward and justification of the system because the unbridled pursuit of private property involves the negation of the ordered, harmonious, industrial society. By rigorous central planning the more excessive consequences of a free market form of capitalism could be ironed out in a consensual manner without the inherent class conflict associated with extreme market capitalism or the total eradication of the market deemed necessary by socialist critics. As Lichtheim puts it, Saint-Simon, 'was both a reaction against individualism and a glorification of the Industrial Revolution (1975, p. 53).

In terms of its ideological staying power, this view of rendering political problems as apolitical technical problems, to be 'solved' by the application of scientific-technical principles, is far from outdated. The very notion of an 'end of ideology' in which value problems are rendered as out of date and superceded by the decline of social classes is contemporary and central to popular belief in the latter part of the twentieth century, and indeed the ideas of Saint-Simon can be seen as precursors of the 'end of ideology' thesis of the post-industrial society (see Chapter 8, on 'Industrial Convergence'). Essential to this thesis is the relative decline in the centrality of class conflict aligned around the relationships of ownership and non-ownership of property. Central also to this argument is that as post-industrial society emerges from either capitalistic, market-induced industrialisation or from centralised planned sources 'the logic' of industrial society leads to a mixture of market and plan-guided economic institutions in which the technical problems tend to be similar and consequently so do their solutions. It is over such issues that one can see the difficulties in separating the 'ideological' from the 'sociological', since the belief that class conflict had declined in such a way as to render political and value decisions mere technical problems to be solved by objective methods has heavy ideological connotations. For example, if sufficient people believe that decisions concerning the management of the economy should be left to professional scientific managers, then they will tend to be politically acquiescent and such beliefs could be then said to sustain the economic and political *status quo*. On the other hand, those who claim that class conflict concerning the distribution of property is the same in its nature and intensity as in the nineteenth century have to answer the question as to whether their ideological position has led them to ignore the vast changes in the occupational structure since the nineteenth century, the vast changes from small-scale entrepreneur-owned and controlled firms to vast joint-stock corporations more concerned with long term investment and stability than quick profits. Indeed the latter question concerning the nature of the corporation and its commitment to profits is one of the key 'ideological' debates whose outcome has important consequences for the one view of contemporary class analysis.

Fourth, Saint-Simon developed the view that the normal condition of the industrial order was one in which vested interest of a class nature was transcended by virtue of a consensual belief system based upon scientific analysis. According to Marx this analysis was basically one of 'Utopian Socialism' since it 'apparently could not, or did not, see the conflict of interests between these major classes of the industrial system and therefore not only treated them as one class with common interests, but left bourgeois property institutions intact in the blueprint for the future society' (Zeitlin, 1968, p. 57).

This latter point leads to the fifth and last point demonstrating the relevance of Saint-Simon. His sympathetic view of central planning was at loggerheads with the *laissez-faire* views of the successfully industrialising English bourgeoisie. This is important since it is only in Britain and the United States that the ideological antagonism towards state interference in the economy had a major influence. It is no coincidence that France underwent a considerable political revolution prior to its embarkation on industrialisation and this revolution meant that the emergent non-aristocratic classes had to justify themselves in terms of political liberties and social and economic engineering rather than their role in already started economic growth. In other words, the role of state interference or planning was never as contentious in other histories of industrialisation as it was in Britain or the United States. Planning *per se* was not immediately associated with socialism nor the bourgeois with the free market in France or indeed Germany. Thus the development of both German and French industrialisation, although involving immense political conflicts with socialistic and proletarian organisations, did not involve the equation of state 'interference' or indeed monopolistic control of the market by both state and vast corporation as inimicable to industrial capitalism. This is significant since many of the political controversies that surround the Anglo-Saxon model of industrialism, especially those concerned with planning the economy and controlling the market, seem strangely irrelevant in the context of Continental nations. It is particularly true concerning the relationships between class and ideology, for many of the peculiarly British and American criticisms of the Welfare State and its identification with creeping socialism are products of their atypical free market industrial origins rather than of any predilection of Continentals towards socialism or communism. Thus Dahrendorf, comparing German industrialisation with the model deduced from the English experience, says: 'At what should, in terms of the English model, have been the heyday of private enterprise and liberal social and political patterns, the state was in Germany, the largest single entrepreneur' (1968 p. 39).

A central role in the later industrialisation of Germany was played by centralised banks, large monopolistic enterprises and cartels, all in a context of considerable protectionism and rationalisation of hitherto local particularities provided by the central state authorities. Of especial importance was the responsibility for social welfare measures accepted and instigated by the highly centralised paternalistic state. Dahrendorf puts the situation well when he states that 'Not even industrialisation managed, in Germany, to upset a traditional outlook in which the whole is placed above its parts, the state above the citizen, or a rigidly controlled order above the lively diversity of the market, the state above society' (1968, p. 40).

This, then, suggests the atypicality of the British and indeed American patterns of industrial development and the compatibility of capitalist development with a high degree of state intervention. The degree to which the technical rationality, inherent in the process of industrialisation characterised by the systematic application of non-animate sources of energy in the factory and in process production, is autonomous – that is, independent of the specific economic organisation of capitalist relations of production – is the key to this question and the central starting point for the analysis of social class. Here again is repeated the crucial significance of Saint-Simon's notion of the industrial order, or in more contemporary language, the 'post-industrial society' which cuts across the notion of the class base of modernism.

Karl Marx

Marx, like all of the major social theorists, sought an understanding of the tension between the individual and society. It is no coincidence that the very processes of industrialisation and the development of the market-induced 'individualism', which brought about the emergence of both sociology and Marxism as attempts to explain and comprehend these very processes, should make this tension one of the central problems for its social theorists. The ideology of *laissez-faire*, the extreme celebration of market society attempted to reconcile the individual and society – as suggested earlier – by imputing a rationality to the individual which would be easily reconciled with the mechanical demands of the market, since the 'maximising' individual, in his interior self, would seek by means of market operations of work, investment and consumption to maximise satisfactions. Since his wants were attainable through the mechanisms of the market then conformity to market rules would ensure this anticipated state. Since the market was the most 'natural' of institutions the rational individual would achieve his true nature by rational actions which were guided by the laws of supply and demand. Acts of gross irrationality were discouraged by these very laws, which held inbuilt punishments, and the laws of the market ensured that the rational actor would receive a just reward, the irrational his due recompense, failure. Because these laws were strictly impersonal, and in the last analysis no more than the individual discrete behaviours concerted in an aggregated way above and beyond the individual, both individual and society were reconciled. Individuals not involved in market activities, such as the dependants of labourers and investors, because of their very dependency upon the economic actor, were also reconciled with the 'hidden hand' by virtue of their very dependence. The market was both impersonal and just and metered out reward and punishment according to the most natural of laws; the individual was thus reconciled with the social order, and accepted his dependence upon its mechanisms. Consequently, interferences with the market or restraints upon its impersonal mechanisms were viewed as a threat to this reconciliation. Whether they were large firms able to dictate the price of commodities outside the context of competition, or individuals who through inherited wealth were able to protect their estates from the forces of market logic, or collections of individuals who through concerted actions were able to change the price of free labour, all were equally culpable of unnatural behaviour restraining trade, and for this reason reducing social welfare.

Marx was considerably influenced by the political economy of the day, which proclaimed the operations of *laissez-faire* markets as the most equitable and natural of reconciliations between individual and social levels. He was much influenced by the philosophical traditions of his native Germany. He shared the view of the philosopher of history Hegel that social phenomena must be studied in their totality, that is, each part in terms of its consequences for all the rest and he shared the view that history must be understood as a process, that is, in a constant state of dynamic change. Hence for Marx and Hegel history and society were part and parcel of the same dynamic process. Social systems were no more than frozen moments in the unfolding of historical development. Marx also accepted Hegel's view that conflict was the key dynamic of historical change. Hegel, however, viewed this dynamic to be in the realm of the idea. Hegel saw the unique essence of being human as man's capacity to carry ideas. Since ideas persisted beyond the life of their historical carriers, he saw history as being a product of the unfolding of conflictive tensions between opposed ideas. Good presupposes the 'logical' opposition of evil, high the opposition of low, the sacred the profane, and so forth. Men, the carriers of these oppositions, objectify them in social institutions; nevertheless the opposition between master and slave remains a dialogue of oppositionary subjectivism fought out on the level of objective observable action. This opposition, this dialectic between rationally constructed ideas and action, seeks some rest in the ultimate state of reason. That condition of absolute reason manifests itself when the oppositions inherent in man's creative quest to overcome his irrationality become bounded and the opposites are reconciled; thus it is only where man's creative unfolding results in an ultimate idea which cuts across oppositions and unites that man can find rest. According to Hegel, the modern state is the final reconciliation of oppositions which have hitherto tormented man's search for truth. Since the State in its objective and external form, epitomised by Crown, judiciary and administration, is above and beyond the petty, sectionalistic bounded interests of men it is able to reconcile all oppositions. The ideal of ultimate reason is reached in the idea of the State; the modern state with universal rights of citizenship reconciles the individual with the whole by virtue of its transcendental reason. As divine arbitrator it is able to grant universal rights, such as equality before the law, and enable the individual to reconcile any oppositions by virtue of his rights to full participation.

Universal rights bestow upon the individual universal access to impartial and impersonal reason. The ideal of the State yields the end of history since history is based upon struggle and the transcendance of the State over the particular thus culminates in the end of history. Man's creative quest for ultimate reason is reconciled with the ultimate objective apparatus, his own collective creation, the modern state.

The astute reader will have noticed the religious connotations of this position. Man the actor is no more than the carrier of the 'spirit' of reason, his very status of bearer of the 'spirit' of reason relegates him as an actor on the world scene to the sidelines. That is to say the realisation of the objective synthesis epitomised by the modern state was only partially mankind's creation since it was, in a sense, innate in the very structure of mind to achieve this synthesis. Man only acted out the process of history in order to achieve that which was predetermined by mind: the explanatory status of mind, thus a transcendental idea like the idea of the ultimate God. Man's creations are nothing more than the acting out of the predetermined 'will' of the ultimate. Thus man is alien to his own creations. The State, the absolute epitome of reason, is acceptable to the individual by virtue of its alien qualities, being above the mundane constraints of petty vested interest and civil strife.

Whilst influenced by this theoretical synthesis, Marx recognised that the sophistication of German philosophy was itself a product of the peculiar nature of social development in Germany. Specifically, the domination of the landed Junker aristocracy, who controlled the state bureaucracy and the army, led to the powerlessness of both the intellectuals and the entrepreneurial middle class and allowed them autonomy only in the realm of ideas. To put the matter crudely, the reconciliation of the situation with the objective constraints of reality was only possible on the level of 'ideas', hence Marx claimed that 'In politics the Germans have *thought* what other nations have done.' It was not that Marx sought by his emphasis upon the real material world to replace the philosophical penchant for idealistic explanations, but rather to cut across a simplistic dichotomy between 'materialistic' and 'idealistic' explanations by posing the limits placed upon creative mankind by the constraints of economy and history. By recognising man the actor on the historical stage as inevitably involved in the process of survival, he posed the importance of work and the relationships of work as the baseline which constrains and limits all other forms of social and cultural development. Consequently purely idealistic solutions to the human condition were mere illusions since the crucial factors of economic survival and production would always restrict the feasibility of such reconciliations.

Marx accepted the systematic nature of society but saw this system as ultimately depending upon the condition of the working relationships – the relations of production and their articulation with the means of production. Thus if the modern state reconciled the individual with his social condition by virtue of its inherent justice, yielded by its universalistic detachment from particular individual and group interests, then, in terms of men's work relationships, it would be expected that conditions of economic abundance and equality of distribution would be exhibited since the State had no specific interests which would lead to inequality in the distribution of scarce resources. In this sense Marx was saying that the material reality of scarcity of large numbers of the population prevented the universal acceptance of the reasonableness and rationality of the modern state. If the State was providing a rational and thus acceptable set of conditions for all its citizens, the formal equality of participation in citizenship, which enabled the population to accept its edicts, would be correlated with a substantive equality in material conditions and access to the abundance of the products of work. If the State was the final product of man's request for reason, then the material conditions of the citizenry would reflect this and the distribution of material goods and services would also reflect this ultimate, disinterested and impersonal rationality. The means of production, factory production geared to a mechanical technology, meant in long-range historical terms the dawn of an era of productive abundance. For the first time, the application of rational methods of science to technological and production problems meant that mankind was potentially liberated from the material constraints of scarcity. The contradiction of the capitalist mode of production exhibited itself at the level of the objective capacity of such rational technological and organisational means of production, the relations of production, to effect the distribution of this capacity on a proportionately rational basis.

History has been a long and tortuous process of mankind's liberation from the material scarcity caused by his dependence upon nature. Natural causes, such as flood, disease and vicissitudes of weather and crops, had long set the backcloth to man's endeavours; his social relations had long been limited by the unpredictable and malevolent forces of natural phenomenon. With the advent of machine power and rational science began an age of liberation and abundance made possible by the overcoming of this dependence upon nature. Material constraints of survival were no longer potential limits upon the ideals that man set himself. Thus Marx was arguing for an age of reason, of rationality akin to Hegel's ultimate synthesis, yet he claimed that the contradiction between the rational means of production and the seemingly irrational relations of production prevented the emergence of this age of reason. The capacity for human freedom yielded by the triumph of rationality in productive methods was restricted by the material scarcity which co-existed with this potential. It is to the existing relations of production that Marx attributed this material barrier to the triumph of rationality.

Marx viewed man's efforts as inherently a social activity. That is to say that from the beginning the endeavour to survive was in the context of interaction on a communal basis. This is crucial, because he rejected a root assumption of the political economy of his contemporaries, namely what could be called their 'methodological individualism'. The economics of his contemporaries, in the tradition of Adam Smith, based their propositions on the assumption of individual rationality. Because of individual actors' capacity to avoid pain and seek pleasure, the workings of the market were made possible since in the pursuit of maximisation of satisfactions individuals would consume, invest and labour according to the rules of rationality. Consequently the laws of supply and demand were predictable and comprehensible and the market society tended to a state of equilibrium. Marx rejected individual units as the reality from which society emerged with the market at its centre from which all else derived, and claimed that man was inherently a social animal and all explanations concerning society and economy had to refer to this social level of explanation. Furthermore, the process of production could only be understood according to social and historical explanations. Since the market was not a 'natural' outcome of individual rationality, it had to be explained historically.

Initially mankind had lived in a state of what Marx called 'Primitive Communism'. 'At the dawn of civilisation the productiveness acquired by labour is small, but so too are the wants which develop with and by the means of satisfying them' (*Capital*, I, pp. 511–12). It is worth noting that here Marx rejects all notions of irreducible human needs. Again he rejects all individualistic core assumptions. For Marx, human needs are derived from their social context. Men only need what they have been taught to need by virtue of economic circumstances. Thus there is no system of human needs outside the context of social interaction. It is in the very process of production that social man develops needs. The level of what is defined as survival is then a social definition and not some set 'biological' quantity. The social being must labour to achieve this survival and the irreducible amount of labour for Marx was labour time spent upon providing the amount of goods necessary for the labourer to go on living, or, in Marxist terms, to reproduce himself. Since man is a social being, he always has to produce more than his own means of reproduction. Children, the old, the sick are all part of any society. Thus those who labour must always produce more than the amount necessary for their own survival. This latter amount of labour time Marx calls 'surplus labour'. Labour therefore consists of two basic parts: necessary labour and surplus labour. The latter must be present in all societies since it is essential for the reproduction of society. Without it society could not perpetuate itself. In primitive communist societies this surplus is collectively used: that is, it is shared between the members rather than being appropriated by specific groups. In this sense primitive communist society is classless. Where surplus produce of labour (i.e. surplus labour) is appropriated by specific non-productive groups then a class society exists. Different economic systems have different systems by which this surplus value is extracted by and on behalf of non-labouring groups. For Marx the State and various bureaucratic devices were none other than the apparatus of extraction of the capitalist mode of production. Put another way, under primitive communism the technical division of labour, i.e. between say men as hunters and women as gatherers, or between the young who provide manual labour and the old who provide wisdom, is not converted into a condition of social division of labour.

That is to say the mere technical divisions which are functional in terms of the maintenance of sexual and age distinctions are not converted into permanent ascribed allocations of occupational rights and obligation over time, since women remain women and raise more women and all grow old this technical division is not converted via the appropriation of surplus by specific minorities into permanent systematic inequality. In this sense, then, capitalism as a means of production brings a historically unprecedented situation of inequality. Since all societies after that of primitive communism have been based upon the exploitation of majorities through appropriation of surplus, capitalism is unique because the very process of production, i.e. the harnessing of inanimate sources of power to systematic techniques of organised production, enables, for the first time, the freeing of mankind as a species from the dependency upon nature and therefore for the first time allows the generation of a sufficient surplus to enable a true communism. Unlike primitive forms which are restricted in the amount of surplus which can be generated by the vicissitudes of nature, i.e. flood, crop failure, movements of animals and weather, this communism would be made possible by the very abundance of the goods and services produced by capitalistic methods of production. Capitalism, however, whilst allowing the modes of production to create abundance, imposes certain relations of production which create an artificial scarcity for the majority. The producers of wealth, those who labour, do not own or control the means of production. The tools and the factories, which are nothing but labour converted into plant via the mechanism of profit, are in the hands of the bourgeoisie, whose very existence depends upon the perpetuation of this systematic inequality. Thus the relations of capitalistic production are in contradiction with the mode of production. The factory brings workers together, the division of labour depends upon their intimate cooperation, unlike feudal production, which tended to be localised in self-sufficient enclaves, yet the relations of production are not truly cooperative since they depend for their perpetuation upon the continuation of capital ownership in the hands of a minority. Furthermore this minority is basically locked in a competitive struggle since the profit system ensures that it must attempt to undercut others in the market, or be forced out of the market by other capitalists. The mechanisms of profit thus force employers to reduce the wages of the labourer to that level which is just sufficient for survival and reproduction of the work-force. Unlike other forms of production, capitalism is unique in that it is unregulated by considerations other than the economic. Its unregulated nature forces the capitalist into actions that lead inevitably to the destruction of the system that creates and sustains him. The forces undermine the capitalist system act in the following way:

(1) Competition leads to crises of over-production, which cause increasingly intolerable periods of economic recession. To gain greater market shares capitalists engage in price cutting and cost cutting, technological innovation; however, the eventual consequence of this competition between capitalists is the production of more goods than the market can absorb. The natural reaction of capitalists confronted with a surplus which cannot be sold is to reduce price further; this they do, but only after they have forced down wages so that profit can be maintained. This forcing down of wages aggravates the crises because it further reduces the ability of the market to absorb the products of the capitalist mode of production.

(2) The competitive struggles drive cut the smaller and the less efficient entrepreneurs so that capital becomes increasingly concentrated into large blocks; small capital is engulfed by large capital. In this way the number of people identifiable with the bourgoisie declines, and the numerical strength of the capitalist class is eroded. This tendency combined with the tendency of the rate of profit to fall makes the political position of the capitalist class increasingly vulnerable to mass action.

(3) The conditions of capitalist production lead to a continuous growth of the proletariat, or industrial labour force, who bring nothing to the market-place but their labour power. The remnants of the feudal classes and the unsuccessful entrepreneurs all swell the ranks of the industrial work-force as the capitalist mode of production progresses and monopoly capitalism emerges. These developmental processes, however, bring into existence new social institutions, the factory and the working-class town, and these institutions place large numbers of people in close association with one another. Marx believed that this bringing together of large numbers of wage labourers had great political potential. The tendency of capitalism was to make ever more transparent the basis of the extortion of surplus which capital achieved via the wage-labour system and production for profit. The potential exists, therefore, for the emergence of a 'class for itself' which would express the interests of wage labour and lead to the overthrow of capitalism.

In the unregulated market there is thus a tendency for the class structure to become more and more simplified and for the two classes, proletariat and bourgeoisie, to become the only significant classes. Moreover the proletariat is seen as the historical actor who will bring about a transcendance of capitalism and the assertion of a substantive rationality based on an equality situation.

Class is then best reserved to characterise the relationship between a social aggregate and the mode of production. Marx's definition of class in capitalist society reflects the centrality of property and the consequences ownership of property have for the relationship of a class to the productive process. On the one hand we have the bourgeoisie, who, owning property, are in a position to dominate the market and organise production to sustain their dominance. On the other hand we have the proletariat, who, owning nothing but their labour power, are compelled to accept their positions of subordination. The ideology of *laissez-faire*, with its emphasis on individual responsibility and its justification of the survival of the fittest in terms of the promotion of social welfare, serves to explain and justify this class structure and suggests that it is irrational to try to interfere with the structure of inequality because such attempts would reduce social welfare. This is a gross simplification of Marx's treatment of class; in actual social situations the class structure reflects the particular stage of the historically unique developmental sequence. Thus the role of the peasantry remains of major importance in any class analysis of French society. Marx distinguished between a 'class-in-itself', which consists solely of all those people occupying similar market positions, and 'class-for-itself', which involves some collective action or consciousness of shared position by the people who share common market situation. It is one of the peculiar features of capitalism that it creates not only an ideology which sustains the dominance of property but also the conditions in which the proletariat can mobilise an alternative ideology in political struggle. In so far as the working class were able to act upon the system and change it into a set of relationships over which they had control, they were fulfilling man's historical mission and bringing history and society under the control of mankind for the first time. In short, then, Marx envisaged mature capitalism as beinging about a clear-cut polarisation of the classes. Intervening classes and status groups would be eroded, thus facilitating a confrontation between the owners and non-owners of the means of production. This must be of a revolutionary nature since the interests of the proletariat must inevitably be the destruction of the system that exploits and prevents them from controlling their own destiny. The framework of capitalism cannot assimilate the proletariat because it drives them inevitably towards increased misery in its desire to attain greater profit yet simultaneously forces upon them a consciousness of the real sources of their misery and indeed a recognition of capitalism's own reliance upon their labour, hence a recognition of their power.

Weber's approach to class and ideology varies from Marx's, but not in his treatment of class as such. Class for Weber was determined by the individual access to life chances in the market. Classes were thus aggregates of individuals similarly located in the economic structure. This area of agreement between Marx and Weber should form a basis for a rejection of all usages of class which do not relate the phenomena under observation to the mode of production. Considerable confusion has resulted from the lack of use of the term 'class' in a consistent way. As used by the Registrar-General, in the collection of statistics for policy purposes, class is defined in terms of occupational labels which bear an indeterminant relationship to the significant features of the mode of production. The phrases 'working-class' and 'middle-class', although useful everyday concepts, relate people more by style of life than by access to life chances. Other categorisations rank 'classes' according to size of income and these differences, while extremely significant, divert attention from questions about the sources and bases of income. Class analysis focuses attention upon the ways in which the economic system of production systematically distributes life chances unequally to different groups.

Weber distinguishes a separate realm of status from class and it is here that we see a divergence from Marx. Marx assumed that the economic determinants of social location would predominate and that class-based inequality would continue to dominate capitalist society. Weber, however, believed that status stratification, i.e. the hierarchical organisation of groups based upon styles of life, or ways of consuming rather than ways of producing, had an independent existence and would continue to be of great significance in capitalist society.

This difference in treatment of 'status' affects the treatment of ideology offered by Weber. Weber refers to the process of ideological justification as legitimation, and stresses the importance of acceptance by the subordinate group of the bases of authority claimed by the dominant group. The higher status group's status is sustained because its life style is highly valued by the lower groups. Claims to legitimacy, therefore, not only have to justify the existence of economic inequality, they also have to sustain social valuations which are essentially arbitrary. Legitimation involves the acceptance of claims and explanations by the subordinate group and a certain voluntary submission to the rights claimed by the dominant group. Ideological justification implies a systematic presentation of social reality, so that no alternative is perceived to exist to the current arrangement. In this way we can see the tendency of Weber to attribute primacy to the political aspect of legitimacy, while it can be inferred from Marx that the economic base determines the political.

Marx's treatment of class as presented here, represents the analysis of class in the model of capitalism. In practice capitalism has shown an ability to cope with many of the strains it has created, and through the manipulation of the State and ideology the dominance or hegemony of the bourgeoisie has been preserved. The State has interfered in the market increasingly, even in Britain and the United States, both as a purchaser of goods and services and as a provider of the basic economic infrastructure. This state intervention has two consequences; first, it has tended to put off the crises of over-production by providing a mechanism for maintaining consumption. Second, it has created new groups in society who, while not property-owners themselves, are allied with the interests of capitalism because they are supported from the surplus extracted by the capitalist mode of production. In the initial stages of the development of the capitalist mode of production the State's role was merely to contain political disquiet and reproduce the social structure which guaranteed the continuing hegemony of capital. Giddens has argued along these lines that the liberal democratic political system is the natural development of capitalism, and the seeming increase in political citizenship is part of an ideological containment which the representatives of the working class or proletariat are incorporated in capitalism. In his words,

> The working class, or the political organisations which represent it, had to struggle to secure full incorporation within the polity of the modern nation state, the result of this incorporation, however, has not been to weaken but to stabilise, or complete, the institutional mediation of power in the capitalist order. Social democracy, in other words, is the normal form taken by the systematic political inclusion of the working class in capitalist society. (1973, p. 285)

It has been suggested that, as capitalism moves into a monopoly phase in which the numbers of the bourgeoisie have fallen and the intermediate groups left over from pre-capitalist society have finally disappeared, and the development of the labour process (Braverman, 1974) has reduced the residual skill divisions in the proletariat, the State assumes a new importance as the creator of social differentiation. In its current stage the political stability of capitalism is dependent, at least in part, on the skill with which the State, acting as a representative of capital, is able to use the surplus generated by the capitalist mode of production to create groups whose well-being is linked to the continuance of the system. The growth of the professional element in the Civil Service might be interpreted in this light.

These new activities of the State have been justified in terms of new ideologies which, while not abandoning the notion of the 'hidden hand' of the market, have identified a distinctive role for governmental intervention designed to make the market function better. Keynesianism is the most important of these new ideologies, and no revolution is involved in the adoption of Keynesianism in the *laissez-faire* context of Britain, because, although marking out an independent role for government, Keynes made the expectations of investors the linchpin of economic welfare and reconfirmed the dependence of social welfare on the behaviour of the entrepreneur. The task of the State was to provide the circumstances in which entrepreneurs perceived that future profits could be predicted safely from current investment and consequently undertook the productive investment necessary for economic growth and social welfare.

In these ways the peculiar abstention of the State in the early phases of British and American industrialisation can be seen to be giving way to a new situation in which the State is becoming a central institution of mature capitalism in these countries. Indeed the State is more typically at the centre of the development of capitalism than at the periphery.

The basic question that confronts the sociologist when he addresses himself to problem of class is not what generates class – Marx has provided a compelling explanation of that – but what enables the propertied class to maintain their hegemony of power, despite the increasing irrationality of the system of production based not on use-values but on opportunities for profit. The beginnings of the answer to this question seem to lie in three areas: in the processes of the generation of explanations of the nature of social reality, ideology; in the way the State operates as a buffer between the mode of production and the relations of production; and in the processes breaking down the unity of the exploited which allow the economic system to continue to be dominated by the criterion of private profit. The chapter on industrial conflict (Chapter 9) investigates the degree to which conflict has been contained because it has been systematically defined as involving purely economic issues, as a bargining process in which everything has its price. To the extent that industrial relations is viewed in this way attention is channelled away from issues of control, or class domination. Giddens suggests the increased role of the State in economic management and particularly in incomes management jeopardises this separation of economism from control and contains the potential for a renewal of class conflict. He concludes, however,

> But how far such conflicts will take the form of a major revolutionary confrontation of the working class with the existing structure of the capitalist state is not a matter which can be inferred from their generic character. . . . There are instances where such an occurrence is conceivable: but these are those (France, Italy) whose development has, for specific reasons, created a class system which is not representative of that of the majority of the capitalist countries. (1973, pp. 292–3)

In capitalist society, class based on relationship to the mode of production and ownership of property remains the basic axis of political domination, and the main mechanism of exploitation. State socialist societies have eradicated class but not exploitation, and capitalism's ideological dominance remains unchallenged by a convincing programme for harnessing rationalised production, without exploitation, shared by sufficient members of the exploited class of capitalism and constituting a basis for political activity aimed at revolutionary change.

Suggested Further Reading

Giddens, A. (1973) *The Class Structure of Advanced Societies* (London: Hutchinson).

Bibliography

Braverman, H. (1974) *Labour and Monopoly Capitalism* (New York and London: Monthly Review Press).

Bendix, R. (1964) *Nation Building and Citizenship* (New York: Wiley).

— (1976) 'Inequality and Social Structure', in M. Abraham, E. H. Mizruchi and C. A. Hornrung (eds.), *Stratification and Mobility* (New York: Macmillan Publishing Co.).

Dahrendorf, R. (1965) *Society and Democracy in Germany* (London: Weidenfeld & Nicolson).

Dawe, A. (1976) 'The Two Sociologies', in *British Journal of Sociology*, vol. 21, pp. 207–18.

Giddens, A. (1971) *Capitalism and Modern Social Theory* (London: Cambridge University Press).

Giddens, A. (1973) *The Class Structure of the Advanced Societies* (London: Hutchinson).
— (1976) 'Classical Theory and the Origins of Modern Sociology', in *American Journal of Sociology*, vol. 81, no. 4.
Gouldner, A. W. (1976) *The Dialectic of Ideology and Technology* (London: Macmillan)
Habermas, J. (1971) *Toward a Rational Society* (London: Heinemann).
Hobsbawn, E. J. (1973) *The Age of Revolution, 1789–1848* (London: Cardinal, 1973).
Lichtheim, G. (1975) *A Short History of Socialism* (London: Fontana).
Marx, K. (1954) *Capital*, vol. 1 (Moscow: Foreign Languages Publishing House).
Polanyi, K. (1963) *The Great Transformation* (New York: Octagon Books, 1973).
Unger, R. M. (1976) *Law in Modern Society* (New York: Free Press U.S., 1976; West Drayton, Middx: Collier-Macmillan (U.K. distributor)).
Zeitlin, I. M. (1968) *Ideology and the Development of Sociological Theory* (Englewood Cliffs, New Jersey: Prentice-Hall).

8
Convergence Theories

There has been much theorising about the nature of the industrialisation process and many attempts to abstract sets of core principles which explain the conditions for the development of industrial society. In this chapter we are going to examine some variants of one approach to the process of industrialisation: this approach has been called the convergence hypothesis. The basic idea of all theories of convergence is that industrialism brings with it certain inevitable changes in the way that social life is organised and imposes common patterns of social behaviour on societies that embark on the path to becoming 'industrial societies'. This can be oversimplified: all societies that industrialise converge, or tend to become alike.

The preceding chapters of this book have stressed the unique features of industrialisation in Britain and how any adequate understanding of British development requires a careful balance between the generalising approach, which ignores the special features of each individual case and the approach which, dwelling on the details of specific cases, refuses to grasp any organising principles. In this chapter we present, first uncritically, the ideas of several authors all of whom have stressed the general features of industrialisation, then we will return to criticise the adequacy of their approaches.

The best-known exposition of the 'convergence thesis' is that contained in Kerr *et al.*, *Industrialism and Industrial Man* (1973). In this book the authors initially set themselves the task of explaining the pattern of worker protest which accompanied industrialisation. After the first stages of their investigation, however, they concluded, 'But labour protest, on a closer look, is on the decline as industrialisation around the world proceeds at an ever faster pace. In the mid-twentieth century, workers do not destroy machines. The protest of today is more in favour of industrialisation than against it' (p. 34).

This led them to turn 'to a more universal phenomenon affecting workers – the inevitable structuring of the managers and the managed in the course of industrialisation. Everywhere there develops a complex web of rules binding the worker into the industrial process, to his job, to his community, to patterns of behaviour. Who makes the rules? What is the nature of these rules? Not the handling of protest, but the structuring of the labour force is *the* labour problem in economic development' (p. 35). These initial investigations also led them to conclude that ideologies and dominant personalities were of less importance than certain processes and trends which occurred everywhere. They argued that ideologies competing to explain the nature of development were giving way to a more rational technology of decision making which removed more and more areas of management, both at the firm level and at the national level, from the political arena as its power to solve 'problems' expanded. They argued that certain universals were more important than these issues of personalities and ideologies. 'There was always a web of rules, and some rules were repeated again and again. There were some quite obvious uniformities in the several patterns of industrialisation. Generally these uniformities seemed to arise out of the uniformity of the basic technology itself' (pp. 36–7).

They then suggest that events accompanying industrialisation are most fruitfully analysed if they are classified according to a threefold classification: universals, related developments and unique developments: 'Thus we identify the universal with the "logic of industrialisation", the related with the strategies of the "industrialising élites", and the unique with specific cultures and environments' (p. 37). The core of their analysis is the relationship they posit between technology and the logic of industrialism.

Having redefined their research problem Kerr *et al.* list eight questions they intend to answer (pp. 38, 39):

(1) Is there a logic of industrialism? What impact does it have on the actors in the industrial production system?

(2) Who directs and plans the industrialisation process and with what consequences?

(3) What are the major special factors which embroider the universals of industrialism in each of its specific appearances?

(4) How does entrepreneurship and business management fit into the process?

(5) How is the industrial work-force obtained, retained and motivated?

(6) How does the industrial workforce experience industrialisation?

(7) How do the workers become organised, and how are institutions regulating the interrelations between the actors in the industrial production system evolved?

(8) Do industrial societies become more alike?

Here we will concentrate on questions one and eight, although these inevitably involve touching on the other questions.

We will start by presenting the argument that Kerr *et al.* put forward concerning the logic of 'industrialism'. It will help if we reverse the order of the treatment that they use and start from their statements (1973, pp. 54–5). 'The industrial society is world-wide. The science and the technology on which it is based speak in a universal language. (Science) is non-national, non local and, although one would not say non-cultural, singularly independent of the form of government, the immediate tradition or the affective life of a people.' Technology spreads out from the most advanced industrial nations in four major ways: first, through the normal channels of trade; second, through military channels; third, through deliberate adoption of tactics of imitation by less developed countries and fourth, through the direct and indirect effects of economic aid and manpower training. Kerr *et al.* are quite explicit about the role of the military in fostering advanced technology (1973, p. 55). 'The character of military defence and the world-wide scope of military conflict have been a significant means of diffusing modern technology. The training of a workforce to build bases and to maintain motor vehicles and aircraft involves the establishment of important beach heads for industrialisation.' It is this diffusion of the world-wide technology which is primarily responsible for the processes which Kerr *et al.* identify as the logic of industrialism (Chap. 1). The spread of this advanced technology creates a series of problems which can only be resolved in particular ways, and it is as the solutions to these common problems are found that the basic institutions of industrialising societies become more alike.

For Kerr *et al.* the process of industrialisation involves the utilisation of ever more complex technology capable of raising the productivity of the industrialising country and thus increasing its welfare. Technology and science are seen as developing independently of the social contexts in which they are employed, and developments occur according to rational principles as the knowledge of the technologists and scientists grows.

How does technological change create social change? Figure 8.1 schematically relates the various social changes to the prime cause, which is the application of more advanced technology. A particular technology dictates the structure of industry; for example, the techniques of modern steel production make it inevitable that large factories are set up. Advanced technology also requires the growth of all sorts of new industries which complement the original basic industries, and thus the industrial structure becomes trans-

Universal technology – changing from simple to complex

↓

A structure of industries

↓

A division of labour – including professionalisation of management

↓

Needs for placement and training structures such as: an education system, a stratification system, social and physical mobility

↓

Growth in the scale of society involving: Urbanisation, Bureaucratisation, Growth of Government role

↓

Labour market structuring; collective bargaining and the emergence of a web of rules

↓

A consensus in society

↓

Pluralistic industrialism

Figure 8.1 The logic of industrialism

formed from small production units exhibiting relatively low levels of technical specialisation to a much more complex and interdependent industrial structure comprised of large units embodying very high levels of specialisation. In this way the industrial structure generated by the technology generates a particular division of labour; it creates a particular system for assigning responsibilities and tasks to particular roles in the organisations. The division of labour is thus the product of technical rationality and reflects the best ways of producing the goods and services feasible at a given level of development. Part of the process of the division of labour is the specialisation of management, a shift from management based on an ideology of property rights to management based on technical competence derived from the new comprehension of production problems which scientific advance makes possible.

The division of labour creates a variety of different jobs which have to be filled, and these jobs require that there be some form of allocative mechanism to ensure that workers fill all the positions in the structure. This need to ensure the efficient allocation of human talent to roles within the industrial structure gives rise to a system of differential rewards to compensate people in a manner which encourages them to contribute their talents to the production process. Thus this need to allocate people to roles gives rise to a system of stratification and this aspect of convergence is considered in detail in the next chapter.

Kerr *et al.* argue that because growth is a high priority once a country embarks on the route to industrialisation traditional barriers to the mobility of human resources have to be overcome. At a minimum level, industrialisation requires a free labour force willing and able to move to the industrial employment which industrialisation creates. To this is added a suggestion that the pressure for growth is so intense that industrialising countries have to utilise the personal talents of the most intelligent members of the population whatever their position might be within the traditional social structure. For this reason Kerr *et al.* argue that industrialisation promotes social mobility, the process whereby the talented offspring of all social groups are able to achieve positions of economic and social prominence if they have important contributions to make to economic growth.

The division of labour and the increased technical content of all jobs, particularly management, create a demand for a particular system of education. Industrialisation requires a comparatively highly educated work-force and especially a section of the work-force that understands the potentialities of the technology embodied in the specialised jobs in the division of labour. Education thus becomes harnessed to the productive system, to servicing the needs of the developing technology, and, as the technology develops according to common principles, so the education system tends to reflect these. Educational provision and access to educational opportunity come to be determined by the needs of the rational technology: education becomes the handmaiden of industrialisation.

The growth of education and the development of industry and the division of labour are usually accompanied by developments in the scale of society. Kerr *et al.* suggest that industrialisation is only possible in the context of a concentration of resources which allow for the benefits of economic specialisation. Thus industrialisation leads inevitably to urbanisation; the creation of factories requires larger labour forces than are available in sparsely populated areas, and the factories demanded by complex technology thus spawn the town as a new form of social living pattern. The growth of the technical basis of management allied to the growth in the scale of productive enterprise creates new problems for controlling economic activities. The solution to these problems is the invention of new organisational forms based on rational principles, which allow both centralised control and the flexibility necessary to integrate the wide range of activities occurring within the business enterprise or the management of the economy.

The growth in scale of industrial society creates a new and expanded role for government. Governments are required to intervene in a substantial range of economic activities, both as purchaser of many of the products of the new technologies – roads, airports etc. – and as the only investor capable of bearing the risk involved in some of the investments associated with high technology. (The British Government's investment in Concorde is an obvious example.) The growth of government intervention, however, does not take place at the expense of the individual, as industrialisation opens up new avenues for individualism.

At this point in the process the problem of social order emerges. How in the new differentiated society, with distinctive social groupings with specific interests peculiar to themselves, can the conflicting interests be mediated and prevented from creating destructive conflict? Basically Kerr *et al.* argue that as industrialisation creates a particular system of production involving opposed social groups it also creates mechanisms for the resolution of these conflicts. Trade unions and other representative bodies emerge to organise worker protest, and there is a general extension of the areas of conflict, which are defused by being defined as purely technical problems amenable to solution by new developments in rational decision making. Over a period of time, Kerr *et al.* argue, the various parties to industrial conflict develop their own sets of agreements which mediate the conflicts, and these mediations eventually amount to a set of basic procedural rules which form a basic web of rules accepted by all parties as legitimately constraining social action. Here Kerr *et al.* are drawing attention to the ways in which collective bargaining serves to incorporate the working class in industrial society.

Kerr *et al.* stress the role of the web of rules in creating social order, and suggest that in developed industrial societies collective bargaining forms a genuine three-party method of rule creation which serves the needs of all three parties and creates sets of mutually acceptable rules.

> Governments have a significant role in determining the substantive rules of the work community or in establishing the procedures and responsibilities of those with this power. In the highly industrialised society, enterprise managers, workers, and the government tend to share in the establishment and administration of the rules. The industrial relations system of the industrial society is genuinely tripartite (1973, p. 52).

Over time the operation of the machinery for rule making gives rise to a concensus which forms the ultimate cement of the social order of industrialism. Industrial society creates a value system capable of sustaining the efforts required by the technical system of production and of providing a rationalisation for the particular social arrangements designed for this end. The central values which integrate industrial society are:

(1) Scientific and technical knowledge and the possessors of that knowledge are highly valued.
(2) Resistance to change is viewed negatively, and change is valued as 'progress'.
(3) The relationship between knowledge and education means that a high value is placed upon education.
(4) A belief in the need for social flexibility, and status which reflects achievement rather than traditional values.
(5) A belief in the need for a plurality of special purpose social groups and in the need for people to belong to many such groups.
(6) A belief in the virtue of consumption which fosters imitation and the adoption of common styles of life.
(7) A belief in the virtue of hard work and a sense of integration in the societal division of labour.

Of this last value Kerr *et al.* say:

> Industrial countries may differ with respect to the ideals and drives which underlies devotion to duty and responsibility for performance, but industrialisation requires an ideology and an ethic which motivate individual workers. Strict supervision imposed on a lethargic workforce will not suffice; personal responsibility for performance must be implanted within workers, front-line supervisors and top-managers. (1973, p. 53)

Having outlined the elements of the 'logic of industrialism', we will now consider the end state to which the logic leads, in spite of the special features introduced by the leaderships of the countries embarking on the path to industrialism. Kerr *et al.* distinguish five types of élites or power groups that have controlled industrialisation:

(1) a middle-class élite,
(2) a dynastic élite,
(3) revolutionary intellectuals,
(4) colonial administrators,
(5) nationalist leaders,

and distinguish six cultural traits where the policy of the élites can alter the impact of industrialism (1973, pp. 108–9). These traits are:

(1) the family system,
(2) class and race,
(3) religious and ethical valuations,
(4) legal concepts,
(5) concepts of the nation-state,
(6) the total culture.

Each élite has to adopt a clear policy towards each of these areas, and there is scope here for differences in approach, as there is in deciding the basic priorities with respect to pace of industrialisation, sources of funds for capital investment, priorities between industries, source of control over managers, the gearing of education to industry, the degree of involvement in the world economy and population policy. Indeed Kerr *et al.* qualify the universal effects of industrialisation thus 'Each of the industrialising élites confronts a specific set of cultural factors and economic constraints which shape the industrialisation process. These tend to impart a unique character in a particular country to the more universal aspects of the industrialisation process' (p. 142). The treatment of élites and special conditions, however, is couched in the language of priorities, and aberrations from a general pattern. The choices open to the élites are not seen as choices between fundamentally different routes to different ends.

Where then are they all heading? Kerr *et al.* answer as follows:

> To predict the future with any accuracy, men must choose their future. The future they appear to be choosing and pressing for is what might be called 'pluralistic industrialism'. 'Pluralistic industrialism' describes a society which is not characterised by class division and the existence of a ruling class justifying its programme in terms of some ideological construction of reality. Conflict about the fundamental direction of society ebbs as the ability of science and technology to provide rational solutions expands. (p. 270)

Technology provides a unifying focus in society and reduces much management to a process of administration, administration conducted by administrators who become increasingly benevolent as well as increasingly skilful. Moreover the relationship of managers to managed alters and a clear-cut dichotomy between the groups is no longer an accurate description: 'there develops a hierarchy of the semi managers and the semi managed'.

Pluralistic industrialism involves the emergence of realistically independent groups with some measure of independent power, able to engage in a process of bargaining which produces a series of compromises that satisfy most people most of the time. However the process of fragmentation of power cannot proceed too far otherwise the needs for coordination and integration crucial to complex industrial society are endangered. In conclusion, then, 'pluralistic industrialism' involves both a decentralisation of power and a degree of strong central control. A strong central government is accompanied by other autonomous social groups. As Kerr *et al.* say,

> The complexity of the fully developed industrial society requires, in the name of efficiency and initiative, a degree of decentralisation of control, particularly in the consumer goods and service trades industries; but it also requires a large measure of central control by the state and conduct of many operations by large scale organisations. (p. 270)

Now we will turn our attention to a different formulation of a type of convergence thesis, that embodied in Dore's (1973) treatment of Japanese industrial organisations. The first point we must bear in mind is that Dore attributes a much less central role to 'technology' in the explanation of the nature of industrial society; more precisely, he makes technology share the stage with two other ideas which he argues are equally important in explaining the actual patterns of industrialism discernible in particular countries. The first important addition is drawn from Stinchombe (1965), who argues that the organisational forms present in a particular industry, and by extension society, are partially a product of the period at which that industry developed.

Thus the structure of the British cotton industry reflects its early origins, while the complex corporate style of the new textile grants, I.C.I. and Courtaulds, reflects not only changes in technology but changes in social values and social technology. Dore argues that some of the differences between Britain and Japan can be explained in terms of the later development of Japanese industry, after the advent of a new sophistication in management which allowed new forms of social control to replace the market control of *laissez-faire* ideologies which governed managerial action at the point of growth of British industry. Japanese firms developed when unions were a fact of life, when imposing the costs of market fluctuations on workers too openly was unacceptable; they developed in an environment posing different problems from those posed by the environment of Britain in the nineteenth century.

This brings us to Dore's second important addition to technology, and this is the spread of new ideas which condition the acceptable form of industrialisation. Japan, as a late developer, has adjusted more fully to changes in organisational technology and ideology as well as technology. Dore suggests that ideology is an independent force, conditioning development, not simply a product of a particular system of production. Dore does, however, seem to believe that there are certain world-wide changes in ideology which condition action within all countries linked into systems of world trade and world politics. The particular development that Dore attaches significance to is the development of a belief in egalitarianism or democracy. In summary, then, Dore explains the Japanese employment system as 'simply one national manifestation of a phenomenon characteristic of all advanced industrial societies – namely the adaption of employment systems to:

(1) The emergence of the giant corporation
(2) The extension of democratic ideals of a basic "equality of condition" for all adults at the expense of earlier conceptions of society as naturally divided into a ruling class and an underclass' (1973, p. 339).

Dore argues that because some countries came late to industrialisation there is what he calls a late-comer effect, which reflects the ability of these countries to learn from the experience of already industrialised countries and adopt organisational forms and institutional arrangements which are more 'developed' than those of the more 'developed' nations. Indeed this is what he suggests has happened in the case of Japan. Figure 8.2 maps out Dore's suggested pattern of development in management systems. Industrialisation, he argues, is tending everywhere to promote 'democratic corporatism', a belief that work-forces have a right to participate in management, or in

Changing Managerial Styles

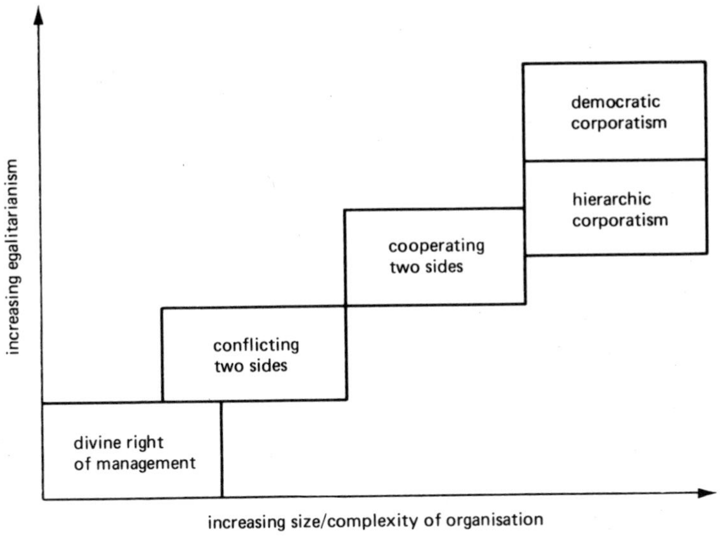

Figure 8.2

From R. Dore (1973) p. 367, *British Factory – Japanese Factory* (London: Allen & Unwin).

decision making, because basically there is a real collective interest which their participation can advance. Corporatism involves two notions: first, that the firm has needs or interests and second, that the employees of firms as well as the investors of capital have a stake in the firms. Hierarchic corporatism involves a claim by management to know what the 'corporate interests' are, and on this basis to the right to exercise hierarchical authority. Democratic corporatism involves a questioning of this managerial superiority and its replacement by direct participation in decision making by all sectors of the corporation.

Dore is circumspect in his analysis of convergence, although he argues a tendency exists for all industrial societies to respond to the emergence of the giant corporation and the strengthening of the power of egalitarian ideologies by moving towards democratic corporatism. He argues that the degree of corporate independence depends on the timing of the growth of the giant business corporations and the extension of state welfare systems and national bargaining structures. He is clear that established developed nations like those of Scandinavia and Great Britain will not permit the same degree of independence to the corporation as has been achieved by corporations in Japan, where the private firms rose to strength before a central state authority was capable of influencing the process. He suggests they will not tolerate the existence of a subordinate non-unionised sector of the labour market, nor the two classes of citizenship which are promoted by private welfare provision.

At this point we will move on to consider the argument that certain basic structures have changed so much and the principles guiding those structures have also altered to the point where it is more useful to create new models for use in analysing actual examples of advanced societies. Although we will concentrate on Daniel Bell's thesis (Bell, 1974), which is based on American experience and views the world through American spectacles, it must be pointed out that both Soviet and Polish sociologists have reproduced similar analyses of developmental tendencies within their countries and Dahrendorf and Touraine have argued similarly for Western Europe. The basic idea of all these writers revolves around their treatment of the role of scientific and technological knowledge in determining the social structure of society. They argue that knowledge is achieving a centrality in social life that it has not previously had and this is resulting in a shift in power and precedence among both social institutions and social groups.

Before outlining the details of Bell's thesis we will justify our inclusion of his thesis in a chapter dealing with convergence theories. Bell explicitly argues that he is not offering a theory of societal convergence based upon changes in the role of technology. He argues that the analysis of given societies requires the distinguishing of three areas of social life which while having a high degree of interdependence also exhibit a high degree of independence. These areas are the social structure, the polity and the culture. The social structure is the focus of analysis in the post-industrial society thesis and Bell distinguishes this area from the other two thus: 'The social structure comprises the economy, technology and the occupational system. The polity regulates the distribution of power and adjudicates the conflicting claims and demands of individuals and groups. The culture is the realm of expressive symbolism and meanings' (1974, p. 12). He argues it is necessary to distinguish analytically these three dimensions because they can be governed by different central principles, and it is in the degree of fit between the principles governing each area that the problems of modern society are located. Moreover while the social structure reflects the presence of certain common agendas of problems between countries, the polity and culture do not necessarily illustrate similar commonality. Indeed he argues that the diversity of outcomes in terms of the integration of these areas will remain and make each society's adaptation a unique social constellation. While noting Bell's cautions about treating his theory as a total theory of societal convergence, we believe there is sufficient parallel between the structure of Bell's argument and others presented in this chapter to call his theory a convergence theory; what is converging is one element of society, social structure: that is, the distribution of economic activity between industries, the evolution of the occupational structure and the stratification system.

What then are the developmental forces in social structure that Bell discerns from his analysis of American society? The forces are related to the method of production used in society for the production of economic goods and services. Bell's thesis is about the transition from industrial to post-industrial society, not from capitalist to post-capitalist society, and this draws our attention to the conception that Bell has of the relationship between the property ownership system, the method of production, and the institutions of power. Bell clearly believes that all three have separate existence and that he is explaining changes along a separable dimension, methods of production:

> Thus the terms feudalism, capitalism and socialism are a sequence of conceptual schemes, in the Marxist framework along the axis of property relations. The terms pre-industrial, industrial and post industrial are conceptual sequences along the axis of production and the kinds of knowledge that are used. (1974, p. 11).

Bell is arguing that industrial society, characterised by Aron in terms of machine technology and the factory, is giving way to a new society characterised by new technology and new institutions. Bell uses the notions of axial principles and axial structures to chart the change from one type of social structure to the next. The axial principle represents the energising principle or touchstone for evaluating social action; it represents the primary logic around which all other logics adapt. The axial structure is the institution or institutions which embody most strongly the primary logic and which express the logic in the form of practical action. The axial structure and axial principle are analytically abstracted from ongoing social reality, and used to make sense of patterns of change, because in actuality they are the organising frame, not only of analysis, but of practical life: social life revolves around them, as the wheel revolves about its axis.

Bell argues that in modern Western society, in the phase of social structure identified as industrial, 'the axial principle of the social structure is *economising* – a way of allocating resources according to principles of least cost, substitutability, optimisation, maximisation and the like' (1974, p. 12), and the axial structure is the business enterprise. Currently priorities in social life are predominantly set by the needs of business, which are established in terms of economic goals defined in terms of cost minimisation and growth maximisation. It is within the arrangement of the social structure which reflects these priorities that Bell discerns the fundamental changes which he sees leading towards a society dominated by a new axial principle and a new axial structure. Bell presents his argument under five heads.

(1) The changing shape of the economy;
(2) the occupational distribution and class structure;
(3) the emergence of a new axial principle: the centrality of theoretical knowledge;
(4) social choice and planning – time scale of awareness and social planning;
(5) decision making: intellectual technology and the control of decisions.

Under the first head he argues that the locus of economic activity is changing. Industrialisation involved a shift from a predominance of economic activities based on extracting benefits from natural resources (agriculture is the obvious example) to an emphasis on activities involving operations transforming these resources into manufactured products. This is the shift referred to by economists as the shift from Primary to Secondary sector. As industrialisation proceeded it advanced bureaucracy, which resulted in a further shift of activities towards coordination and the provision of services; this started the growth of white-collar and service activities, which become increasingly important. This is the growth of the tertiary sector. Bell suggests that this shift in activity is continuing and the important growth now is not in service activities, spawned by manufacturing industry and providing coordinative services, but in government services and the extension of education, health and welfare services.

The shift in emphasis from manufacturing activities towards service activities has resulted in a shift in the occupational distribution: fewer people are now employed in manufacture, and the white-collar groups that represent the employment of the newer economic sector have been growing rapidly and are predicted to continue growing (Bell, 1974, p. 134).

From a total of about 5.5 million persons in 1900 (making up about 17.6 per cent of the labour force), the white-collar group by 1968 came to 35.6 million (46.7 per cent) and will rise to 48.3 million in 1980, when it will account for half (50.8 per cent) of all employed workers. Within this group the group of professional and technical workers has risen from 3.8 million in 1947 to an estimated 13.2 million in 1975. Bell focuses his attention within this group of knowledge workers on the smaller core of scientists and professionals who fully embody the new knowledge: these make up about 2 million workers in 1975. Bell argues this new knowledge élite is gaining in importance in the stratification system, and that possession of knowledge increasingly replaces possession of property or political power as the basis for high status in the social structure.

This brings us to Bell's third head: the emergence of theoretical knowledge as the axial principle in place of economising. Bell argues that post-industrial society is organised around knowledge, and that knowledge is used for social control and the directing of innovation and change; moreover the knowledge has new and special properties which enhance its significance.

> What is distinctive about the post industrial society is the change in the character of knowledge itself. What has become decisive for the organisation of decisions and the direction of change is the centrality of theoretical knowledge – the primacy of theory over empiricism and the codification of knowledge into abstract systems of symbols that, as in any axiomatic system, can be used to illuminate many and varied areas of experience. (1974, p. 20)

Bell argues that a new intellectual technology is developing, aided by the development of machines like computers, which pushes the division of labour far into the realms of intellectual life. The new knowledge is knowledge which is developed by teamwork and requires teamwork to apply to the problems of social control, firstly in the realms of the control of physical technology but latterly in areas like the management of the national economy. Post-industrial society is characterised by the substitution of an intellectual technology based on algorithms – or sets of problem-solving rules which are calculating and instrumental – for intuitive judgements based on ideologies and reflecting emotional and expressive values. It is the growing reliance of society on this burgeoning knowledge which leads to the emergence of the technocrats as new members of the élites of society.

The growth of knowledge allows prediction of the future in a manner previously impossible, moreover it brings with it an awareness that decisions of the past, based on short-time horizons, have created social costs in the long run which far outweighed their initial benefits. Bell elaborates his fourth dimension:

> Every modern society now lives by innovation and the social control of change and tries to anticipate the future in order to plan ahead. This commitment to social control introduces the need for planning and forecasting into society. It is in the altered awareness of the nature of innovation that makes theoretical knowledge so crucial. (1974, p. 20)

Bell argues that post-industrial society is characterised by a future awareness which contrasts sharply with the present awareness of industrial society; not only is the time dimension of decision making broadening, however, but also the number of interests which have to be compromised satisfactorily before action can be taken.

Finally Bell argues that post-industrial society is creating a new technology for decision making which allows the potentials of the new knowledge to be harnessed to social ends. He stresses the politicisation of wider areas of decision-making, suggesting that the existing power structures are being rapidly eroded and that the new knowledge technology allows the replacement of ideological panacea by genuinely acceptable compromise based on accurate technological assessment.

Clearly, then, the axial principle of society is, according to Bell, undergoing a fundamental change and as the central values of society are changing so too are the social institutions which embody these values. While the private firm remains the dominant institution of Western society, and will probably continue its dominance to the end of the century, it is giving way to new knowledge-based institutions: the university, the research divisions of government and the professions. These institutions express the logic of post-industrialism in their adherence to the value of knowledge as the guide to action.

Bell argues that post-industrial society raises new sets of issues and its significance is that firstly, it strengthens the role of science and cognitive values in society, and creates needs for the institutionalisation of these values; and secondly, by increasing the technical components of decision making it increases the political significance of the holders of knowledge. Bell then points to tensions set up by these changes in social structure and argues that post-industrial society brings to the forefront crucial issues about the relationship between bureaucracy and intellectual freedom and between the technological knowledge professionals and the literary or cultural knowledge élite. Bell argues repeatedly that the central clash in post-industrial society revolves around the confrontation between the technological determinism flowing from the social structure and the demands for personal freedom and participation in decision making flowing from changes in cultural values. Bell appears to believe that the new knowledge professionals have a distinctive set of values which are bringing about a transformation in decision making and a broadening of the criteria used to decide priorities in decision making.

Touraine (1974) shares with Bell a belief that society can now most usefully be described as post-industrial, and he believes also that it is through the changed role of knowledge and social planning that the break with previous societies is made. He argues that growth today stems from a whole complex of factors, not simply the accumulation of capital, and indeed increasingly depends on knowledge and the ability of society to call forth creativity. Touraine argues that the most informative way of characterising post-industrial societies is as programmed societies, which draws attention to their production methods and economic organisation. At this point Touraine's analysis begins to diverge from Bell's, although he also attributes a peculiar significance to the university in the evolution of post-industrial society.

While Bell points to the contradiction between the cultural values of participation and the values of technocratic decision making, this is the centre of Touraine's analysis as he strives to analyse the structure of domination in post-industrial society and relate patterns of class struggle to this structure. In this concentration on class Touraine's analysis parallels that of Dahrendorf (1959), who argued that society had become post-capitalist as class conflicts no longer revolved around issues of property, but around issues of authority: the fundamental divide is between those who hold positions of authority and those who do not, or between, in Touraine's language, the programmers and the programmed.

Touraine argues (1974, p. 7) that the massive investments of the large enterprises are now made on the basis of expansion and power and this has profoundly transformed the traditional forms of social domination in three ways: firstly, by the production process imposing a life style which matches the objectives of the dominant group; secondly, by an extension of cultural manipulation in which the large enterprises influence needs and attitudes directly; and thirdly, by the growth of the political aggressiveness of these enterprises as they strive to subordinate their environments to their purposes. The new dominant group is the technocracy, centrally concerned with the problem of the opposition between development and consumption.

> The technocracy is a social category because it is defined by its management of the massive economic and political structures which direct development. It conceives society simply as the totality of the social means needed to mobilise this development. It is a dominant class because, in proclaiming identification with development and social progress, it identifies the interests of society with those of the great organisations which, vast and impersonal as they are, are nonetheless centres for particular interests. (Touraine, 1974, p. 53)

The emergence of the technocracy makes the struggle for control of knowledge and information critical and shifts the potential for change from the zone of production and property. We are leaving a society of exploitation and entering a society of alienation (Touraine, 1974, p. 61).

The conflict centres around the creation of knowledge and is particularly acute in the universities and professions. This conflict reflects the tension on the one hand between rationality and technological requisites, and on the other between personal autonomy and self control.

All the treatments of the development of industrial society so far covered share one fundamental feature: they all stress the role of technological change as the independent factor which creates problems for the social structure and leads to modifications of the social institutions central to the process of providing economic benefits to society. The most fundamental criticism of all hinges on this treatment of technology as an independent force in social development. While using varieties of system theory to describe the transitions occurring in industrial and industrialising countries, all these theorists treat technology as an input from outside the system to which the system must adapt. This is explicit in Kerr *et al.* (1973) notion of world-wide technology and implicit in Bell's treatment of knowledge élites. The theories also postulate the emergence of decision-making technology, including intellectual algorithms and organisational structures, which are neutral with respect to the goals of social action and are simply the formally most rational ways of achieving the benefits promised by the new physical technologies. These theorists link the development of this new technology to the development of new social groups who embody distinctive sets of values about how they should conduct themselves when they finally gain a role in the determination of social priorities. These new social groups are motivated by an ethic of social service and guided by a longer term vision than the previous groups controlling the political system.

There is no reason for treating technology as an independent variable without careful justification. There may conceivably be some sense in which science proceeds according to a logic of its own, with discoveries and advances reflecting the idiosyncracies of individual scientists and occurring either according to some random pattern, or conceivably as a reflection of some underlying structure to the scientific universe which can only be revealed by peeling away successive layers one at a time. Technology cannot possibly be seen to develop in this way. Technology is the product of the scientific knowledge available, the definition of social problems to be overcome and the relative costs of the factors of production, capital, labour and raw materials. Technology is thus very much a social product, and ought not to be relegated lightly to the role of an external influence to which a society adapts. As soon as we conceptualise technology as a marriage of science and the relative costs of the factors of production we see that a central feature of any technology must be the degree to which it embodies the existing power structure, as this is one determinant of the relative costs of the factors of production.

Since the cost of scientific research escalated and the growth of intellectual knowledge made scientific research a team activity, science has required external sources of financing. The old adage that he who pays the piper calls the tune has obvious relevance here. The major sources of finance for scientific research, as so clearly documented by Bell himself, are the government and the major corporations responsible for economic production. Although there is some so-called free money that researchers can get to fund pure research the bulk of funds are granted to researchers who promise to tackle problems of direct interest to the providers of the funds. The government's funding of research for defence purposes is only the most obvious case. Medical research is concentrated not in the areas where most human suffering could be alleviated, but in areas where the potential market for the drugs produced by the giant oligopolist drug producers is most promising. Doctors might prefer to work in other areas of research where the social payoffs are higher, but the choice becomes drug company research or no research. Moreover the direct control of funds is only the crudest way that science's priorities are decided by outsiders. Science may create a culture of its own, scientists may be socialised into a service ethic, but the scientific sub-culture is a sub-culture: it lives in a broader culture and its priorities reflect in a variety of subtle ways the basic values of the host culture.

If as we have suggested science and technology embody social values and institutionalised power relations are reflected in technology through factor prices, a critical question becomes, who controls the new knowledge and how and for what purposes? To treat 'knowledge' as neutral is a prelude to blindness to a range of possible answers to these questions. It is clear that theorists of the type of Kerr *et al.* and Bell believe that 'knowledge' is creating a new social class who must be admitted to the process of goal setting in society, whether as one of many groups, pluralistic industrialism, or as the dominant group as a meritocratic élite. Knowledge is certainly a form of property and as such has a certain power, but while the owners of knowledge are unorganised, they, like unorganised labour in the nascent markets of capitalism, are ripe for exploitation. As unorganised labour was disciplined by the existence of alternative labour willing or forced to accept capitalist terms, so is unorganised 'knowledge'. Also, as Marx pointed out, large capital tends to swallow small capital. Touraine's analysis points the way here and guards against assuming that 'knowledge' can always be contained by existing dominant groups. Knowledge embodied in a distinctive social group is a more difficult form of property to control than capital embodied in physical plant, and any analysis of the development of industrial society must address the problem the political potential of this new social grouping. At the very least it demands new forms of social control, if existing power groups are not to be usurped.

Related to this misleading treatment of science and technology as value-free and world-wide systems of knowledge is the treatment of ideology embodied in both Bell and Kerr *et al.* For both theories ideology is seen as a misleading structure of thought which can exist only so long as people are ignorant of the true relationships between events: once such knowledge is developed it spells the 'end of ideology' (Bell, 1960). Weber's treatment of formal and substantive rationality ought to have averted this fallacy, but both Bell and Kerr *et al.* lose sight of substantive rationality. Weber's reliance on the charismatic breakthrough of great men may be disturbing, but at least he saw that while the spread of systematised knowledge would improve problem solving there was no way that systematised knowledge could provide an agenda for social action. If the agenda for social action is not a purely technical problem, then there remains a role for ideologies which provide not only explanations of the nature of society but also blue prints for a new society reflecting new priorities. The predominance of the gods of materialism in all countries embarking on industrialisation needs explanation, and cannot be assumed away as part of a structure of 'natural needs' that operate universally, unless forcibly restrained.

This brings us to the related criticism, again most relevant to Bell and Kerr *et al.*, that these theories of industrial convergence assume the existence of discrete nation states and the belief that the appropriate system for analysis in the national social system. In the context of industrialisation this seems a dangerous error. Feldman and Moore (1969), using the same basic functionalist system model, suggest that industrialisation can only be understood as part of a broader social system and this certainly points to certain possibilities which are otherwise precluded. Frank (1971) has suggested that the underdeveloped world is linked by exploitative relationships with the developed world and that the developed world can only maintain its position by a continuance of that structure of dependence. The form of exploitation changes, but as long as the undeveloped world remains tied to the developed world the mechanisms of exploitation ensure the balance of advantage stays with the developed world; the form of exploitation changes from stealing natural resources to stealing human resources and monopolising the most lucrative development projects. The influx of Asian doctors in Britain is an example of the first; the dominance of English multinationals in countries like Belise is an example of the second. If, as this type of analysis suggests, there is some form of exploitative world economic system, industrialising countries may become like the developed world today, but only because this allows the developed societies to develop still further: there is no inherent logic which means the societal structures of the various countries will ever become alike.

This treatment of the developed–underdeveloped world as a unity allows a further point to be made about technology. Kerr *et al.* assumed technology spread because of its inherent superiority: if the role of advanced technology in the underdeveloped world is carefully scrutinised there is strong evidence that the borrowing of technology from the advanced world has hindered economic growth, because it reflects the relative price of capital and labour in the United States, not the relative prices in the underdeveloped countries, and results in too much capital being combined with too little labour for the maximisation of the economic welfare of the underdeveloped country.

Finally there is the problem of the relationship between the technological and economic base and the superstructure erected upon that base. Convergence theories have tended to concentrate unduly on the processes whereby the technological base influences such superstructural features as the stratification system, education system and political system. If the relationship is seen less simply as an interaction between base and superstructure then many of the developments associated with technology take on a new significance and can be interpreted as part of the process of ideological control which dominant groups use to protect their established power against threats posed by altered economic circumstances. As Ross (1974) argues, Bell's analysis of post-industrial society and the problems he envisages for the stability of the technological élite may more accurately be seen as an analysis of the problems of advanced capitalism as its legitimations come under increasingly critical scrutiny.

Indeed far from technology and particularly knowledge technology marking the 'end of ideology' there is a very important sense in which the claims for value freedom associated with the new decision-making methods are a mystification which serves to disguise the extent to which the new technology is the servant of old masters. If, as we have argued, technology is a social product, a harnessing of science to the social purposes of the owners of capital, then a central task for a sociological analysis of economic development is to make clear how this is achieved and why a belief in technical progress masks the unequal distribution of the benefits from such progress.

We have already examined the impact of industrialisation on various social institutions and suggested the inadequacy of a theory which proposes that there is only one fit between a given production technology and such institutions as the family and social stratification. There is usually a range of acceptable adaptations and accommodations which can preserve a unique character to the industrialisation process. The intervention of the developed world in the process of industrialisation, both directly through economic and political imperialism, and indirectly by providing models for emulation, has ensured a degree of similarity between countries that was previously totally lacking. Technology has been exported from the developed world both via the ever-expanding activities of the multinational corporations and via deliberate politically notivated technological aid. There is a real sense in which the automobile plants, the steel works and the chemical industries in various countries are similar environments, and tend to exhibit the same systems of managerial authority and economic reward as well as the same technical transformation processes. It is also probably the case that for the vast majority of the population in industrial societies the similarities in life chances are greater than the differences which flow from the different processes of social control. However, the notion of a convergence resulting from necessary adaptations to common problems seems an inadequate theory to guide the understanding of the processes of transition involved in industrialisation. The transition can only be adequately understood when the interaction between political power and economic change is analysed, and the transition is seen to reflect not only technological imperatives but also the political choices of the significant social groups involved in the change. In each case we need to know how the economic and technological changes are related to the power bases of the dominant groups and how far the changes create new social groups with new bases of power, who have to be accommodated by the existing groups if they are not to totally replace the existing group. The analysis of industrialisation in Britain attempts to illustrate this type of analysis.

Suggested Further Reading

Giddens, A. (1973) *The Class Structure of Advanced Societies*, chaps. 8, 9, 14 (London: Hutchinson).

Kerr, C., Dunlop, J. T., Harbison, F., and Myers, C. A. (1973) *Industrialism and Industrial Man*, 2nd ed., postscript (Harmondsworth, Middx: Penguin Books).

Kumar, K. (1977) 'Continuities and Discontinuities in the Development of Industrial Societies', in R. Scase (ed.) *Industrial Society: Class, Cleavage and Control* (London: Allen & Unwin).

Bibliography

Bell, D. (1960) *The End of Ideology* (New York: Free Press).
— (1974) *The Coming of Post Industrial Society* (London: Heinemann).
Dahrendorf, R. (1959) *Class and Class Conflict* (Stanford: Stanford University Press).
Dore, R. (1973) *British Factory – Japanese Factory* (London: Allen & Unwin).
Feldman, A. S., and Moore, W. E. (1969) 'Industrialisation and Industrialism: Convergence and Differentiation', in W. A. Faunce and W. H. Form (eds.) *Comparative Perspectives on Industrial Society*, pp. 55–71 (Boston: Little, Brown).
Frank, A. G. (1971) *Capitalism and Underdevelopment in Latin America* (Harmondsworth, Middx: Penguin Books).
Ross, G. (1974) 'The Second Coming of Daniel Bell', in *The Socialist Register 1974* (London: Merlin Press).
Stinchcombe, A. (1965) 'Social Structure and Organisation', in J. G. March (ed.) *Handbook of Organizations* (Chicago: Rand McNally).
Touraine, A. (1974) *The Post-Industrial Society* (London: Wildwood House).

9

Conflict in Industrial Society

While we do not suggest that pre-industrial society was in any way conflict-free, we will deal in this chapter with forms of conflict which by definition can emerge only after the advent of the industrial production system. Moreover, we will pay attention primarily to organised collective action and in particular to the most visible expression of such collective action: the strike. We will start with a brief resumé of the role of industrial conflict in Marx's treatment of capitalist society and Durkheim's analysis of industrial society and then proceed, after a discussion of some conceptual and measurement problems, to an attempt to present competing explanations of what has been defined as Britain's strike problem (McCarthy, 1970).

For Marx conflict was the universal situation in existing societies. Capitalism established new forms of conflict, which mirrored the new classes created and reproduced by the capitalist mode of production. 'Our epoch, the epoch of the bourgeoisie, possesses, however, this distinctive feature: it has simplified the class antagonisms. Society as a whole is more and more splitting-up into two great hostile camps, into two great classes directly facing each other: Bourgeoisie and Proletariat.' (Marx and Engels, 1967, p. 80).

The crucial mechanism which created these two opposing classes was the labour market and the relative power of the two groups as they fixed the terms of the labour contract. The bourgeoisie were already the possessors of some capital, acquired via trade or other non-productive activities, the proletariat were the possessors of nothing but their labour power. The worker was thus in a very poor bargaining position because he had no resources to see his family through should he fail to find gainful employment immediately. The bourgeoisie exploited this superior power, which stemmed from their ability to wait without threat of starvation, to force down the wages of the labourer. Moreover, should one labourer resolve to resist accepting employment on the employer's terms, there was an excess supply of labour which meant that there would probably be other labourers willing to work at the employer's rate, and thus augment the employer's capital. Profit was the motivator of the bourgeoisie, and profit was realised by the creation and expropriation of surplus value. This profit, when accumulated, formed the capital which reproduced and extended the capitalist mode of production.

Surplus value existed because the labourer was forced by his weak initial bargaining situation to accept wages which represented less value than his labour power created. Capitalism was the system where this surplus value was expropriated by the owners of property and was converted into capital, in which guise it perpetuated the power disparity between bourgeoisie and proletariat.

The proletariat, consequently, had an interest in attempting to alter the power balance in the labour market. Initially, immediately following the establishment of labour markets and manufacturing industry, the proletariat were scattered and faced employers as atomised individuals. This minimised their ability to resist the power of the employers. Marx, however, believed there were certain inevitable tendencies which would lead the proletariat to organise and, using the power of collective action, resist the power of the employers and eventually topple that power. Trade unions were seen as relatively futile as a way of resisting the labour-market power of employers but potentially important as vehicles of education in the creation of class solidarity and fostering of consciousness of common class interest. 'The real fruit of their battles lies, not in the immediate result, but in the ever expanding union of the workers.' (Marx and Engels, 1967, p. 90).

The centralisation of production, arising from economies of scale and the concentration of capital in fewer hands, brought workers together in larger numbers as it created both large factories and urban areas which overcame the workers' isolation, the isolation which was initially the major source of their weakness in the labour market.

The organisation of capitalist industry tends to reduce all labour to unskilled labour and thus reduces internal divisions of the working class, which means that in the new concentrations of working-class employment the common class interest forms the basis for collective action, or collective resistance to employers. These collective interests are brought most sharply into the consciousness of the working class by the recurrent crises of capitalist society. The crises stem from the inability of capitalists to sell all that they have produced and as the capitalists' response is to cut back production and sack their surplus labour this makes workers' wages and survival even more precarious. As Marx puts it in the *Communist Manifesto:*

> The essential condition for the existence, and for the sway of the bourgeois class, is the formation and augmentation of capital; the condition for capital is wage-labour. Wage-labour rests exclusively on competition between the labourers. The advance of industry, whose involuntary promoter is the bourgeoisie, replaced the isolation of the labourers, due to competition, by their revolutionary combination, due to association. The development of Modern Industry, therefore, cuts from under its feet the very foundation on which the bourgeoisie produces and appropriates products. What the bourgeoisie, therefore, produces, above all, is its own grave diggers (1967 edition, p. 93).

In summary, Marx saw capitalism as producing conflict because of the division of society into two predominant classes, the bourgeoisie and the proletariat. This conflict was a political conflict and involved centrally the distribution of power in society, power which stemmed from property ownership. Theoretically, conflicts about the actual content of the employment contract were irrelevant except as they promoted consciousness of the political position of wage labour. In practice as Hyman (1971) has shown, Marx saw that trade union actions and conflict strategies in nineteenth-century Britain were not promoting working-class political consciousness. This aberration Marx explained in terms of the incorporation of the British working class in the capitalist system.

Marx concentrated on illustrating the form of inevitable class conflict in capitalist society, not on explaining conflict in industry. This highlights a major dilemma in sociological treatments of conflict in industrial societies: the degree to which the various spheres of society are independent of each other. Marx and Marxists insist on the centrality of the mode of production as a conditioning factor on all social action in society. Therefore analysis of conflict which ignores the fact that conflict at the place of work is part of a wider conflict about the distribution of power in society is a mystification of reality and obscures rather than clarifies our understanding of the nature of such conflict. Other theories are not so clear in their insistence that conflict is always related to the mode of production, even in its wider sense, which includes basic issues of political power. We will return to this later when we consider Dahrendorf's (1959) arguments about changes in conflict in the twentieth century.

For Marx industrial conflict, or conflict confined simply to bargaining between a single employer and his employees, is either a preliminary to class conflict, where employees of many employers, perceiving the nature of their exploitation, struggle to overthrow the capitalist system, or alternatively an expression of false consciousness. Industrial conflict involves false consciousness when the protagonists among the working class believe that a solution exists within the property relations of the existing system. Marx believed, or wanted to believe, that the second type of situation would give way to the first.

Like Marx, Durkheim did not separate conflict from a broader treatment of the structure of society. An earlier chapter has outlined the role Durkheim attributed to the division of labour in the transition from pre-industrial society characterised by cohesion stemming from the 'collective conscience' to more complex industrial societies where the role of the collective conscience has waned and cohesion or solidarity flows more from consciousness of mutual inter-dependence. The division of labour promotes social solidarity in the normal case for Durkheim because the performance of

> each special function does not require that the individual close himself in, but that he keep himself in constant relation with neighbouring functions, take conscience of their needs, of the changes which they undergo etc. The division of labour presumes that the worker, far from being hemmed in by his task, does not lose sight of his collaborators, that he acts upon them, and reacts to them. He is, then, not a machine who repeats his movements without knowing their meaning, but he knows that they tend in some way towards an end that he conceives more or less distinctly. . . . (1964, p. 372).

However, Durkheim was aware that industrialisation in nineteenth-century Europe had not promoted a division of labour which was spontaneous and provided the basis for a moral community in which the individual was involved and to which the individual deferred. There were two major forces which prevented social solidarity from establishing itself on the basis of the organic division of labour. The first of these forces was merely the rapidity of the change from pre-industrial society, which had in the process created new market boundaries no longer comprehensible to the producer, and these market changes were accompanied by the separation of the producer from the consumer so that the balance between production and consumption could no longer be guaranteed. The old systems of familial relationships which had served previously to regulate the relationship between individuals were insufficient to regulate new economic activities and had not been replaced yet by any new source of moral regulation. As Durkheim puts it in the *Division of Labour:*

> If the division of labour does not produce solidarity in all these cases, it is because the relations of the organs are not regulated, because they are in a state of anomy. But whence comes this state?
>
> Since a body of rules is the definite form which spontaneously established relations between social functions take in the course of time, we can say, a priori, that the state of anomy is impossible wherever solidary organs are sufficiently in contact or sufficiently prolonged. (1967, p. 368).

In the absence of such regulation there would be a continual process of the equilibration of conflicting interests, which involves as much conflict as cooperation as the new rules are created. Indeed in *Suicide* Durkheim argues that anomie is constant as a result of the economic changes and the recurrent crises.

> There the state of crises and anomy is constant and, so to speak, normal. from top to bottom of the ladder, greed is aroused without knowing where to find ultimate footholds. Nothing can calm it, since the goal is far beyond all it can attain. Reality seems valueless by comparison with the dreams of fevered imaginations; reality is therefore abandoned, but so too is possibility abandoned when it in turn becomes reality (1952, p. 256).

It might appear from the treatment so far that Durkheim thought that time and the constant intermeshing of the parties would inevitably produce a moral framework which would defuse the conflict between employer and employee. This was not, however, Durkheim's belief and he enjoins us to remember that between employers and their newly created factory employees 'this antagonism is not entirely due to the rapidity of these changes, but in good part, to the still very great inequality of the external conditions of the struggle. On this factor time has no influence' (1964, p. 370).

This provides the link with the second cause of conflict in industrial society, and a cause which unlike anomie is not seen as a transitory phenomenon. The second cause of conflict is conditions in society which prevent the division of labour from involving a fair or felt fair distribution of individuals to positions within the division of labour. 'In short, labour is divided spontaneously only if society is constituted in such a way that social inequalities exactly express natural inequalities' (1964, p. 377), or alternatively, 'Perfect spontaneity is, then, only a consequence and another form of this other fact, – absolute equality in the external conditions of the conflict.' (1964, p. 377).

Conflict in industrial society is thus exacerbated by a division of labour which is forced upon particular elements of that society and which involves the subordination of particular people to other groups whose superiority is not morally accepted by the subordinate group.

Durkheim actually says,

> If one class of society is obliged, in order to live, to take any price for its services, while another can abstain from such action thanks to the resources at its disposal, which, however, are not necessarily due to any social superiority, the second has an unjust advantage over the first at law. In other words, there cannot be rich and poor at birth without there being unjust contracts. (1964, p. 384).

Where these external inequalities influence the allocation of individuals to positions in the division of labour there will be fundamental conflict between the occupants of the superior and inferior positions in the division of labour. Moreover as the remnants of the collective conscience weaken, 'as labour becomes more divided and social faith grows weak, these same injustices become more insupportable, since the circumstances which give rise to them reappear very often and also because the sentiments which they evoke can no longer be as completely tempered by contrary sentiment' (1964, p. 385). In other works Durkheim points towards the issue of equity or fairness and suggests that the development of the division of labour inevitably makes the issue of the distribution of rewards and access to opportunities to acquire the necessary training for highly rewarded positions more and more central. 'The task of the most advanced societies is, then, a work of justice.' (1964, p. 387).

Conflict thus comes from two sources: rapid change and the disruption it causes to the institutions of social regulation, and social inequalities which have no basis in justice but which fundamentally interfere with the sponteneity of the division of labour.

Durkheim paid some attention to the development of mechanisms which would eliminate the conflicts in society. The first was the elimination of external inequality by the State legally restricting inheritance. For Durkheim this was a minor problem compared with the second problem of creating the new moral community to regulate men's activity in complex society. Here Durkheim looked to the development of occupational corporations to unite all the agents of the same industry. It was only in some such intervening institution that Durkheim believed moral order would be re-established and the interdependence of the division of labour would become apparent and thus form the basis of a strong organic solidarity. 'What we especially see in the occupational group is a moral power capable of containing individual egos, of maintaining a spirited sentiment of common solidarity in the consciousness of all the workers, of preventing the law of the strongest from being brutally applied to industrial and commercial relations' (1964, p. 10).

Most treatments of Durkheim's view of industrial society have not given sufficient emphasis to the importance of inequalities in promoting and sustaining social disorder.

Weber's contribution to the understanding of industrial conflict is very important and relates centrally to his treatment of the bases of domination. As we noted earlier, Weber argues that neither force nor expediency formed an adequate basis for the coordination of a corporate group: the dominant group always seeks to establish its authority, or its legitimate right to issue orders. This claim is always conditional upon the acceptance of the group whom the dominant group is trying to coordinate in pursuit of its goals. As long as the subordinate group accepts the legitimacy of the dominant group no fundamental conflict can exist. When, however, the dominant group's claim is challenged, there exists immediately the basis of conflict, because the goals of collective action have been those of the dominant rather than the subordinate group and social arrangements reflect the interests of the dominant group. Weber was quite clear that nineteenth-century capitalism was based upon the successful claim of the bourgeoisie to legitimacy in terms of rational legality. Industrial capitalism's rationality was the substantive rationality of the capitalist class; the working classes, therefore, did have fundamentally different material interests and where the legitimacy of the bourgeoisie faltered, conflict would become manifest as the working class came to believe that they possessed sufficient power to resist the demands of the dominant group. Weber's treatment of authority leads to an emphasis on the mechanisms which tend to suppress the conflicts that would otherwise arise from a system of productive relationships which systematically favour one group at the expense of the majority.

We will now examine two case studies which can provide some insight into the processes by which particular industrial conflicts emerge and take the form of collective action. These studies are both from the twentieth century: the first is part of Warner's studies of Newbury port (Warner and Low, 1946) in the 1930s, and the second is Gouldner's study of the gypsum plant after the Second World War. (Gouldner, 1954*a* and 1954*b*). Both describe the processes by which the interpenetration of community and work is broken down and the conditions of wage labour becomes the dominant experience of the work forces.

Before considering these cases in detail we will present an organising device (Figure 9.1) to help ensure that we know what aspect of the conflict process we are discussing.

Smelser's value-added model (Smelser, 1962) can be adapted to industrial conflict, where it can serve a useful function in promoting systematic analysis and alerting the investigator to the relationship between various elements in the process of generation and expression of industrial conflict.

Following Figure 9.1 it is clear that there is no conflict unless the structure of the situation is such, as in capitalism, to create conflicting interests. The next stage in the process, if manifest conflict is to emerge, is the presence of some source of strain in the situation which unsettles established patterns of accommodation: the periodic crises of capitalism would generate such strain. At this stage the conflict remains latent and gives rise only to unorganised

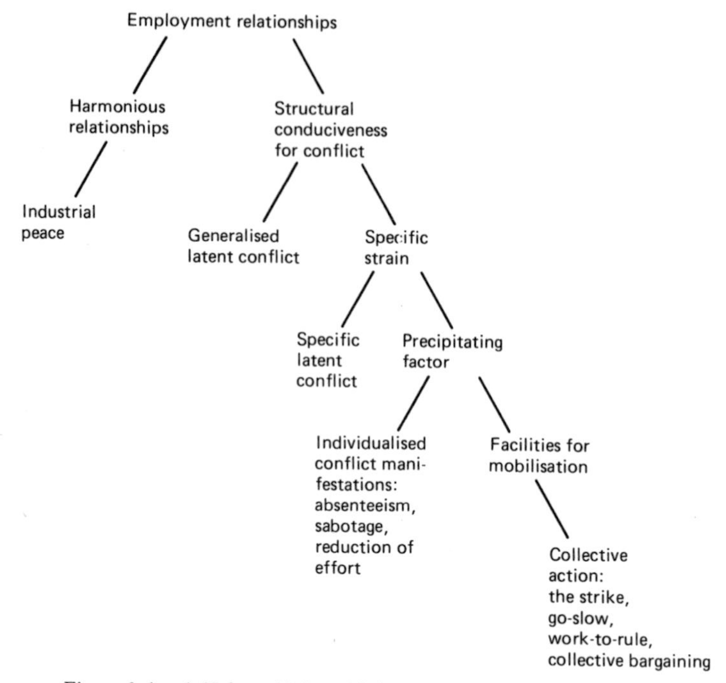

*Figure 9.1 A Value-added model for analysing industrial conflict**

*A debt is acknowledged to R. Loveridge, who used a version of this device in lectures at the London School of Economics in 1968–9.

manifestations of conflict, such as increased absenteeism, which is a form of withdrawal from the situation. At the third stage some event occurs which crystallises as an issue about which conflict can be expressed. What occurs following such a precipitating factor depends on the conditions for mobilisation, that is the extent to which there are

(1) leaders available to organise collective action;
(2) facilities available to allow the activation of the workers commonly affected by the issue;
(3) possibly an alternative explanation to management's as to the cause of the precipitating factor and an alternative solution to the management-proposed solution.

Without all four pre-conditions, strikes cannot occur, for without mobilisation conflict must remain basically atomised and take the form of individual absenteeism, lateness or sabotage. Throughout the rest of the chapter use will be made of this descriptive device to organise the treatment of the various theories of the strike.

Warner headed a team of anthropologists who were investigating the community structure of a small New England town during the 1930s. During their investigation the first signs of unionisation occurred in the town's shoe industry and culminated in a strike. Warner and Low (1946; Eldridge, 1973) were interested in showing how the strike could emerge only after certain developments in the relationship between the economic system and the community have taken place, developments which effectively remove the control of economic activities beyond the boundaries of the local community, and therefore free them from the controls and limitations the common membership of a face-to-face community could impose. Their analysis, therefore, concentrates on the structural conduciveness which creates industrial conflict. They describe the changes under six heads: first, a change in technology from manufacture or handicraft to machine-based mass product. Second, the related change in the division of labour as individual and highly skilled jobs were replaced by fragmented and routinised unskilled labour. Third, the replacement of ownership of the factories by local prominent families with ownership by New York financiers. Fourth, a change in the structure of markets for the products of the industry in which virtual monopoly of the local regional markets by the town's firms is replaced by a national market in which the town's factories compete as one of many sources of supply to the nationwide shoe chains. Fifth, the replacement of kinship and neighbourship ties and relationships of mutual self-help, by the formal organisation of an industrial union. And sixth and finally, the transformation of the former structure of economic relations based on localised élites and status distinction by the absorption of the local factories into the national system of economic life, where they become subject to the forces of the wider capitalist economic productive system.

The personification of the capitalist entrepreneurs as Jewish emigrés was of some importance in explaining the actual process of the strike, but the essential processes Warner and Low point to are those which accompany the creation of any national economic system. Warner and Low pay particular attention to the deskilling process of mechanisation, which destroyed an age-graded status structure that differentiated the skilled from the less skilled, and offered a career for the working man in which his social status grew as his work skills increased, reflected in a differentiated pay structure.

'The workers of Yankee City were able to strike, maintain their solidarity . . . and in a sense flee to the protection of the unions because the disappearance of craftsmanship and the decreasing opportunities for social mobility had made them more alike with common problems and common hostilities against management.' Warner and Low thus argued that 'strikes' come about when the bureaucratisation of industry at the hands of monopoly capitalists removes the control of economic activities from the community within which production takes place; the systematisation and rationalisation of production create the conflict between producer and consumer roles and between local labour and national and international capital. They are thus drawing attention to the fact that organised collective action and particularly the strike can only occur at certain stages in the development of the economic system of society. At prior stages the economic was cross-cut by the social, the religious and the political and this tended to prevent industrial conflict from becoming organised. The break with community ties also tended to create the necessary conditions for working-class mobilisation for conflict.

Gouldner's study of the gypsum mine highlights similar features of the transformation of the relationship between employment and the community. Oscar Centre, prior to the end of the Second World War, had possessed most of the features of a *Gemeinschaft* or traditional community. Work relationships reflected community values and the authority system of the manager was based on stressing traditional bases of legitimacy and down-playing task-based or rational-legal bases of legitimacy. The established manager succeeded in maintaining the authority system of management by utilising the traditions of the community and creating reciprocal personal loyalties among his work-force. This system was possible because the market discipline of competition was suspended during the Second World War while the Government bought, on a cost-plus basis, all the gypsum board the factory could produce. Following the war the discipline of profitability re-asserted itself and led central management to define the plant's performance as substandard. A new manager was appointed to sort things out and as a response to his belief in the lack of individual motivation among his workers he instituted a system of depersonalised bureaucratic rules which attempted to ensure adequate conformity to the performance needs he identified for the company. This created a situation which was structurally conducive to conflict, as it replaced the multi-stranded relationships of the employment relationship prior to and during the war by a purely market relationship in which labour was treated in an impersonal manner.

Over several years the increased bureaucratisation created an atmosphere of hostility and resentment and when a methods engineer was imported to supervise the installation of new plant the process had proceeded to the extent that collective action was now possible. The actual precipitating factor which led to the strike was a relatively trivial incident in which the methods engineer insulted a worker. The final solution to this first organised manifestation of conflict was the extension of bureaucratic rules via the institution of the formal labour contract. Gouldner defined the strike as a 'breakdown in the flow of consent', a withdrawal by the work-force of the legitimacy previously accorded management. As Eldridge puts it (1968, p. 65), 'The social disruption, which the strike reflected and symbolised, is seen as a consequence of trying to "free" the labour contract from the social "givens" which made it effective in the first place, namely, the shared traditional beliefs and values in the community from which workers had derived their complementary expectations.' The solution of both factions among the workers was to attempt to re-establish social givens, either the traditional givens, or new legally protected givens embodied in the labour contract.

Before examining the argument that manifest conflict is a transitional phenomenon, which becomes contained and regularised by the creation of conflict resolving institutions, we will briefly turn to some problems of definition and the problem of the relationship between structural conduciveness and social action. Although we are concentrating in this chapter on the strike it is crucial to remember that the strike is only one manifestation of industrial conflict. Figure 9.2 outlines the types of ways in which conflict can be generated by industrial employment: it outlines the types of structural

Level of manifestation / Type of conflict	Structural	Idiosyncratic
Individual	Role conflict	Personality clashes
Collective	Conflict about substance of bargains	Conflicts arising from the application of agreements to particular groups in particular ways
	Conflict about modes of establishing bargains	

Figure 9.2 Types of conflict situations and typical manifestations

conduciveness rather than the concrete manifestations of conflict. The form that conflict takes depends on how the individual actors interpret the situation, whether they consciously devise strategies designed to remove the source of the blockage to their interests, and whether these strategies involve collective direct confrontation with their employers or employees.

It is very important to realise that conflict can be expressed in a series of behaviours. Taylor and Walton (1971) have discussed sabotage as an expression of conflict. Henry (1976) has argued that the trade in goods taken from the place of work can be interpreted as a response to the conflict between the individual's needs and the opportunities present in his work situation. Handy (1968), in a study of absenteeism and turnover in the coal industry, suggests that in some situations absenteeism is a deliberate conflict strategy, while in many situations turnover, absenteeism and accidents may be seen as a withdrawal responses from intolerable conflict. The strike has been the dominant weapon in the armoury of the working class, but it is accompanied by other less extreme weapons, such as the go-slow, the work-to-rule, or the restriction of output. The last five years have seen three new tactics of conflict; the work-in, the guerilla strike and the flying picket. The first is self-explanatory; faced with managerial decisions to stop operations several groups of workers have taken over the plant and operated it themselves: the Upper Clyde Shipbuilders' example created the fashion. The guerilla strike has not been fully developed yet, but involves the withdrawal of key personnel at random from their work, and creates chaos disproportionate to the costs it imposes on the union. The flying picket is not in fact a new form of conflict, but a new tactic for ensuring that strikes are not broken by scabs crossing the picket lines. Developed by the coal miners in 1972, it ensured that there were sufficient pickets to enforce the close-down of power stations although the local strikers might have proved insufficient on their own.

It is crucial to remember that when strikes are used as an index of industrial conflict the nature of their relationship to the underlying phenomenon should be made explicit. Much time has been devoted to distinguishing between official and unofficial strikes and between constitutional and unconstitutional strikes, and while for certain policy issues this may seem sensible, here it is argued that these distinctions are not very illuminating. At this point too it seems appropriate to caution against the too easy adoption of official definition of causes of strikes. Strikes are classified by the Ministry of Employment according to the major issue involved, but, as Gouldner's *Wildcat Strike* (1954) shows, the major cause reported may simply be the precipitating factor and obscure the real causes of the conflict. Thus the majority of British strikes are reported as about wage issues but this may simply reflect the symbolic centrality of the wage and a tendency on management's side to believe that every grievance can be solved by an increased wage.

Extreme caution should be exercised in the interpretation of strikes, and their meanings are only to be understood in the context of an analysis of the power structure within which they occur. This may mean that attempts to compare international strike records are fraught with insuperable problems of interpretation unless they involve total comparisons of the modes of production involved and the historical patterns of social development associated with such modes of production. Typically such comparisons isolate industrial conflict and suggest it has some independent consequence for the economic performance of the countries concerned. For all their shortcomings, in Western societies strikes remain the central expression of conflicting interests in industry, and strike trends can, therefore, if treated carefully, provide strong evidence for or against theories about the development of patterns of industrial conflict, especially if the analysis is careful to distinguish between (1) developments which might reduce underlying structured conflicts of interests, (2) developments which mediate the interpretation and expression of those underlying issues and (3) the relationship between developments in structure and developments in consciousness.

The two examples from Warner & Low and Gouldner (1954*a*, 1954*b*) both illustrate some of the issues which Marx, Durkheim and Weber suggest lead to the expression of industrial conflict in capitalist or industrial society. Now we will look at the treatments of the development of industrial conflict which argue that following the initial period of violent readjustment the parties to the conflict will shake down into new patterns of accommodation which channel conflict away from the direct confrontation of the lockout or the strike. The central mechanism, to which is usually attributed the ability to resolve conflicts and create an over-arching unity, is the collective bargaining system. Basically we will examine two major statements of this thesis, firstly the Ross–Hartmann version and secondly the Kerr *et al.* (1973) version. Ross and Hartmann (1960) in *Changing Patterns of Industrial Conflict* argued strongly that the strike was 'withering away' particularly in northern Europe and to a lesser extent in the United States. They based their position on statistical measures in two major series used to measure conflict: the percentage of union members involved in strikes, and the average duration of strikes taken for three essentially arbitary periods; 1900–1929, 1930–7 and 1948–56. Ingham (1974) has reanalysed their data, questioned whether it supports the kinds of claims they make, and suggests the data only really supports the tentative conclusion that the strike may have declined in Scandinavia since 1948. The actual details of Ross and Hartmann's statistics, while critical, are less interesting than the basic structure of their explanation and their theory of the accommodative potential of advanced industrial societies. This rests on five interrelated developments: first, the increased sophistication of management and the development of new organisational technologies; second, the growth of the state as a major employer and as a supervisor of standards in the labour market; third, a shift by the labour movement from emphasis on industrial action to emphasis on political action; fourth, and most contentiously, the declining inclination of rank-and-file members to strike; and fifth, they draw attention to the notion of the growing maturity of trade unions which parallels the increased management sophistication. Lester (1958) had already elaborated this thesis that as unions developed away from their struggles for establishment they tended to become more and more firmly wedded to an orderly form of bargaining behaviour, governed by a web of understandings which ensured that issues were not pursued to the point of hostility but were compromised on an acceptable basis through collective bargaining.

The major thrust of Ross–Hartmann can thus be reduced to an argument that as a result of constant interaction over a prolonged period of time the parties to industrial conflict, the unions and management, come to adjust their behaviours and develop a sophisticated understanding of their mutual interdependence which enables them to transcend their day-to-day points of disagreement.

Ross and Hartman's thesis is mirrored in Kerr *et al.*'s treatment of the evolution of the industrial relations system under the impact of industrialism, and while allowing for historical variation Kerr *et al.* suggest that technology and competitive pressures induce a degree of similarity between countries. Kerr *et al.* argue that 'Industrialisation requires and industrial jurisprudence at the workplace and in the work community. In short, each industrialising society creates an industrial relations system.

'Industrial relations systems reflect both uniformities and diversities. All industrial relations systems serve the functions of defining power and authority relationships among managements, labour organisations, and government agencies; of controlling or channelling worker protest; and of establishing the substantive rules themselves' (1973, p. 227). In particular they argue that one of the significant groups of rules which all industrial relations systems develop is one of rules concerning the procedures for the resolution of disputes. There are two major developments in these rules: first, they tend to limit stringently the resort to force, including the strike and lockout, and the established procedures are designed to substitute for open conflict; second, increasing use is made of professionals, and in particular there is a growth of neutrals (like the Advisory, Conciliation and Arbitration Service set up in 1974, charged with mediating in the conflicts between the two parties over particular employment relationships).

There are two variants of the institutionalisation theme which we will consider before examining the closely related theories of conflict like that of Fox and Flanders (1969) which revolve around notions of the breakdown of institutionalisation. Dahrendorf (1959) has argued that capitalist society has altered fundamentally: the central axis of conflict has ceased to be the ownership of property and become instead the possession of authority. Industrial conflict now revolves around issues of authority rather than power and this is paralleled by similar shifts in other spheres of social life so that where once there was a rift between the propertied and propertyless, which united the propertyless and made possible class action, now the various spheres of social action are relatively independent of one another and conflicts in the various areas cross cut one another. Industrial conflict becomes, in this way, divorced from other social conflicts and loses some of its potential for social change.

Ingham (1974) attempts to explain the difference in strike records between Britain and Sweden in terms of the institutional framework of the labour market in the two countries. He attempts to explain the differences in the institutionalisation in terms of important differences in the industrial infra-structure between the two countries. (Industrial infra-structure is defined to mean the features of a society's economic and technological system which shape the organisation of, and the social relationships between, those groups engaged in the process of production.) Conflicts between unions and employers then produce the specific institutions of normative regulation, and these determine the number of conflicts which result in strikes. Ingham argues that societies vary in their degrees of (1) industrial concentration, (2) complexity of technical and organisational structure and (3) product differentiation and specialisation and that these variations explain the ease with which institutionalisation occurs. Where there is an infra-structure with a low level of concentration, a high level of complexity of organisation forms and low product specialisation, institutionalisation is hindered because the lines of conflict between capital and labour tend to be lacking in clarity and consequently fail to provide an adequate basis for purposive and voluntary normative regulation. In Ingham's words, 'A fragmented infra-structure makes for a weak and fragmented normative structure unless the latter is imposed and supported by authoritarian political measures' (1974, p. 43). In Britain, he argues, the conditions created by the infra-structure are conducive to conflict because they amount to complexity, differentiation, decentralised bargaining, and these prevent clear and stable lines of dispute from emerging. This complexity is largely attributable to Britain's emergence as the first industrial nation and the diversity of goods and services British entrepreneurs supplied as they profited from the burgeoning markets at home and abroad. On to this wide spectrum of industries, established before mass or process production techniques and before the organisational forms pioneered by the American national companies allowed simultaneously both greater control and decentralisation, were grafted additional industries as these developments were incorporated into British management practice. The complexity of production facilities was matched by a similar complexity of bargaining structures reflecting the differing abilities of employers to reject workers' demands for a degree of self-determination. The contours of bargaining ceased to reflect any logical divisions in economic activity and this led to lack of normative regulation and hence strikes.

In Sweden, by contrast, Ingham argues that the industrial infra-structure encouraged centralisation of bargaining and the emergence of clear and stable lines of conflict between managements and workers. He attributes the inhibition of strikes to three factors (1974, p. 56):

(1) The Swedish industrial infra-structure and its centralised institutions produce a relative equality of organisational power between capital and labour and this, through fear of escalation, reduces strike activity;
(2) the 'visibility' of each side's power and intentions means that strikes are not frequently used as bargaining strategy or method of assessing strength and weaknesses;
(3) the centralised institutions and the nature of their power relationship have favoured the development of a very formal and comprehensive system of normative regulation which inhibits strike action by providing alternatives.

There are problems with Ingham's approach, but it does attempt to incorporate both a structural and a normative element in its explanation of the incidence of strikes.

Kerr and Seigal's (1954) theory of strike proneness of certain industries similarly revolves around the issue of normative control. They argue that the high incidence of strikes in logging, mining, docking and seafaring, and textiles, can be explained in terms of the low degree to which the workers in these industries are bound into the communal activities of the broader society and consequently do not share fully common values about what is acceptable behaviour. Additionally in these industries there are no cross-cutting ties to complicate the essential class nature of industrial conflict and the optimum conditions for fostering class solidarity are present. Grievances tend to extend in scope to all the employees in a particular employment relationship. So not only is normative control lacking, but also the optimum conditions for collective action are present. Kerr and Seigal hypothesise that the conditions which account for strike proneness are transitional and industrialisation in time erodes the isolation of these industries and brings them under normative control. The Kerr and Seigel formulation has been very influential, but the evidence is not very convincing, especially when the period subsequent to 1956 is included: variation between the same industries in different countries are often greater than variation between different industries in the same country, and the new strike-prone industries, like the motor industry, do not conform in any intuitively appealing manner to the notion of structural isolation.

Now we will turn our attention to the form of the breakdown of institutional order theme which became the industrial relations' orthodoxy of the late 1960s. Embodied in the Donovan Commission's analysis (1968) and explicitly articulated by Fox and Flanders (1969), the idea was advanced that British industrial relations had become disorderly because the web of rules which lay behind collective bargaining and provided the institutional expression of the moral consensus or normative order of society was no longer adequate to contain the conflict generated by the processes of production. The Donovan Commission argued that British industrial relations were bedevilled by two systems of industrial relations: the formal and the informal. In Fox and Flanders's words:

The former, of which the industry-wide agreement is the keystone, flies in

> the face of the facts by assuming industry wide organisations powerful enough to impose their decisions on their members. The latter, which is increasingly the reality, rests on the wide autonomy of managers in individual enterprises and the independent power of work groups. The assumptions of the formal system still exert, however, a potent influence over men's minds, and prevent the informal system from developing into an effective and orderly method of regulation. (p. 151).

Fox and Flanders take issue with the argument that trade unions are too powerful and need curbing by legal restrictions. They argue that unions can only provide the kind of labour discipline which is necessary to provide industrial order if they also have the power to make employers take their members' interests into account when making decisions. They refer back to the argument put forward by C. W. Mills (1948) that union leaders are actually 'managers of discontent', and defuse many issues and concentrate energy and attention on a small number of grievances and issues which are resolvable within the structure of capitalist industry. They quote Mills to this effect; a trade union leader 'organises discontent and then sits on it, exploiting it in order to maintain a continuous organisation. He makes regular what might otherwise be disruptive, both within the industrial routine and within the union he seeks to establish and maintain' (1969, p. 155). In Britain the necessary power is often missing and Fox and Flanders argue that trade unions may not be strong enough to be able to act effectively as managers of conflict and therefore play their essential part in the process of compromise and assessment of priorities in conflict on which order in industry rests.

Fox and Flanders argue that the key to theoretical understanding of the situation in the late 1960s was Durkheim's concept of anomie, or normlessness, resulting from a breakdown in social regulation. However they defined normlessness not as the absence of normative order, but as produced by an excessive proliferation of different normative systems which are unrelated and divergent. Put simply, there are too many people going in too many directions at once for overall order to prevail. They say, 'Every system of industrial relations is a normative system regulating employment relations, in short, a system of job regulation' (p. 156), and go on to say, 'In other words, an accepted normative system provides a framework of comparisons and constraints within which otherwise unlimited aspirations can be shaped with some concern for social proportion. (p. 158).

Although order in itself may not be the highest social good and certainly no normative system can be regarded as sacrosanct, society cannot exist without some normative regulation providing for the integration and predictability of expectations and behaviour. Although order is necessary, they argue that in a pluralistic society this order is in tension with the competing claims to power and their associated advocacy of particular normative systems; they continue

> What matters is that historically collective bargaining has been the principal method evolved in industrial societies for the creation of viable and adaptive normative systems to keep manifest conflict in employment

> relationships within socially tolerable bounds. This it has done because the rules it produces, as expressed in collective agreements and in unwritten understandings, are supported by a sufficiently high degree of consensus among those whose interests are most affected by their application. (p. 160)

They argue that collective bargaining has been predominantly preferred because it involves both parties to job regulation in the process of establishing the rules – both procedural and substantive – which govern the employment relationship. The stability of the collective bargaining system rests on an equilibrium in the struggle for power; when power distributions change, the ability of the system to reconcile conflicting interests is called in question. This is the hub of the situation in Britain, they argue.

> In these circumstances collective bargaining institutions which previously sufficed to maintain social order, or as much of it as was desired, may no longer be able to cope with the increased input of conflict unless they are radically reformed. This is precisely what has been happening in Britain over the post war years, and the main effect, as we will show, has been an increasing fragmentation of normative regulation. (p. 161).

The major causes of the fragmentation are aspirations which no longer accord with norms current in collective agreements and the entrance to the arena of new areas in which groups have aspirations, and desire a say where previously they had none. The causes can interact and where very prevalent result in the fragmentation and breakdown of existing systems. The system of normatively accepted reference points breaks down and naked market power becomes the arbiter of disputes. Put simply, strategically placed groups win concessions which other groups who identify with these groups are unable to achieve and the overall belief in the fairness of the method of conflict resolution becomes shaky as the unsuccessful groups withdraw their support for the basic ground rules, realising that the ground rules are biased against them.

Fox and Flanders's evidence of disorder was the growth in unofficial, unconstitutional and small strikes during the 1960s (see Silver, 1973, fig. 1). They were seeking to explain why small groups of workers were acting unilaterally to try to achieve their own particular groups' ends rather than acting through the mechanisms of representative trade unions. The explanation rests on the failure of the regulative mechanisms to adapt as fast as conditions altered under the impact of accelerating technological, organisational and social change. So new aspirations emerged from the new conditions of work which the old normative rules did not recognise, and moreover the new conditions of work put 'power' in to the hands of shop-floor operatives where previously it had resided in full-time trade union officials. Payment-by-results systems contributed by fostering the growth of shop-floor leaders and providing a constant source of new aspirations. Moreover the conditions of relatively full employment brought to the fore the issue of the distribution of resources within the working class, or the problem of establishing which groups of labour should benefit most, and early incomes policies drew attention to this (see the similarities and differences here with Hyman's treatment, (Hyman and Brough 1975) and increased aspirations which were not met. Fox and Flanders argue that since the Second World War the industrial relation system has been subjected to inflationary fragmentation caused by awakening aspirations both for greater self-control (the extension of claims to craft-like autonomy by other groups) and by the failure of traditional standards to contain the substantive aspirations of workers.

Fox and Flanders suggest there can be no solution to the industrial disorder in the absence of some new social consensus. Despite their failure adequately to adapt Durkheimian analysis and the way they ignore his treatment of inequalities in power as a barrier to moral unity (Goldthorpe, 1969), Fox and Flanders's conclusion that conflict will increase unless a new source of ground rules is discovered remains a critical insight. Their particular solutions may not appeal, leaving unchanged as they do, the fundamental principles of capitalism. However, as they say, 'Nothing less than the forceful articulation of common norms by an authoritative source can restore order' (1969, p. 179).

Fox and Flanders's analysis has been criticised on the grounds of the overly conservative nature of their prescriptions. Indeed the strategies suggested for constructing a new social consensus, and thus basis of social order, are not consistent with their alleged debt to Durkheim. Durkheim saw organic solidarity as arising spontaneously from a certain form of the division of labour, not as a result of deliberate policies by a central state authority. If the analysis is recast in a different vocabulary it would indicate that their analysis does not fall simply because their concrete proposals are unlikely to solve the problem they identify. The central conclusion could be reworded thus, 'The existing ideologies of the powerful have lost their ability to persuade workers to accept their lot, and either a new legitimation is put forward by the powerful which recaptures the workers' loyalty, or there will be disorder until the system of productive relations is replaced with a new system, with new ideologies capable of sustaining worker commitment to that new system of production.'

Before we conclude by briefly trying to assess whether the wave of large official strikes which followed the Industrial Relations Act (1971) can be interpreted in terms of a Durkheimian analysis better than they can in a Marxist analysis we will turn our attention to the work of Hyman, whose article and two books (Hyman, 1973, 1975, and Hyman and Brough, 1975) constitutes the most challenging treatment of industrial conflict in Britain and are claimed to represent a Marxist analysis. The focus of Hyman's analysis is firmly conflict, not the strike or any other particular manifestation.

Hyman's explanation of the upsurge of the overt expression of conflict in the sixties and seventies is based on an analysis of the changing problems faced by capitalism as a system of production after the Second World War. Resting heavily on Glyn and Sutcliffe's (1972) analysis of the crisis of the declining rate of profit, Hyman proceeds to argue that this incipient crisis, brought about by the decline in profitability, leads to distinct changes in industrial relations, especially as it is linked to development in the structure of capital which create new problems for management in their quest for profit (1973, p. 111). The escalating costs and complexity of capital equipment are one important cause of change; the growing size and interdependence of companies another. Together these create an urgent need for planning; and planning, to be effective, requires predictability and control. Such pressures impinge most powerfully on labour costs and labour utilisation: the aspects of companies' economic environment over which management have the greatest direct influence. These developments, which intensify management attempts to reassert control over the employment relationship and resulted in the prevalence of first productivity bargaining and then measured daywork, as at British Leyland, are matched by developments in the problems of the management of the economy by the State. As Blackburn (1967) argues, this is inevitable as long as responsibility for investment remains in the hands of the rich, because the whole social process of investment and accumulation depends upon the fostering of conditions favourable to the private accumulation of profit. Employers thus came to look to government to forsake their absentionist role, and argued that 'voluntarism' is incapable of solving the particular problems of the current national crisis in 'the national interest', and what is required is intervention by government, and perhaps additionally by the law, to control wages so that investment can be got right and the crisis in profitability can be overcome. These developments led to the introduction of the various pay policies and incomes policies, by which government have intervened in the labour market to attempt to curb wage demands.

Before considering Hyman's treatment of how incomes policy fits into the threatened breakdown of the dominant value system (Parkin, 1971) or ideology, we will briefly state Hyman's position on the inevitability of conflict in capitalism and the impossibility of resolution within existing relations of production. Capitalism is fraught with fundamental internal contradictions which cannot in the long run be papered over and by the ideological hegemony of the ruling class (Hyman & Brough, 1975, p. 251). The contradictions inherent in modern industrial relations, it is abundantly evident, are irresolvable within the framework of capitalism, and

> Without a transformation of the structure of class domination, of property ownership and of employment relationships, state intervention and management and governmental planning cannot engender a genuinely rational social organisation whereby the system of production and distribution is consciously subordinated to the collective decisions of societal members. (Hyman and Brough 1975, p. 250).

It is here that Hyman's difference with Fox and Flanders lies, Hyman arguing that normative aspirations flow inexorably from the structure of power which is reflected in the relationships of production and, while that structure creates fundamental conflicts of interest, ideological systems can only mystify and obscure the conflicts in the short run and never establish a genuine normative consensus. Fox and Flanders on the contrary seem to argue that a genuine consensus is possible. Using Lockwood's distinction between social integration and system integration (Lockwood, 1956; Eldridge, 1971) Fox and Flanders concentrate on social integration and the state of order or conflict in relationships between actors, while Hyman concentrates on system integration or the state of order or conflict between parts of the social system. One of Hyman's problems is to explain why system disorder does not inevitably lead to social disorder and why the last few years have seen increasing social disorder without increasing consciousness of the causes of that disorder, namely the system contradictions of capitalism.

The key to the level of manifest conflict in industrial relations is the degree of opaqueness of class relations and power relations in society, or put more directly the success of the ruling class in containing working-class aspirations to areas where the aspirations can be met without fundamentally challenging the distribution of property and privilege. Hyman draws on Gramsci's notion of hegemony and Parkin's notion of the subordinate value system to explain how it is that working-class consciousness fails to become capable of constructing an alternative explanation of society to that offered them by the existing privileged groups. Building on the work of Lenin, Hyman (1971) analyses the processes whereby the trade union movement fosters a trade union consciousness which restricts the aspirations of workers and leads them to accept the contours of capitalist market structures. Many trade union leaders, he argues, become incorporated into the power structure and accept the pluralist view of the nature of society and consequently shy away from any confrontation which threatens the political stability of the nation. It is argued that it was this fear of constitutional crisis which corroded the resistance of the trade union leadership in the General Strike of 1926, and it has been argued that one of the significant developments of the Yorkshire miner's militancy in the 1970s was that there emerged a willingness to carry industrial action to the point where it did actually threaten political stability. In general, however, trade unions, rather than fostering an awareness of the fundamental contradiction between working class interests and capitalism, have accepted an accommodating role and restrained their bargaining to issues which initially did not threaten the basic wage relationship. The recent developments in the management of the economy have made the concentration on the cash nexus a potentially problematic way of containing working-class opposition because with the intervention of the state and the breakdown of traditional understandings about fair wage relativities the brittleness of the cash nexus (Westergaard, 1970) becomes more and more exposed and open to challenge.

Incomes policy actually contains a contradiction because it suggests that there is and should be a rationale for relativities between groups of workers. This is necessary if claims based on relativities are to be rejected as unjustified as part of the strategy of wage containment, but it has also added nails to the coffin of the traditional sets of beliefs about what constituted a 'fair' structure of pay between different occupations. The traditional structure's only rationale was custom and practice and could not logically be justified according to any generally acceptable principles. Thus incomes policy and the ill it was introduced to cure, inflation, interact to exacerbate the breakdown of traditional patterns of accommodation in industrial relations. According to Hyman:

> These two related aspects of many recent disputes – the questioning of levels of pay which were previously taken for granted, and the adoption of

> new and more ambitious 'orbits of comparison' – constitute an important component of the dynamic of the heightening of strike activity. In part this is a natural response to rapid price inflation which has had the predictable effect of weakening the hold of traditional frames of reference for judging pay. It may also be related to the experience of 'incomes policy'. (1973, pp. 105–6).

The crisis in profitability of modern British capitalism and the rise in money wages have led the employers to believe that a policy of curtailment of free collective bargaining is necessary if the system of production is to survive. Thus the material interests of capital have found expression in state intervention in the labour market designed to restrict the growth of incomes and stimulate the growth of output from the private sector. The actual measures of the State, embodied in the various incomes policies, have, at the same time as they have partially served the material needs of employers, undermined the legitimating ideology of the dominant group and thus precipitated responses among the employees which, while not representing a unified challenge to the social order, have created a series of events which threaten its continuance. As Hyman and Fryer see it, the increase in industrial conflict in the last few years is explained thus:

> Typically, workers do not question the dominant ideology when formulated in abstract and general terms; yet in respect of their concrete and specific experience they fail to endorse its implications. Hence they may adopt cynical attitudes towards those in authority, and engage in actions (going on strike, for example) deprecated by those whole-heartedly committed to the prevailing ideological perspective. This then involves trade unionism in a profound contradiction: workers have adopted aims and methods intolerable to the custodians of the social and moral order, even though no explicit or coordinated challenge to this order is intended. (Hyman and Fryer, 1975, p. 199).

Beynon, in *Working for Ford* (1973) stresses the way in which industrial conflict in current employment situations continues to be constrained by the frame of reference of the leaders of the workers. At Halewood, despite a continual battle with management about control over working conditions, and about the role of the union as representatives of the working class, Beynon argues that consciousness of the fundamental cause of the conflict with management is limited, and there is no articulated class consciousness which 'explains' the conflicts in terms of the broader political economy of capitalism. The conflict between management and workers which ebbs and flows around the line, and control of conditions on the line, gives rise only to a factory consciousness not to a class consciousness. In Beynon's words,

> Struggle over line speeds, lay offs, victimisation and the like fostered the articulation of a highly developed form of factory class consciousness. This class consciousness has been termed a *factory* consciousness because as an ideology its cutting edge is essentially limited to the confines of the area of production. (p. 107)

Thus for writers like Beynon and Hyman the important question in analysing industrial conflict in Britain today revolves around the relationship between the actual position of the working class and the consciousness of that position and how it is articulated or not articulated in politcal and industrial action designed to fundamentally alter the mode of production. Hyman explicitly argues that industrial conflict is not a sufficient teacher: 'There is very little evidence to support the romantic belief that participation in a major industrial struggle naturally generates an "explosion of consciousness" with lasting consequences' (1973, p. 126). Hyman is clearly concerned (1973) with the task of fostering a class consciousness which is capable of transcending the boundaries of the factory, of the labour market, or any of the other structures of capitalist society which currently serve in various ways to defuse the potential of that consciousness. However at the level of prediction Hyman is more cautious, and while arguing that the contradictions of capitalism are increasingly causing problems in industrial relations, as the policies designed to serve the material interests of capital undermine the traditional ideological acceptance of the structure of inequality, he concludes one of his articles:

> Which direction is followed in the future development of trade unionism and working class consciousness depends on the conjuncture of a complex array of factors. If it is academically unsatisfactory to regard the outcome as indeterminate, this is nevertheless the only realistic conclusion. 'History is at its least automatic when it is the consciousness of the proletariat that is at issue'. (Hyman and Fryer, 1975, p. 201)

There seems to be a measure of agreement about the causes of conflict and the factors leading to the ebb and flow of the overt manifestation of basic conflicts. Conflict stems from the inegalitarian distribution of power, and the inegalitarian structures of access to positions of power, and from the distinctly different interests of the dominant and dominated groups. Sociologists have documented repeatedly the continuation of structures of inequality which bear no relationship to 'needs of society or to 'distributions of natural abilities'. Property remains the major determinant of a person's fate in the distribution of power. There have been changes in the distribution of property, more in some societies than others, but the fate of the industrial worker in industrial societies continues to rest in the hands of groups of managers whose interests cannot be assumed to coincide with the interests of those they manage. The problem is not so much to account for why there should be conflict in industrial society, but why there is so little fundamental conflict expressed in overt industrial or political action.

The ebb and flow of manifest industrial conflict has been explained similarly by sociologists identifying primarily with either Marx or Durkheim or Weber. All essentially are drawing attention to the key importance of the successful creation of a body of beliefs about the necessity for the world to be organised in a particular way, or the creation of a belief in the 'fairness' of a particular pattern of social relationships. The analysis of all three founding fathers makes the role of beliefs of this nature crucial to the understanding of social stability.

British industrial relations over the decade since the late 1960s can only be understood in terms of the relationship between consciousness and action, or between belief in the need for particular governmental action and acceptance or non-acceptance of that action. During the last decade the State has been forced to introduce a series of measures for which acceptance has not been easily won, incomes policy can be interpreted as an attempt to re-create some sense of moral unity of purpose and some shared ideology about the nature of British society. There is disagreement about whether the 'moral unity' is being created at the behest of the ruling class, or genuinely as a cooperative process between classes. And in this way the treatment of industrial conflict mirrors the general conflict within sociology between accounts which stress the irreconcilable conflicts between classes generated by the capitalist mode of production and accounts which stress normative agreement between opposing groups about the limits within which conflict will be contained.

A satisfactory account of British industrial relations must analyse both changes in the political economy of British capitalism and changes in the ideologies actors in the industrial relations system use to understand those changes, and then use to guide their attempts to change the system. The changes in British capitalism which have led away from a policy of minimal state intervention and a justificatory ideology based on *laissez-faire* beliefs have created strains at both the organisational and ideological level. The challenge for all who do not wish to see a fundamental change in the organisational basis of society is the problem of how to create the shared systems of values between all actors which can halt the fragmentation of the last few years. That is what the Social Contracts of 1975 and 1976 attempted. Belatedly the trade union leadership adapted to the new crises and once again sought to operate as 'managers of discontent'.

Suggested Further Reading

Eldridge, J. E. T. (1973) *Sociology and Industrial Life* (London: Nelson University Paperbacks).

— (1975) 'Industrial Relations and Industrial Capitalism', in G. Esland, G. Salaman, and M. Speakman (eds.) *People and Work*, pp. 306–24 (Edinburgh: Holmes McDougall; The Open University Press).

Hyman, R., and Fryer, R. (1975) 'Trade Unions', in J. B. McKinley (ed.) *Processing People*, pp. 150–213 (London: Holt, Rinehart & Winston).

Bibliography

Beynon, H. (1973) *Working for Ford* (Harmondsworth, Middx: Penguin Books).

Blackburn, R. (1967) 'The Unequal Society', in R. Blackburn and A. Coburn, *The Imcompatibles* (Harmondsworth, Middx: Penguin Books).

Dahrendorf, R. (1959) *Class and Class Conflict* (Stanford: Stanford University Press).

Donovan Commission (1968) *Royal Commission on Trade Unions and Employers' Associations 1965–1968 Report* (London: H.M.S.O.).

Durkheim, E. (1952) *Suicide: A Study in Sociology* (London: Routledge & Kegan Paul).

— (1964) *The Division of Labour in Society* (New York: Free Press Paperbacks).

Eldridge, J. E. T. (1968) *Industrial Disputes* (London: Routledge & Kegan Paul).

— (1973) *The Sociology of Industrial Life* (London: Nelson University Paperbacks).

Fox, A. and Flanders, A. (1969) 'The Reform of Collective Bargaining: From Donovan to Durkheim', *British Journal of Industrial Relations*, 7, pp. 151–80.

Glyn, A., and Sutcliffe, R. (1972) *British Capitalism, Workers and the Profit Squeeze* (Harmondsworth, Middx: Penguin Books).

Goldthorpe, J. H. (1969) 'Social Inequality and Social Integration', *Advancement of Science*, 26, pp. 190–202.

Gouldner, A. (1954*a*) *Patterns of Industrial Bureaucracy* (New York: Free Press).

— (1954*b*) *Wildcat Strike* (Yellow Springs, Ohio: Antioch Press).

Handy, L. J. (1968) 'Absenteeism in the British Coal-mining Industry: An Examination of Post War Trends', *British Journal of Industrial Relations*, 6 pp. 27–50.

Henry, S. (1976) 'It Fell Off the Back of a Lorry', *New Society*, 35 (26 Feb.) p. 699.

Hyman, R. (1971) *Marxism and the Sociology of Trade Unionism* (London: Pluto Press).

— (1973) 'Industrial Conflict and the Political Economy: Trends of the Sixties and Prospects for the Seventies', in *Socialist Register 1973*, ed. R. Miliband and J. Saville (London: Merlin Press).

— (1975) *Industrial Relations: A Marxist Introduction* (London: Macmillan).

— and I. Brough (1975) *Social Values and Industrial Relations: Study of Fairness and Inequality* (Oxford: Blackwell).

Ingham, G. K. (1974) *Strikes and Industrial Conflict* (London: Macmillan).

Kerr, C., and Seigal, A. (1974) 'The Inter-Industry Propensity to Strike – An International Comparison', in A. Kornhauser, R. Dubin and A. M. Ross, *Industrial Conflict* (New York: McGraw-Hill).

Kerr, C., Dunlop, J. T., Harbison, F., Myers, C. A., (1973) *Industrialism and Industrial Man*, 2nd ed. (Harmondsworth, Middx: Penguin Books).

Lester, R. A. (1958) *As Unions Mature: An Analysis of the Evolution of American Unionism* (Princeton, N.J.: Princeton University Press).

Lockwood, D. (1956) 'Some Remarks on the Social System', *British Journal of Sociology* 7, pp. 134–43.

McCarthy, W. J. (1970) 'The Nature of Britain's Strike Problem', *British Journal of Industrial Relations* 8, pp. 224–36.

Marx, K., and Engels, F. (1848) *The Communist Manifesto* (Harmondsworth, Middx: Penguin Books, 1967).

Mills, C. W. (1948) *New Men of Power: America's Labour Leaders* (New York: Harcourt, Brace).

Parkin, F. (1971) *Class Inequality and the Political Order* (London: McGibbon & Kee).

Ross, A. M., and Hartman, P. T. (1960) *Changing Patterns of Industrial Conflict* (New York: John Wiley & Sons).

Silver, M. (1973) 'Recent British Strike Trends: A Factual Analysis', *British Journal of Industrial Relations* 11, pp. 66–104.

Smelser, N. J. (1962) *Theory of Collective Behaviour* (London: Routledge & Kegan Paul).

Taylor, I., and Walton, P. (1971) 'Industrial Sabotage: Motives and Meanings', in S. Cohen (ed.) *Images of Deviance* (Harmondsworth, Middx: Penguin Books).

Warner, W. L., and Low, J. W. (1946) *The Social System of a Modern Factory* (New Haven, Conn.: Yale University Press).

Westergaard, J. (1970) 'The Rediscovery of the Cash Nexus', *Socialist Register 1970* (London: Merlin Press).

Author Index

Subject Index